An Unof

Inside the conflict

MATTHEW KENTRIDGE

dp

DAVID PHILIP
Cape Town & Johannesburg

The world contemplates the great spectacle of combat and death, which is difficult for it to imagine in the end, because the image of war is not communicable – not by the pen, or the voice, or the camera. War is a reality only to those stuck in its bloody, dreadful, filthy insides. To others it is pages in a book, pictures on a screen, nothing more.

— Ryszard Kapuściński: *Another Day of Life*

First published 1990 in southern Africa by David Philip Publishers (Pty) Ltd, 208 Werdmuller Centre, Claremont 7700, South Africa

© 1990 Matthew Kentridge

ISBN 0-86486-160-5

Printed by Clyson Printers (Pty) Ltd, Maitland, Cape, South Africa

Contents

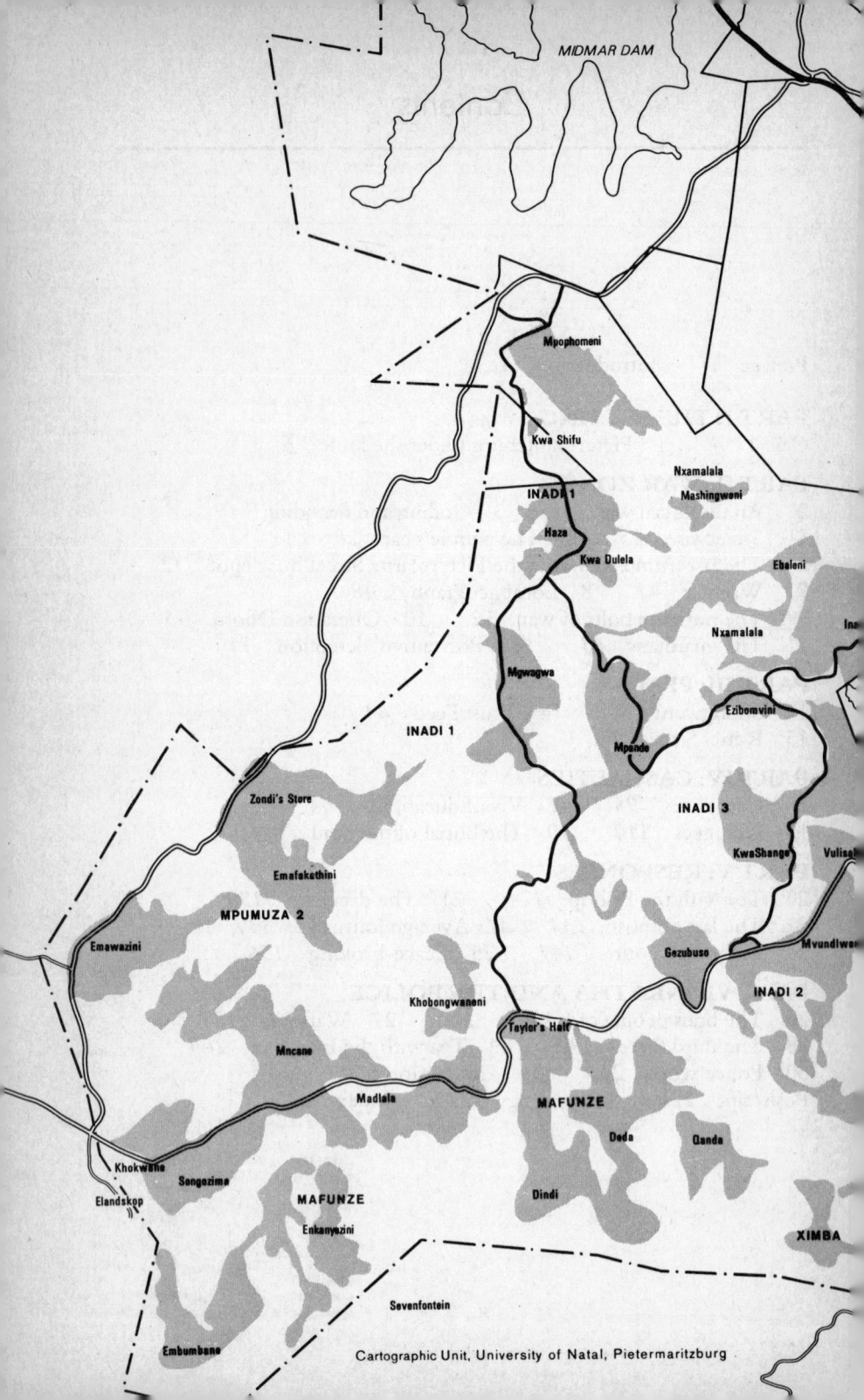

MIDMAR DAM

Mpophomeni

Kwa Shifu

Nxamalala
Mashingweni

INADI 1

Haza

Kwa Dulela

Ebeleni

Nxamalala

Ina

Mgwagwa

Ezibomvini

Mpande

INADI 1

INADI 3

Zondi's Store

KwaShange

Vulisel

Emafakethini

MPUMUZA 2

Emawazini

Gezubuso

Mvundlwe

Khobongwaneni

INADI 2

Taylor's Halt

Mncane

MAFUNZE

Madlala

Deda

Qanda

Khokwane

Songozima

Elandskop

MAFUNZE

Dindi

Enkanyezini

XIMBA

Embumbane

Sevenfontein

Cartographic Unit, University of Natal, Pietermaritzburg

PIETERMARITZBURG

Swartkops
Mbubu
Sweetwaters
Mbubu
Mpushini
Zayeka Mvubukazi
MPUMUZA 1
Papyipini
Landauville Caluza
Smero Siyamu Harewood
Esigodini Madakaneni
EDENDALE
Georgetown Machibisa
Dambuza
Wilgefontein Imbali
Nhluthela
Inyandu
Nhlazatshe
Pata
Noshazi Mount Partridge
Sinathing

WILLOWFOUNTAIN

NEW POLITIQUE

Sobantu

Scottsville

Ashdown
Plessislaer
Slangspruit

Ambleton

Shenstone

| 0 | 2 | 4 | 6 |

Kilometres

Preface

I am grateful to all the people who granted me interviews. I would like to thank John Aitchison and the staff at the Centre for Adult Education at the University of Natal, Pietermaritzburg, for making their time, knowledge and facilities available to me unstintingly. My special thanks go to Georgina Hamilton for her hospitality, for introducing me to contacts, for setting up interviews when I was unable to do so and for discussing the subject with me at length. Thanks also to Lynn Middleton and Vernon Solomon for their hospitality in Natal. I thank Mark Orkin and Daan Matheusson at CASE; Edwin Cameron; and Janet Hersch, all of whom in different ways helped see the manuscript through to its final draft. Finally, my thanks to my editor Russell Martin and to Alison Hill for producing the book.

★   ★   ★

Because I do not speak Zulu I conducted my interviews with people whose first language is Zulu, in English. I have quoted them verbatim because I thought it unnecessary to impose formal rules of construction on the language used. This is the way English is spoken by many South Africans and it is an entirely fluent variation.

★   ★   ★

Many of the acts or omissions attributed to individuals or groups in this book are only allegations unless the contrary is stated. They have not been proved in court. The incidents related in this book strongly suggest why this is so. Those who have brought cases or agreed to testify in court have been harassed and even killed before they had a chance to present their evidence. The allegations made are based on affidavits, newspaper reports and eyewitness accounts and I have included them because in my opinion they are reliable.

Introduction

On Wednesday, 28 March 1990, South Africans woke up to the fact that something very ugly was happening in Pietermaritzburg. Headlines trumpeted the news in huge bold print: 'Natal on the boil'; 'Thousands in impi attack'; ' "War" in Maritzburg'.

The violence in Natal dominated the media for a week. Papers, journals, even the television news, were crammed with stories of murder, dispossession and displacement. A force of up to 12 000 men, many carrying guns and some even armed with submachine guns, attacked the same areas again and again, KwaShange, Gezubuso, Vulisaka, KwaMyandu, Caluza, Ashdown – these obscure place-names kept appearing in a grim litany of mayhem and destruction. Together with stories of lawless mobs rampaging through hills outside Pietermaritzburg came reports of police partisanship towards armed Inkatha supporters; of police failing to respond to urgent calls for assistance; of police telling residents to leave besieged areas as they could provide no help.

Spokesmen for the two chief actors in the conflict, Inkatha and the UDF, traded accusations as their members traded spear thrusts and gunfire. A high-level delegation from the South African Council of Churches called on Chief Mangosuthu Buthelezi, president of Inkatha, who denied that his organisation was responsible for the killings and instructed the delegation to meet rather with the UDF and ANC, in his view the instigators and perpetrators of violence in Natal. For their part, the UDF and ANC published eyewitness accounts which sought to prove, categorically, that the new eruption was solely the result of a fresh attempt by Inkatha to invade non-Inkatha territories and so redraft the political geography of the region.

In parliament, the government was galvanised into action. The State President, F W de Klerk, announced a development plan for the region to be worked out over a period of years. The Minister of Law and Order, Adriaan Vlok, said that the police were doing everything possible to contain the violence, but they were seriously undermanned. The State President conferred with the Minister of Law and Order and the Minister of Defence. Two thousand troops were sent to Natal, and the government went to great lengths to convince the general public that they were responding with firmness and determination to events around Pietermaritzburg.

Among the public at large, and even in the editorial columns of certain newspapers, the prevailing reaction was one of bewilderment. That this should be so was singularly ironic – in the South Africa of 1990, where nothing is as it was a few months ago, let alone a year ago, the single, continuous political strand is the endemic conflict between Inkatha and the UDF in Natal.

There is a process of forgetting in the public consciousness, an attrition of memory which results in the failure to relate current events to their constitutive histories. The violence in Pietermaritzburg and Mpumalanga at the end of March was not a self-explanatory, discrete occurrence, but part of a long internecine struggle which has gripped the Natal Midlands for more than two years. In this region the bitter warfare between Inkatha and supporters of the UDF and COSATU has claimed well over two thousand lives, wrecked family and community relationships, turned tens of thousands of people into refugees, and caused incalculable mental and physical damage.

It is only now that the government is beginning to perceive the violence as something more than a local tribal infraction. For the first time the government is conceding the significance of the political cleavages which underlie the fighting, and there is now a tacit acknowledgement that the conflict has taken on the dimensions of a regional civil war.

But there is more to this fight than politics; over the years the feuding has taken root to such a degree that there is now no area of people's lives that is free of its baneful influence: schools, work, transport, recreation, all are affected. And while all wars have common features, it is here, in its particular impact on people's lives, that one locates the differences which set this conflict apart from others. Any chronicle must therefore focus as much on these details as on the broader political rupture behind the fighting. For this reason, in the chapters which follow I have cast my beam wide to seek out the specific characteristics which together constitute the unique personality of this unofficial war.

PART 1
The setting

Case 1

The windows had lost their panes and the gaps were filled with uneven squares of cardboard, damp and wilting from the recent summer rains. In the small, dark room light penetrated through chinks in the boarding. The woman sitting in a corner leaned back against the wall. Her name was Gladys Sangweni and she had an idea that she was about 75 years old. The air was heavy and still, and the smell of floor polish hung about the room as familiar as breath. She wished she could take her chair outside into the yard and breathe in the scent of the hillside grass but it was not yet safe to leave the room.

Outside the dogs were still barking frantically and poultry in the next yard squabbled in alarm and confusion. The sounds meshed with the harsh and continuous noise of men crying out, shouting taunts, roaring with anger. Behind them the voices of women were raised in a long wail of communal keening and excitement. The noise grew and fell as the tide of battle drifted closer or further from the house. The old woman sat impassively waiting for it to end – she was used to the constant attacks by now; she had already lost her windows to the invaders.

She waited, surrounded by her possessions, most of them now no more than a dull gleam in the murky interior: a stove, a rack of utensils – she had had the kettle for 50 years – the bed raised high on bricks and covered with a faded quilt. A radio from the 1960s stood on the starched white tablecloth, its plastic cover was dry and cracked, and a child had once snapped the aerial. In a corner, flanked by low-backed wire-seated chairs there was a foot-pedal sewing machine which she had not used for many years. She had a Bible somewhere too. On the bed there was an album with a few photographs and many more postcards and cuttings from magazines which she had gathered over the years. Three mats in green and yellow, white and red, woven from supermarket bags, lay on the floor and on the door she had strung a calendar, new with the year.

The sounds of conflict began to ebb away; she could now hear snatches of conversation, high-pitched and garbled. Doors banged closed as people returned to their houses, and next door a metallic scrape signalled that a window had been opened.

Gladys Sangweni moved to the door and went outside. She was blinded by the glare, and shielding her eyes she worked her way round to the outside toilet, holding on to the wall with one hand for guidance. The yard was lush and muddy. A hen moved from one clump of grass to another, stepping fastidiously through the puddles, and a listing banana palm stood in one corner, barren of fruit and declining.

The plot itself had been levelled out of the hillside and formed the top shelf in a series of terraced steps which dropped into a valley before climbing again. An earth wall stood between house and hill; from the hillside the yard and house lay open like an arena. Above the house was only waving grass, and on the brow a police mobile unit was just visible as a brown mound surmounted by a pennant on a long aerial, like a Hindu prayer flag.

The hen moved away as the old woman returned around the side of the house. She still kept one hand on the wall for support, walking carefully to avoid the mud. Now, however, four men stood on the hillside watching her silently. They wore dark clothing and each carried a gun. With the rustle of a mamba, a few loose stones broke away from the hill face and fell into the yard. Gladys Sangweni turned towards the sound. The men smiled but she could not see their faces. They stood out against the sunlight as ominous silhouettes. She reached for the doorknob, her movements clumsy with age and fear. The men raised their guns. The old woman struggled with the knob which was loose and did not easily catch or release. The men waited. She pushed harder. Then impassively, almost gravely, they fired, and fired again and again. Gladys Sangweni fell heavily against the door, one hand still pressed to the wall while her feet slithered and kicked in the mud. Inside the house the calendar was jerked off its nail and dropped to the floor. Soon she lay still, her throat and nostrils stopped with blood and earth. The men continued shooting, chipping plaster off the walls and making the earth spurt around the body. Abruptly they stopped and ran swiftly up the hill to the road and vanished over the brow. The neighbours arrived at first slowly – with caution – and then people came pouring into the yard; a car was summoned. Above the mobile unit the police flag hung small and limp.

1

Pietermaritzburg under the knife

I inserted a forefinger into the bullet hole in the wall and scratched at the powdery plaster. It felt damp and grainy. When I withdrew my hand, a grey crust was lodged under my fingernail.

From the yard I looked up and across the hill. At the top I could see the police unit and over the shallow valley there was a good view of Mpumuza. In the foreground was the shell of a large house, now just a series of wide holes surrounded by a little wall. Behind the house there were cows in the long grass and further back there were small clusters of rural dwellings – mud walls surmounted by a corrugated-iron roof. In front of each house was a small cultivated plot dominated by mealies. A few figures wandered along distant paths and the cry of a cockerel came floating across. To me it seemed disingenuously peaceful; somewhere among those houses were concealed the four men who had killed Gladys Sangweni.

I made my way through the mud patches back to the car. A girl of about 6 trailed after me. She was holding the remains of a plastic tommy-gun which she pointed at me warily from time to time. Near the car other children were squatting among the puddles looking for frogs, and a thin yellow dog limped around sniffing my tyres.

Later that morning, in an office at the University of Natal, Pietermaritzburg (UNP), I paced the green regulation carpeting, trying to order my thoughts. I pondered the processes of war that could lead to the barbarous and meaningless execution by firing squad of a woman who, in the course of a long life, had caused harm only to chickens. Bloodlust is both a spontaneous and a cumulative state of mind: the four men who killed Gladys Sangweni were probably battle-befuddled and deranged with adrenalin. They were probably also suffering from the well-entrenched delusion that anyone in enemy territory is ripe for killing, and had performed this murder with less compunction than they would feel in clubbing off the head of a lizard.

Nhlanhla looked in on his way home. He worked as a fieldworker at the University and was an activist in the townships. He had recently been released after being detained for six months and was now bound by a restriction order, but this had not impaired his powers of observation and analysis, or his ability to know what was going on, and where. He was a tall, thin man with restless fingers which moved through the air as though playing a ghostly piano. He had a dry and ironic sense of humour, and had taken it upon himself to show me around. I told him about my visit to Gladys Sangweni's house, and my theory about the killers' state of mind. He shrugged. 'They may be deluded, but not so much that they don't know an easy target when they see one,' he said sardonically.

Nhlanhla went off, possibly to catch a bus into Edendale, to go to his home of the day, to have a meal and swallow a couple of beers, or possibly to fight for his life at an ugly fracas at the bus ranks in down-town Pietermaritzburg. This fresh danger, a relatively late addition to the list of hazards faced by black people in Pietermaritzburg, was becoming increasingly prevalent.

In the meantime I attacked the mound of documentation on the desk to try to make some sense of this messy conflict. I had recently arrived in Pietermaritzburg to do field-work; at the time I was still attached to a British university. Even at that early stage, however, I was beginning to realise that I would rather write something on this local war than my planned Ph.D.

I pulled a pad towards me and began to make notes.

The protagonists: First the United Democratic Front (UDF), an umbrella body composed of affiliated organisations around South Africa. At its foundation in 1983, some 600 organisations affiliated to the Front; the number rose subsequently. The UDF is both the largest extra-parliamentary opposition grouping in the country and the single largest recipient of government repression. In the eyes of the state, the UDF was seen as the internal arm of the then banned African National Congress (ANC). Youth organisations, township civics, educational, student, women's, cultural and sporting organisations and associations are all represented within the structures of the UDF. Politically, the UDF is committed to the abolition of apartheid and to the construction in its place of a free, democratic and non-racial South Africa.

Active supporters of the UDF who are members of affiliated organisations are known as activists, or comrades. The two terms are not mutually exclusive – a comrade can be an activist and vice versa – but it is convenient to use 'activist' to refer to people who hold some kind of political office in a UDF-affiliated organisation, and 'comrade' when referring to rank-and-file members and supporters. In the Pietermaritzburg townships the leaders of the various UDF organisations are elected either because they are able fighters, or because they are politically astute. However, the leadership is transient and discontinuous because no sooner does a leader emerge than he is detained, restricted or killed.

In the fighting around Pietermaritzburg, the ranks of the comrades have been infiltrated with a smattering of people known colloquially as the *comtsotsis*. They are small-time gangsters and criminals who have allied themselves to the comrades' cause for one reason or another. They license their illicit activities with political slogans. The comrades have tried to curb the activities of the *comtsotsis* using more or less effective disciplinary methods.

On 24 February 1988, the UDF was effectively banned. The organisation was only unbanned in February 1990, having fought for two years underground.

Allied with the comrades is COSATU, the Congress of South African Trade Unions. COSATU is a national federation of trade unions, representing workers in all sectors of commerce and industry. COSATU unions claim a paid-up membership of close to one million workers. COSATU is chiefly concerned with workers' issues, such as unfair dismissals, wage bargaining and poor working conditions, but unionists have been compelled to take up broader political issues as well because the protection and enhancement of the lives of workers does not stop at the workplace. COSATU also endorses the aims of the Freedom Charter, and espouses a socialist economic dispensation for a post-apartheid South Africa.

On 24 February 1988, COSATU was prohibited from engaging in any political activity. This restriction, too, was only lifted two years later.

From the beginning of 1989, the amorphous term Mass Democratic Movement (MDM) was used to delineate the alliance of extra-parliamentary political organisations which endorsed the Freedom Charter. Both the UDF and COSATU are part of the MDM – in many respects the term MDM was first used in the context of the effective banning of the UDF and COSATU. However, in Pietermaritzburg the MDM has never been cited as a participant in the war. Rather, one talks of a conflict between the UDF–COSATU and Inkatha because the fighting involves people from these specific organisations.

COSATU and the UDF have obvious points of political congruence, and in Pietermaritzburg have entered into a *de facto* alliance, as COSATU members and UDF supporters have been attacked indiscriminately by Inkatha members. Faced with a common enemy, activists and union officials have tried to coordinate a common response.

Opposing the UDF and COSATU is Inkatha. It was established in 1975 by Chief Mangosuthu G Buthelezi, who has been president since its inception. Inkatha is described as a Zulu national cultural liberation movement, but it is also a political party. All the members of the KwaZulu Legislative Assembly (KLA), the parliamentary body in the KwaZulu homeland, are members of Inkatha. Although it controls the self-governing, but non-independent homeland of KwaZulu, thereby participating in state apartheid structures, Inkatha claims to be an anti-apartheid organisation, committed in its charter to non-violent opposition to the South African government. For his involvement in the homeland system, Chief Buthelezi has been labelled a collaborator, stooge and a government puppet, but he justifies his stance on the grounds that opposition from within is more effective than opposition from without. Chief Buthelezi and Inkatha, like the state, have regarded the UDF as the internal wing of the ANC, and, again like the state, are implacably opposed to it.

Chief Buthelezi is a charismatic figure and has been granted audiences with various Western political leaders. Both Buthelezi and Inkatha are popular in white South African business circles for their vocal endorsement of capitalism; and to many white South Africans, and some black, Buthelezi is seen as a beacon of hope for a moderate future. Chief Buthelezi, in addition, is extremely sensitive to any comment, be it ever so mild, which he feels might impair either his or his organisation's dignity.

Inkatha is organised like a pyramid: members at the base; above them are local Inkatha branches; then regional committees, and so on up the echelons to the apex, which point is reserved for the president, Chief Buthelezi himself.

The armed Inkatha members who have been involved in the Pietermaritzburg fighting are known as vigilantes both by themselves and by their detractors. To the latter, Inkatha vigilantes are part of a phenomenon which became common in the South Africa of the 1980s. Vigilantes are organised, violent groups of men who espouse conservative political views and are committed to the destruction of all progressive organisations and individuals. These vigilantes act either in collusion with the police or on their own, with the police apparently turning a blind eye to their activities.

In describing themselves as vigilantes, however, Inkatha members mean that they are merely sober citizens, forced, on those occasions when police protection proves inadequate, to defend themselves against attacks by radicals.

Of the two definitions, the first is more widespread.

Vigilante leaders are drawn from a variety of sources: Inkatha members with a particular penchant and talent for combat; chairmen of local Inkatha branches; as well as chiefs of rural areas and their indunas, or headmen. Chiefs and indunas are salaried civil servants paid by the government of KwaZulu, and as such are also members of Inkatha. These Inkatha leaders are generally known as warlords because they command armies of men and exact allegiance and obedience on roughly feudal lines: in return for military loyalty the warlords provide their men with money, food, drink and some political assistance such as the granting of licences and the favourable allocation of land. Officially, Inkatha denounces the use of the word 'warlord', declaring it to be a heinous insult coined by the enemies of Inkatha for propaganda purposes. Unofficially, there have been alternative reports that the warlords themselves are secretly rather proud of and gratified by the label. When confronted with it, their manner of denial is more self-deprecatory than outraged and insulted. The fraternity of warlords, however, is not completely unified. There have been reports of fighting between different groups of vigilantes and rumours of bad feeling among their leaders.

Allied to the vigilante forces of Inkatha are the members of the United Workers' Union of South Africa (UWUSA), the trade-union arm of Inkatha. UWUSA is at perennial loggerheads with COSATU, its older, larger and stronger rival. Although UWUSA members have attacked and been attacked by COSATU members, as a separate political entity UWUSA has played little role in the Pietermaritzburg conflict.

On 24 February 1988, neither Inkatha nor UWUSA was banned or restricted.

In this conflict the police constitute a third force. The police have deployed hundreds of men in the Pietermaritzburg area, dividing their forces between ordinary policemen on patrol, stationed at police stations in Pietermaritzburg and outlying areas; riot police; security police; and special constables. The last-mentioned are known by everyone except the police themselves as *kitskonstabels,* or 'instant constables'. This faintly derisive nomenclature derives from the fact that the *kitskonstabels* receive just six weeks' training before being sent out into the townships 'to maintain law and order'.

Given that their function is to keep the peace between the major antagonists, the police have done a remarkably poor job. Since September 1987 over two thousand people have died in the Natal Midlands, and the average number of deaths per month is still on the rise. To many people this implies not just bad policing, but an actual policy of keeping the pot on the boil. The allegations of police collusion with Inkatha against the UDF are legion. Both Inkatha and the police deny these accusations of complicity and bad faith – Inkatha, in fact, accuses the police of siding with the UDF against *them* – and yet the reports continue to come in of police escorting vigilante armies, of warlords briefly arrested and then released, of complaints against Inkatha being neglected or ignored. Activists point out that Inkatha vigilantes seem to be completely immune from detention, that Inkatha rallies somehow do not contravene regulations pertaining to illegal gatherings, and that Inkatha, of all the anti-apartheid organisations in the country, has not been affected by the state of emergency except in the positive sense of benefiting from the disarray of its rivals.

Political pundits tend to characterise the war as one between Inkatha–UWUSA and the UDF–COSATU, with the police as more or less cynical outsiders. Inkatha, in the main, holds with this description. In their official statements they interpret the fighting as part of an ANC-orchestrated strategy to destroy them. The UDF, however, rejects this analysis as being far too glib. Activists see the war as one between Inkatha–the police and all non-Inkatha organisations and individuals. The war is part of an Inkatha strategy to eliminate all progressive organisations in Natal. Whether the state is actively promoting, or actively abetting this enterprise, is a question left open.

The UDF explains its reading of the situation on the basis that although many UDF–COSATU supporters have been killed over the past two years, most of those attacked by Inkatha have been apolitical township residents as well as a number of passive Inkatha supporters. Anyone who is UDF, anyone with a family connection to the UDF, no matter how remote, anyone not prepared to register with Inkatha and take up arms on its behalf, is considered a hostile enemy meriting punishment.

John Aitchison, head of the Centre for Adult Education at UNP, has produced a statistical study which supports the contention that most of those killed have not been directly connected to either of the opposing parties. Aitchison has numbered the dead and found that between January 1988 and March 1990, altogether 1 753 people were killed, of whom a large majority were either comrades or non-aligned individuals who, the UDF claims, were slain by vigilantes simply because they were not supporters of Inkatha.

★   ★   ★

I took these notes and tacked them to the pinboard behind my head. It was a start at least, but having a rough idea of who, still told me little about how or why.

PART II
War zones

2
An unofficial war

'So is it really a war? Or is that just a rhetorical device?'

I was in Johannesburg talking to people about Pietermaritzburg. I was trying to explain something about the townships, that it was not a case of normal life plus some fighting, but that 'some fighting' had become normal life. They wanted to know whether the conflict could be characterised as a civil war, or whether that was simply sensational journalism designed to capture attention.

I could provide no straight answer to the question. By definition the fighting in the Pietermaritzburg area is a war because it is an armed conflict for political dominance, a fight for political and ideological power between two warring parties. Both sides are contending for territorial sovereignty although the stakes are necessarily limited; they are not challenging the state. But it is evident that the outcome of this war will have an impact on whatever post-apartheid state eventually does emerge, and so in a sense the parties are taking out political insurance for the future.

On the other hand, where are the generals, the weapons, the long-term strategies, the standing armies? The Inkatha warlords are like mini-generals in command of small troops of bodyguards cum vigilantes, but in the main, armies are mobilised spontaneously to deal with discrete situations and disband automatically after the immediate battle is over. There is an overall objective – to take control of the region – but neither side employs any consistent military strategy. On the UDF side, leaders and strategists are neutralised by Inkatha or the police before they can really place their stamp on the conduct of the war. The war itself is a case of attack and reaction; attack and retaliation. Every incident makes some sense at the micro level, but at the macro level matters are less clear.

'Calling it a war or not has less to do with semantic precision than with one's political and cultural position,' I suggested. 'If you take most white South Africans, you find they have a pretty meagre idea of what's going on around Maritzburg. One of the reasons they're so uninformed is because of their reluctance to come to terms with the implications of the word "war". It's uncomfortable, it sticks in their throats and demands some kind of action, so they dismiss the fighting as a piece of intra-tribal feuding because that's easy and banal, and unthreatening. But it also reflects a specific cultural perception of war. Despite the war in Namibia and Angola and the pervasive ideology of militarism in the media and in advertising, most whites experience war vicariously and through a series of clichéd media images: war comics, war films – predominantly Vietnam movies these days – or clip shots on the TV news of Arab-colonial buildings in Beirut crumbling under mortar shells. There's always a sense that war is somewhere else, a foreign phenomenon which doesn't encroach on ordinary, normal life.'

'But what about the expansion of the security industry: guards in supermarkets, security patrols in every suburban street, every third person armed?' my interlocutors asked.

'That's a neurotic reflex, not a reflection of a state of war. The obsession with security is just the outward sign of a general sense of insecurity and unease. It's a buffer against random, rather than systematic, violence. You find the same thing in New York and other big cities. At a dinner party the other day a woman said to an American visitor who asked exactly that question: "Oh sure, we have a little crime, a little urban terrorism, but we're hardly at war!" She was right, of course, but the corollary is that when there is a real, live war like the one in Pietermaritzburg, whites don't recognise it. Like so much else pertaining to blacks in South Africa, it's invisible to them.

'The form of the war is too low key; the weapons are too crude. There are stones and iron bars instead of submachine guns, shotguns instead of ground-to-air missiles, and petrol bombs instead of carloads of Semtex plastic explosive. But the fact of the matter is that more people have died in Pietermaritzburg in the last eighteen months that in 20 years of fighting in Northern Ireland. That's why it's ridiculous to write off what's happening as faction fighting or gang warfare.'

'But isn't the violence at least containable?' I was asked.

'That's an easy fallacy. You may think so, and the police certainly think so, but to the people who live there, "containable" is just so much complacent garbage. Wars are won or lost, or they go stalemate like this one. If you contain a war it makes things easier for people outside – they feel more secure – but it doesn't do anything for the people on the inside.'

Back in Pietermaritzburg the next day I thought further about the problem of giving a name and a denotation to violence. For the groups involved, the description they employ is an entirely political choice. The police, for example, cannot tolerate having the situation around Pietermaritzburg described as a war. 'War' implies that there is a complete breakdown of the normal channels for defusing and controlling social conflict. In South Africa only the South African Defence Force is legally entitled to wage war and it is the role of the South African Police to prevent any other groups from doing so. Therefore to refer to an area of the country as a 'war zone' amounts to an explicit criticism of the police on the grounds of incompetence and a witting or unwitting failure to perform their proper functions.

Consequently the police use the word 'unrest' to describe political violence in black areas of the country. It is a weaker word than 'war', implying little more than the odd seethe and surge of discontent, easily managed – nothing to worry about. In Pietermaritzburg's townships and outlying rural areas such discontent shows little sign of abating. This means either that the police are not able to manage the unrest, or that managing it meant allowing it to continue. Groups with scant respect or admiration for the police are inclined to condemn them on these grounds.

Not surprisingly, Brigadier Büchner, erstwhile head of the security police in Pietermaritzburg, has a different line on the matter. He believes that even the word 'unrest' is too strong as a description of the current situation. 'By March 1988 major unrest-related conflict had been brought under control,' he told me. 'What we are seeing now is a cycle of retribution and revenge which accounts for the monthly death rate of 40 people a month – let's not quibble, call it 50 people. Now this is criminal violence, it's no longer politically motivated, so by rights it should not appear in the unrest reports at all.'

The state does its best to ignore the existence of this embarrassing war, and its effect on the population of the region is consequently neglected by the authorities. This is an unofficial war and as a result is treated as such by the state. Glib expressions of concern, short-term efforts at containment, and a generally lackadaisical attitude to the most serious political eruption in South Africa in decades indicate an official indifference to the whole affair; an indifference which can easily be interpreted as contempt for the victims. The hundreds of people who have died do not excite pity or self-examination in official circles; they are cyphers, existing only as figures in the official unrest reports. What the government wishes is to prevent its white constituency from discovering that it has allowed a full-scale war to occur within the borders of the country for two years and more.

While the propaganda purposes behind the official account are patently transparent, those behind the accounts of the UDF–COSATU and Inkatha are only slightly less so. Conversely, they do describe the conflict as a war, but each takes this position to emphasise the rampant political authoritarianism of the other. Chief Buthelezi believes Inkatha to be the victim of unwarranted warlike aggression of other black groups intent on its destruction. In a composite interview reprinted in the first volume of the 1988 edition of *Clarion Call*, the official journal of Inkatha, Buthelezi pointed out that 'there will, of course, be little prospect of peace as long as certain individuals and organisations are committed to annihilating

Inkatha. Inkatha believes it has the right to defend itself. We will not be intimidated out of existence. I am a black leader leading in the midst of violence. I am a leader of angry people.'

By 'certain individuals and organisations', Chief Buthelezi obviously meant the UDF and COSATU, both taking direction from an expatriate group whom he calls 'the external mission of the ANC'. Both the UDF and COSATU see themselves as the victim of an unprovoked and hideous aggression at the hands of Inkatha warlords and vigilantes. Writing in the February 1988 edition of the *South African Labour Bulletin*, a collective of Pietermaritzburg activists said this: 'As violence escalated in the Pietermaritzburg region during 1987, it became clear that Inkatha vigilantes were determined to smash progressive organisations and to establish themselves, by force if necessary, as the only organisation with mass membership in the region.'

Earlier, in November 1987, COSATU and the UDF were equally frank about the responsibility for the war, declaring in a joint memorandum: 'The overwhelming majority of the violence is perpetrated by Inkatha-supporting vigilantes. They are responsible for what is literally a "reign of terror" in the townships.'

Perhaps it is this similarity of outraged rebuke by both major protagonists in the conflict which really convinces us that a war is being fought. In a war there are no aggressors; ostensibly no side ever initiates an attack or sets out to invade or destroy the enemy. If an attack is made, it is always 'retaliatory', otherwise both sides are simply defending themselves from their opponent's hostile depredations. The South African army itself is a case in point – even when it made cross-border pre-emptive strikes, or invaded sovereign states such as Angola, it was still known as the South African *Defence* Force.

These political and semantic considerations apart, there are ultimately two good reasons for describing the conflict as a war. The first is simply one of descriptive convenience. But the second and important reason is that any other word tends to trivialise and diminish the extent and effects of the conflict. In the townships, the people who actually have to live through it all talk with natural ease about 'being at war'. They have no political or ideological brief – they use the word because it fits their experience.

In the settlements around Pietermaritzburg residents do not have the luxury of experiencing war vicariously. Insecurity is not some neurotic indulgence but a fact of daily life, as palpable and inevitable as breathing. The people here have adapted their lives to the demands of the war. Alertness and caution inform every act.

The war is not a foreign phenomenon consigned to a distant border. In these ravaged areas the war zone is everywhere. Every road, ditch, yard, river, house and hillside is a war zone. Buses, taxis, privately owned cars, police vehicles – all these constitute arenas of battle. More than that, each person carries the war around with himself or herself, locked into a flowing core of hatred, or adrenalin, or concern, curiosity, pity, pomposity, hypocrisy, fear, or sheer grief. There is no escaping this war, it occupies no defined space or time, it does not knock off in the evenings or at weekends. Even areas which are relatively quiet know little peace. People there are in constant anticipation of the next attack – like a troubled sleeper hounded by some nocturnal dog, waiting for the next harsh and unrhythmical bark.

3
Coding and decoding

In the Pietermaritzburg townships the familiar, the safe, the everyday have become unfamiliar, dangerous and bizarre. Memories and expectations habitually associated with people or places are now suspect as old connotations become obsolete. The material world looks the same but that is partly illusion. In the same way, the old words are no longer sufficient and new ones are needed.

Comrades, with greater or lesser community backing, have taken it upon themselves to find the new terms, appropriate to their current circumstances. They have played havoc with the map of the region, renaming areas according to the political affiliation of the residents.

The theatre of operations in the present war occupies a space of approximately 374 square kilometres. Conflict has chiefly occurred in the Edendale valley west of the city, and in the adjoining rural area of Vulindlela, a part of KwaZulu which stretches far to the west and north of Edendale. With the exception of a brief period at the end of 1987, this vast region has always been an Inkatha stronghold.

At the mouth of the Edendale valley there are two large urban townships: Ashdown, with a population of 8 500, and Imbali, with a population of 35 000. Stretching along the valley is a complex of some twenty villages on freehold land. This is Edendale, and it is here primarily that the old names, the old means of identification, have been replaced.

Nhlanhla spread the map out across three desks pushed together. With one hand – long fingers splayed out like a piano player – he held the paper down, while the other picked its way across the surface from place to place. 'This was Harewood, now we call it Ulundi because it is Gatsha's territory, Inkatha is strong there. But here, where it is Dambuza, we call it Angola because it is a UDF area and this is the name of a popular anti-apartheid country. Now we call Nhlazatshe by the name of Sharpeville, and the comrades in Smeroe and Georgetown call their place Tanzania. Macibisa is Lusaka, Pata is Maputo and Wilgefontein is Cuba; Taylor's Halt is also Cuba.'

White South Africans might find these names fanciful, or even alarming. On the tongues of the township residents they sit easily and are used unselfconsciously. It is not mandatory to use them but many people choose to do so. These new names provide the comrades and residents of the townships with a sense of reassurance, perhaps spurious, but nonetheless felt.

Writing in the *Weekly Mail* in January 1988, Lakela Kaunda says the following:

Some youths are keen to return to normal life.

Those at Siyanda Secondary School in Mpumuza, near Sweetwaters, are a good example. After hearing rumours that their school may not re-open next week, the pupils quickly convened a meeting and convinced their parents that they were prepared to return to school.

The following day they cleaned the lawn and fixed the broken windows, but not before renaming the school 'Tanzania High'.

They have since been informed by the school inspector that the school is definitely open.

At least not everything that happens in our Pietermaritzburg is negative these days.

In this instance 'normal life' is equated with 'Tanzania High'. Under its old title, the school had been a site of conflict and insecurity for students, but in changing its name they scrubbed away the old, negative associations and reappropriated it.

The imposition of a new name attempts to create a new reality, one which cancels the previous experience and inserts, in its place, a new, ordered environment.

*   *   *

But life for the township residents is not uniformly oppressive and distressing and people are not without levity, nor have they lost their sense of irony. There is a section of Ashdown which lies near the Duze River – the houses are separated from the filthy and polluted water by an intractable buffer of thorns, rocks and sharp flints – which is known as 'Beachfront'. In a state of war it is not just the names of places that undergo change; people too discover, generally to their dissatisfaction, that they have been branded with new terms of identification. Khaba Mkhize, editor of the *Echo* supplement to the *Natal Witness*, and self-confessed raconteur about the townships, takes this phenomenon very seriously indeed. 'What is the fighting about in Maritzburg?' he poses. 'Politics? Forget it. The thrust of the war is still the same: senseless butchering over name labels.' According to Mkhize, the momentum of the war has been sustained long after its natural, political life by the practice among the antagonists of insulting and taunting each other beyond endurance.

Colloquially, the comrades are called the *amaqabane*. This is a Xhosa word denoting friend or comrade. Both sides use this word, first coined, in fact, by the comrades themselves. The Zulu word *amaqaba* meaning barbarian, sounds similar, but its usage is not widespread, nor has it sullied the positive associations with which many township residents have invested the word *amaqabane*.

By contrast, the comrades have coined a range of insulting terms for their Inkatha enemies. The most widely used, and the one most likely to provoke a state of rage in the person thus labelled, is *theleweni*, meaning 'the one who pours us over a cliff'. In many instances, when Inkatha members have laid waste to people and places, they claim to have been provoked by this insult.

Another taunt which the vigilantes particularly dislike is *klova*. Even Mkhize, a township etymologist second to none, is not entirely sure of the meaning or provenance of this word. 'Just listen to the way it sounds', he says. 'Try it out in your mouth. *KLova*. It's a violent combination of sounds. Look at the shape your lips make. They purse up in contempt or distaste. But if you say someone's a *klova* you also mean he's a fool, or rather a bumpkin, an unsophisticate, someone who swallows his toothpaste because he doesn't know better. When the *amaqabane* call Inkatha people *klova*, they mean they're like children, they haven't grown up to the twentieth century yet.

'And I've forgotten to mention the *asilutho*', he continued, 'the fence-sitters. It means "we are nothing." Both sides don't like that. It's better to keep quiet and say nothing than to say you are *asilutho*.'

Inkatha does not participate in the name game. They do not rename their areas, nor have they a repertoire of choice invective with which to malign their opponents. Inkatha has repeatedly stressed this asymmetry which neatly juxtaposes, in their view, their own good intentions with the *mala fides* of the comrades. The comrades, not surprisingly, are not impressed with this argument. In their view the level of threat faced by the two sides is not equal, so the need for Inkatha to find names to demarcate friendly from unfriendly territory is not as great. As for the insults, Nhlanhla laughed and gestured ironically: 'It's not our fault they have no imagination,' he said.

In fact the taunts and the reactions they provoke are not a particularly humorous aspect of the war. Wendy Leeb, a researcher at UNP, makes a sombre observation in this regard. 'Young people, and I have seen children three years old doing this, will suddenly and inexplicably seek out those who threaten them. The only explanation I can offer, and it is based on personal observation and questioning, is that the stress of being afraid becomes too much and there is a feeling of "let's get it over with." So you'll find children deliberately going out of their way to taunt and provoke the enemy, milking a situation for its maximum danger. It's a terrifying fatalism. Of course a lot of them don't even know what the words mean, but they know what effect they will have.'

In any war the protagonists establish a series of codes exclusive to themselves which are used to define and distinguish the different antagonists from one another. Using a certain code (a word, phrase or article of clothing), or failing to employ that code when confronted by one group or another, may be considered a hostile act.

In his book *Another Day of Life*, Ryszard Kapuściński, the Polish foreign correspondent and writer, describes a journey from Luanda to Benguela in Angola in October 1975, the month before independence from Portugal was granted. At that time the battling forces of UNITA, the FNLA and the MPLA were spread out haphazardly across the countryside. The road to Benguela was controlled at various places by one side or another. At each point of control the soldiers established a roadblock. Kapuściński describes the traveller's dilemma as one of recognition and greeting: first you had to identify which force had control of the roadblock, and then greet them correctly, using the mode of address sanctioned by that force. This was particularly difficult as the soldiers from all three rival armies looked the same and wore no insignia of identification. Consequently the greeting became a gamble, a verbal Russian roulette. Get the word wrong and you die.

Kapuściński describes one such gamble. Knees buckling with fear, heart in his mouth, he made his guess and mumbled the word, '*Camarada!*'

If the sentries are Agostinho Neto's people, who salute each other with the word *camarada*, we will live. But if they turn out to be Holden Roberto's or Jonas Savimbi's people, who call each other *irmao* (brother), we have reached the limit of our earthly existence. In no time they will put us to work – digging our own graves. In front of the old, established checkpoints there are little cemeteries of those who had the misfortune to greet the sentries with the wrong word.

While their experiences may be a little less vivid – there are no makeshift cemeteries at the roadside, for example – the residents in the townships around Pietermaritzburg share this feeling of helplessness, this sense that one's life is a guessing game with no set rules. White South Africans, for whom the exercise of language, the answering of questions and the daily round of comments and guesses hold no terrors, would be hard-pressed to imagine the sensation of pure terror, the knife-edge of adrenalin to the guts felt by a black South African in these townships when confronted by a hostile group and forced to account for himself. How can one begin to appreciate the feelings of a person whose life, thoughts, achievements count as nothing against the arbitrary cluster of words which constitutes his or her response? The first answer is the one that counts, and there is no second chance.

In an article in *Frontline* magazine, in February 1988, Khaba Mkhize describes an uncanny encounter with a friend.

Yesterday as I was knocking off a man was waiting for me. He pleaded earnestly: 'I know Mkhize you know many contacts. Can you organise me a baby's hand [a gun]?'

He explained, 'It is dangerous to walk at night. Look, today I will be knocking off at 8.00 p.m. and how safe will I be? Where I stay you meet someone at night who greets you "Qabane, Qabane, heyta!"

'Whatever you do you may receive a bullet hole. Some people who are not comrades now masquerade as comrades. But if you deny you are a qabane then you are in trouble if the strangers are in fact comrades. To be silent is also dangerous, because each side interprets that as insolence. To say nothing is futile. It means you are impimpi (informer) for the other group.'

One morning, in their office in the *Natal Witness* building, I asked Khaba Mkhize and his colleague Lakela Kaunda whether they had any more to say on the subject. 'OK, it doesn't even have to be a confrontation situation,' said Mkhize. 'Say you're in a taxi, no hostility, no bad vibes, but you happen to make a comment about "Gatsha." If you're in a Kombi full of Inkatha people you're finished. To them he's Inkosi Mangosuthu G Buthelezi, Shenge for short. If you're with *qabane*, you're all right. The moral is that unless you know who's who, you just shut up and sit tight.'

'Perhaps less so now, but certainly for many months the fear was constant,' Lakela confirmed. From the clutter on the desk she excavated an article of hers which had appeared in the *Natal Witness* in February 1988. 'Listen to this – Mr Thulani Mgaga of Mpumuza laments: "When we are at work we pray that the knocking off time does not come. When it is time to go home you drag yourself to the bus stop. As you alight at home you wonder and fear what will confront you. When the sun sets, you feel tears well in your eyes for you do not know whether you are next on the list or not." '

She set the article aside and continued: 'But times have changed a little. We shouldn't go overboard about the confusion. These days people can read the signs, the little details that save people – or kill them. If you're careful you can tell who belongs to what. For example, T-shirts. The *qabane* wear yellow T-shirts with UDF or COSATU slogans on them. Inkatha people wear khaki, or sometimes UWUSA T-shirts. Of course you don't want to get caught wearing the wrong clothes in the wrong area.' She shuffled the papers in front of her and came up with an old copy of *Echo*. 'Take this letter – Mrs Mabuyi Shenge (she's an Inkatha member) writes: "I have seen *amaqabane* beat up Inkatha members and tear UWUSA T-shirts off women's bodies and they had to go topless in the city." But it happens on both sides; for example, a young man was killed in Ashdown in 1987, only because he was wearing a UDF shirt.

'You can also learn a lot from manner of speech, how people talk to each other. If you speak deep Zulu you are Inkatha, but the *amaqabane* speak *tsotsi taal* (English, Afrikaans, some Zulu, some slang words from God knows where) and they greet each other with *Heytha!*'

I checked up on this concise greeting and found that at one point *Heytha!* was a standard way of hailing friends and acquaintances in the townships, but has now become so loaded with political implications that it is used with circumspection. Similarly, the toyi-toyi, a foot-stomping chant of songs and slogans which groups of people give expression to as they snake their way about the townships, has become an ambiguous symbol. In the past it was an expression of vigour, of resistance and of hope but now it heralds more warfare, more bloodshed. The toyi-toyi is particularly associated with the *amaqabane*, but Inkatha members use it as well, the two forms being distinguished by the slogans shouted. 'If you're wise you don't wait to find out who's on the march, you just run for cover. You never know if you could be a target or not,' Lakela said.

These words, slogans, mannerisms and modes of dress colour the lives of people living in the townships. In general these new forms of speech and behaviour evolve spontaneously with the exigencies of the conflict, but at times they are simply the product of a macho bravado.

'Bravado?' said Nhlanhla, when I suggested this to him; 'sure, maybe, but it helps us beat fear.'

4
Streetwise

It should be clear that nowadays in the townships one has to be streetwise in order to survive. But 'streetwise' is not just an over-used catchphrase. Streets and roads in particular assume an importance undreamt of by the urban planners who first set them down. They no longer serve merely as routes of access from A to B, but now demarcate and enclose areas of political control. Artificial, administrative boundaries established for reasons long forgotten, unchallenged and unnoticed, now take on a new and macabre material reality. Lines on a map – postal routes – grow invisible walls and become fortresses. Geography is not just a description of physical terrain, but yet another code which has to be learned, remembered and observed. Areas into which, two years ago, people would pass without a second thought, now become alien and threatening. It can be dangerous to visit old friends and neighbours who live nearby but nonetheless across a boundary line. Maintaining friendships involves a calculated risk.

In this territorial war different areas fall under the sway of one or other of the warring parties, separated sometimes by a whole hillside of rural land, but more often by a road or even a track. Consequently the business of living becomes a highly self-conscious activity. All the old certainties that regulate social activity are undermined. Even the simplest tasks and decisions become matters for careful contemplation; people have to pick their way gingerly through a morass of considerations and caveats. Quite as debilitating as the insecurity enveloping such a life is the sheer aggravation and inconvenience of it. Residents have to remember who controls which area (for patterns of control are unstable and tend to shift disconcertingly and without warning) and by extension they must be judicious in their choice of route when moving through the townships or going into Pietermaritzburg.

The first months of the war were spent in fighting to establish which side held control over which area. In a few regions it was clear from the first which political grouping held the upper hand but for the most part active Inkatha members, supporters of the UDF and COSATU as well as a majority of non-aligned people had previously lived together without much friction. As the war escalated, this liberal, tolerant attitude became untenable when Inkatha and the UDF launched themselves at each other and the community at large discovered that neutrality was not an option.

A struggle for political control developed in each area, culminating in victory for one or other side when the enemy abandoned houses and possessions and fled to safer regions. In some cases whole townships fell under the sway of a single party. When this happened the large arterial roads linking the different townships were converted into boundaries, a no man's land along which people could move, but not cross.

At the height of the war in 1987–8, tension between some adjacent areas became so intense that residents from each enclave found themselves unable to cross the separating road simply to stand at the bus stop on the opposite side. As a result all commuters from one area, whether going into or away from town, had to take the same bus. At certain times of day whole busloads of people would be carried miles away from their intended destination before they reached a relatively safe area in which they could alight, cross the road, and wait for a different bus to come along, one that would take them back past their homes, in the right direction.

Where Inkatha or the UDF occupied areas on each side of a major road, commuters of the other party found themselves in a difficult position. Even if passengers were free at their point of departure to take the bus from whichever side of the road they chose, they were not free to make a single uncomplicated journey from one point to another. If the road ran through an especially hostile and dangerous area they would change buses to make a detour around the danger zone.

Clearly a road which belongs to one side alone is a valuable asset, slowing and handicapping the enemy, but for the most part access routes in the townships are uneasy buffer zones, under pressure, but controlled by neither side.

In some townships neither side was able to establish control. Instead a stalemate was reached and the area was divided up into small yet very specific spheres of power. In Imbali, Inkatha tried to wrest complete control of the township but without success. Here the boundaries between the two sides are no more than the narrow, pitted sand roads, perhaps partially tarred, which wind through the township. Unlike the broad band of asphalt which maintains a substantial physical distance between parties on either side of a main linking road, these thin strips of sand and stone are under constant attack, and control shifts regularly from one side to the other. Patrols rove along the margins at night, ready to call out their respective armies at short notice.

The inability of the two sides to penetrate enemy territory meant more than ever that the boundary roads came under attack as the field of operations was restricted to the borders and the fiercest battles were waged up and down roads, rather than within residential areas. In addition, this gave the two sides the added advantage of using cars, buses and taxis as vehicles of war.

5

The people's car

As a corollary of the military importance of roads, modes of transport become war zones in themselves. Cars, taxis and buses can be alternatively weapons or targets of attack. Some cars are involved simply because of their colour. For example, any yellow vehicle is associated with the police and is therefore automatically suspect. On one occasion a researcher in Shongweni, unwisely driving a yellow Toyota, stopped a child to ask directions. The frightened child said, 'Why do you ask me this? Your people are going there already.' Disappearing up the road was the yellow back-door of a police van, metal grill banging as the vehicle cornered sharply.

Colour aside, cars take on an identity of their own and become well known or infamous around the townships, depending on the political notoriety of their owners. For example, Khaba Mkhize regards himself as a top candidate for political assassination. Mkhize's political fortune fluctuates with his editorials and at one point few days would pass without a group of Inkatha members or UDF comrades confronting him about this or that offensive sentence. In order to emphasise the tenuousness of his daily existence Mkhize says, 'Look, times are tough. You have to do your job, and you have to preserve yourself so you can do it. In eighteen months I've changed my car fourteen times. After a month, maybe two, I get nervous. Who's out there watching? Maybe I hear a warning, saying, "Khaba, watch out, be careful how you drive, where you go." Then I go to a friend and I say, "Look, man, please help me out here. Give me your car, take mine." We swop; I can relax just a little bit and then it's time to change again.'

Not all car owners are as much in the public eye as Mkhize, however. 'I can put it this way, first you get the private individuals with their cars. There's nothing so special about that. If we need a lift, maybe we ask them but no one pays much notice. They drive to work, they come home. ...' As we paused at the red light, Nhlanhla, in the passenger seat of the blue Honda, sat forward and picked at the Third Party sticker in the left corner of the windscreen. We were on our way into Edendale and Nhlanhla was taking the opportunity to enlighten me on the subject of transport.

'Does that mean that these people can drive around freely wherever they want to go?' I asked.

'There's a war on,' he replied sharply. 'If you live in one place you can't just drive over to visit the enemy unless you want to give them your car as a free gift. But if you understand me, what I am saying is that these people do not fright too much, their cars will not be burnt in the night. But there are some cars which everybody knows are comrade cars and Inkatha will try to destroy them as much as possible. The area must be very safe before you can park such a car. Now with Inkatha, the warlords drive fancy vehicles. If you see them coming you run unless you have protection. And these warlords don't drive alone, there are always two or three cars with them for the transport of vigilantes. These guys kill from inside their cars; they just lean out and shoot through the window. Sometimes they pick people up in the street and force them into their cars. "Come for a little drive with me, bra," they say. You find the body next day in the veld. But likewise, you don't take your car into Inkatha places, not even to drive through.'

'But surely a car offers some protection,' I commented naively.

Nhlanhla ticked off his points: 'First, they can stone; then they can stop you with the roadblock, but anyway you can't move fast along the roads, especially where it's rural.' His point was well made. Along those rural tracks, more hole than road, a mob could surround, shatter and gut a car before it had picked its way through the first rut.

'And what about taxis?' I asked. 'Do they take sides or are they neutral?' We were moving again and unwittingly I found myself at the centre of a complex tapestry of Kombi taxis, braking, overtaking and weaving in and out from lane to lane.

Nhlanhla nodded and clicked his fingers. 'The Zolas are one other thing completely,' he said emphatically. 'Zola' is the colloquial term used by black commuters when speaking of the new wave of black taxis which emerged as the key urban transport phenomenon in the South Africa of the late 1980s. 'Zola' refers to the Free State athlete Zola Budd and is something of a back-handed compliment. Nhlanhla explained it as follows: 'So you see, first it is because they are very speedy like Zola, but then it is also because they always try to take on too much and the third reason is because they knock people down.'

Returning to the political affiliations of taxi drivers, he commented, 'The most they want is to stay away from the war, but how can they do that? They like to say, "Anybody can ride anywhere in my taxi as long as he pays," but this is not possible. So it all depends on where he lives and whether that place is Inkatha or UDF.'

We drove past the turn-off to Imbali. The Edendale road broadened into a double-lane highway with a wide grassy strip separating east- and west-bound traffic. 'Like in Imbali,' he continued, gesturing through the window to the invisible township on our left. 'At first there were Inkatha and UDF taxis there, but now it's just Inkatha.'

'Were they chased out?'

He shrugged. 'Some of them, but most of them just changed sides.'

Past the ugly red-brick fortress that is Edendale Hospital on the left, and past Plessislaer Police Station hidden in the gum trees on the right, we turned left onto a dirt road. The junction was marked by a small store, its entrance obscured by children and rusty metal advertising hoardings. A group of people, one a black policeman, sat outside on a railing, passing round a litre of Coke. 'He's from Plessislaer, he's all right,' Nhlanhla said. We began to climb, moving into Dambuza, an established UDF strong-hold. As we slowed at a turning a gold Mercedes Benz pulled ahead and disappeared behind a screen of dust and flying mud. 'Inkatha,' said Nhlan-hla laconically.

'Is that a warlord?'

'Just an Imbali councillor. He changes cars often, but he's had this one quite a few months.'

'I thought Dambuza was a no-go area for Inkatha,' I said.

'I don't know where he's going,' Nhlanhla replied without interest. 'Or if he'll get there,' he added.

We stopped so he could greet some friends. The unfamiliar vehicle drew cautious stares from the crowds on the roads who moved in thick bands and parted with reluctance to let cars through. 'Now, there,' he said, pointing to a nondescript Toyota coming towards us, 'that's security police. Check the aerial. But I know this car and these guys. They always come here, I don't know what they think.'

'Do you know all the Security Branch cars in the townships?'

'Sure, in Edendale, Ashdown, Dambuza, we know them. We also know what clothes they wear, which one has a suede jacket, which one wears brown leather, which one has a moustache, which one has a red face. And the black security police, we know them too — very well.'

Just as township residents grow to know the vehicles of the security police, so the police in their turn learn to identify cars too, especially those used by comrades. However, whereas the latter gather information over time and through bitter experience, the security police favour a more direct approach. In the last week of February 1989, a group of activists from Ashdown drove a white Golf to New Prison in Pietermaritzburg, intending to visit a comrade held there in detention. As they arrived a white security policeman (in a blue suit and brown tie) detached himself from his colleagues and came over to the car. He leaned in at the driver's window: 'Who's the owner of this car?'

The driver was not prepared to divulge this information. 'No one. This is a People's Car,' he said defiantly. The policeman laughed and moved away.

Coincidentally, that very night, as the white Golf was returning along the Duze River to Ashdown, a bus driven by a well-known warlord came up fast from behind and pulled in sharply to cut it off. The driver of the Golf braked and swerved to the left, taking the car down a short slope and into the river. There were two adults and three children, all younger than 10, in the passenger seats. As they scrambled out they were set upon by a group of men wielding knobkerries and whips. Above the swish of the sjambok, and the cries of pain and alarm, the assailants' shouts and taunts sounded loudly: 'Whose car is this? Where's your People's Car now? We'll finish your shit for you, *qabane*!'

$$\star \qquad \star \qquad \star$$

Finally, there is the phenomenon of the burnt car. This is a familiar sight around the townships – immobile carcasses of machines. They are further casualties of war; an act of destruction designed to complete the ruination of the enemy. Often the cars are looted before they are burned: wheels, engines, seats, sometimes even windscreens are removed, leaving only the chassis to blister and buckle in the intense heat. Many residents live lightly now. Their belongings are scant, their needs few. Dispossession and devastation occur overnight and people do not have money to burn.

6

The last trump sounds
at the Pietermaritz Street bus depot

Friday night in the Edendale valley. Out among the hills sounds of music and laughter came lightly pitched through the darkness. Most people were already home; there was a hot weekend ahead. But Phineas Mdluli, a bus driver working for the Sizanani Mazulu Transport Company, was on shift. He brought his few passengers out along the rural roads of Vulindlela, and by the time he turned off the main road and drove slowly down the track to the Taylor's Halt depot the bus was empty. In the cabin, Mdluli drank a cup of tea and listened to the day's news on the radio. A mechanic with bleary, stinging eyes pumped diesel into the tank. Mdluli called up the Pietermaritz Street depot on the walkie-talkie. 'Leaving now,' he said, swinging himself up into the driver's cab. Four elderly women boarded and settled themselves near the front, first checking that their seats were not torn or loose, and a number of other passengers climbed aboard as Mdluli prepared to set off.

Mdluli drove smoothly; the women chatted. At Gibson's Gate two cars pulled out from the shoulder of the road as the bus went past. Mdluli noted the lights in his rear-view mirror. The cars began to accelerate until they were sitting tight on his tail. One car pulled out as if to overtake. Mdluli lost sight of it but when it reappeared out of his blind spot he could see at once that it was too close. He pulled over to the left but the car stayed with him, forcing him onto the sandy verge. He felt his tyres spin but he accelerated and managed to pull the bus into the centre of the road. The cars dropped back momentarily but were on him again like crocodiles.

At KwaMadlala a group of men had erected a roadblock. They stood beside their lanterns laughing and waiting for the bus to plough into the bollards and scrap metal strewn across the road. Mdluli reacted fast; he pulled the bus round in a tight U-turn, almost overturning as he did so. The two cars stayed with him and forced him off the main road onto a pitted sand track leading up into the hills. The bus was light and unbalanced and it bounced in and out of ruts and potholes like a golf ball. Mdluli could see practically nothing now. He was driving by instinct and moreover he knew that the road ended soon and there was nowhere to turn. The white car on his left flank pulled alongside him — it was sleek and fast and manouevred easily.

The first bullet smashed his window and the second killed him. The bus ran down an embankment out of control and overturned at speed. The cars sped off and the hysterical passengers worked themselves out of the bus with difficulty. Mdluli was splayed across his seat and the driver's cabin stank with the smell of blood.

A year later, in the back seat of my car, Ephraim, Mdluli's friend and colleague, told me the story. His eyes were blank and he picked at his teeth with his one long nail which jutted from his left-hand baby finger. Otherwise his nails were pared down to the quick. 'What about the police?' I asked lamely.

'The police. ...' He located some particle that had been eluding him, positioned it on the end of his tongue and spat it out of the window expressively.

Jacob, sitting next to him, finished the sentence. 'The police claimed that he was transporting a mob and that this was "retaliation." But this is rubbish if you check the ticket sales, he was only carrying a few people. No one has been charged or even arrested. Everyone believes that the induna David Ntombela was involved – people recognised the car as his car – but he's too powerful. The police won't challenge him.'

I had driven to the Pietermaritz Street depot at noon. I was looking for Ephraim, a shop steward with the Transport and General Workers' Union, a COSATU affiliate. He had driven buses along the streets of the townships for years and there were questions I wanted to ask him. The lazy guard at the gate was bored by my enquiries and sent me inside past rows of parked white-and-green buses to the reception desk. Ephraim, accompanied by two other men, found me quickly and led me back outside. He scratched his thick wrestler's neck with his fingernail and explained that there was a problem. 'We need a safe place to talk,' he said. 'We're off shift but management might start asking questions if they know you're talking to us.'

The three men tossed around alternative venues for a while but we finally settled on my car, parked discreetly down the approach road. They chose to sit cramped in the back while I twisted my neck round from the driver's seat to listen, my notebook balanced on the handbrake. The third man picked a copy of the *Weekly Mail* off the passenger seat and read the paper until he fell asleep. Ephraim and Jacob shared the talking.

'I can say that bus drivers are important,' Ephraim began, 'not because I want to brag about myself but because without the bus drivers people can't move. They can't get to work or go home.'

'Which is where the trouble started,' said Jacob.

'It's just as he says,' Ephraim affirmed. 'The first thing that happened was the stayaway, I think it was in June—'

'May,' Jacob cut in.

'Thank you. In May the UDF and COSATU called for a stayaway to boycott the whites-only election. It was very successful but Inkatha and their running dog, UWUSA, tried to get people to ignore it. The point is that we ourselves went on stayaway which meant that there was no transport into town, so Inkatha blamed us for the success and that's when the attacks started. But you can't understand these things without you understand your history. First off, UWUSA, the son of Inkatha, started recruiting people from among the drivers. I knew about this because I came to work and found people carrying guns on the company premises. They claimed that this was for protection, but protection from what? These are big boys; they don't need guns unless they're looking for a fight. Now, by any standards this is not acceptable, but these people were not fired. Most of this was happening out at Sweetwaters where Inkatha is very strong and where they can control a man's life like a dog on a chain.

'These UWUSA boys would abscond from the company on weekends and go on marches with Inkatha. At one point we got in reports that UWUSA people wearing company uniform were chasing kids. This could lead to problems with the UDF and with the whole community. I called a meeting, I spoke to them, I said: "Gentlemen, you are putting all of us in trouble by doing these things." They insulted my name and walked away.'

Jacob nodded. 'I can say myself that what Ephraim says to you is true. During that month of May and for months after that, bus drivers were attacked again and again – shot, stabbed, stoned, beaten, threatened... . This is not an easy job because if I can put it to you like this, you have a duty to your passengers and you have a duty to your family if only to stay alive. In May two drivers were shot. One UWUSA member was killed at 5 in the morning down at East Street. All the UWUSA people left their jobs, and after that we noticed that Inkatha cars were following buses, and of course when that happens it is just a matter of time before the blood starts flowing. They wanted us to stop operating, to sour our relations with the community, but we cannot be intimidated.'

'Perhaps you don't realise', Ephraim said in accusing tones made the more harsh by the deep gravel of his voice, 'that these people were our colleagues, they were our friends. It is not easy to look down the barrel of your friend's gun.'

'One of our drivers was beaten up, left paralysed early in the morning,' Jacob resumed, 'so drivers who were off shift began riding escort on the buses. We would sit in the front, in passenger seats near the driver, and watch everyone who came on board. If anyone started to threaten the driver or the other passengers, or if we could see he was armed, we would throw him off the bus. If he got hurt we could not help it. Sometimes the passengers would react spontaneously to protect the driver if someone was causing trouble. Then we started having problems with the police. They would stop all buses and search for weapons. They confiscated assegais, knobkerries, pangas, bush knives – all our weapons of protection. What could we do? We had no guns.'

'As this gentleman has put it, it is quite true,' Ephraim confirmed.

The two men continued to speak for some time, passing their story back and forth like a soccer ball. Matters came to a head after the murder of Mdluli in January 1988. The drivers at Sizanani Mazulu Transport came out on strike on the grounds that their working conditions had become intolerable. As Ephraim put it, 'We had been patient a long time, but I don't choose to be a lamb to the slaughter.'

The drivers refused to drive through Zone 4, Vulindlela, an Inkatha stronghold where most of the attacks had occurred. After a one-day strike they confined themselves to working short hours, from 5 a.m. to 5 p.m. instead of the usual 3 a.m. to 10 p.m. working day. The management of KwaZulu Transport, the holding company, reacted by issuing all striking drivers with dismissal notices, but the initial uncompromising stance was softened after consultation with union representatives. 'It was fine words,' Ephraim said dismissively. He spat again through the window. 'Management agreed to put in bullet-proof windscreens, two-way radios in all buses, and they said they would ask the police for escorts and protection. So we went back to work. Of course none of this happened.'

Less than a week later, Patrick Magwaza, an off-duty driver, was shot at his home at Taylor's Halt. As his colleagues heard of the shooting they returned to the Taylor's Halt depot, handed in their equipment and left. The next day a meeting was called at Taylor's Halt. The drivers arrived wearing COSATU T-shirts. The meeting was hardly begun when a contingent of riot policemen arrived – young white men, loud and nervous. 'They took our names and the registration numbers of our cars,' said Ephraim. 'One of them came up to me, and with the barrel of his gun he pulled up my T-shirt so that the barrel and the shirt were right up under my nose. The meeting was disrupted, we all went home but I heard they stayed at the depot for hours, drinking and playing cards.'

Over the next week, few buses ran; workers walked. 'We wanted management to lay charges against David Ntombela, but they refused,' said Ephraim. 'They said it was a matter for "the authorities." Management was even saying to us that we brought the trouble on ourselves because Inkatha remembered the stayaway and this was their retaliation. They were talking as if we and UWUSA were just two sides in a soccer match, playing a game. And their attitude was the same as saying, "Come on. You're wasting time. Finish up quickly and get back to work."

'Tell me, is that something reasonable? At the end of the day, you see, management had us over a barrel. What could we do? Who can afford to lose his job these days? Apart from that, we don't like to make the community suffer because we are in danger. We refused to drive any Special Hires for Inkatha – you know, taking Inkatha people to rallies and so on, but management claimed they were losing money because of this, and last September we started again.'

'But that was a big mistake,' Jacob said gloomily. The third man snored softly.

'Why's that?' I asked. 'Did you start taking strain from the UDF because of it?'

Ephraim scraped his nail across his stubbly beard. 'I think we are walking on eggshells here,' he said at last. 'I need to consult with my colleagues first. Perhaps you could see me some other time.' He opened the car door, and he and Jacob left politely but without ceremony, taking their slumbering companion with them.

I contacted Ephraim a few days later but he still refused to discuss matters pertaining to COSATU and the UDF. This was fair enough and we made an arrangement to meet two weeks later for a tour of the depots. In the meantime I consulted other people and other sources and discovered that the relationship between COSATU bus drivers working for KwaZulu Transport and UDF comrades in the townships was not uncomplicated. The tension stemmed from the fact that although the drivers were sympathetic to the comrades, and shared a common adversary, the nature of their job required them to drive into Inkatha territory and to provide a service for Inkatha members.

In the days of the war when boundaries were tight and the battle lines drawn in indelible ink, this criss-crossing of borders by bus drivers was seen by certain comrades as treacherous behaviour. The comrades regarded the buses, the passengers and the drivers as fair game. This did not help the cause of political solidarity between the two groups, but in general the drivers have adopted a philosophical attitude towards those comrades who attack them. 'It's the difference between being caught in the crossfire and being the actual target,' said one driver who finally consented to comment on the matter.

The problem is that sitting in the midst of the crossfire is the most dangerous position of all. When a bus is under attack the wired-in driver's cabin provides scant protection even if the attackers claim only to be interested in the passengers. Furthermore, this explanation is disingenuous: there have been many occasions when the drivers have been singled out for attack, providing an example of what happens to neutrals in this conflict.

Sometimes comrades refused to pay the busfare. 'We don't pay money to KwaZulu,' they said scornfully. 'Gatsha is a rich man – he can give us a free ride.' Occasionally the *amaqabane* would hijack buses and demand to be taken to destinations of their choice. Some of these demands were acceptable to the driver and even the passengers, but others were not. In all cases the driver had to smile and consent.

In December 1988, in Macibisa, the *amaqabane* shot a driver in the head and carved up a passenger with long-bladed knives. The comrades issued an ultimatum to all drivers, warning them not to work outside the areas in which they resided. The nature of the reprisals remained implicit but were clear enough nonetheless. The *amaqabane* were anxious to close off the various areas as much as possible. This would restrict the passage of residents in their own strongholds, but more important, it would keep marauding Inkatha warriors at bay. Many drivers sympathised with the strategy behind the ultimatum. However, it is impossible to obey and is generally ignored. They still travel the Edendale valley roads, driving from area to area, and many of them end the day's work cut and bruised in stone-dented buses.

★   ★   ★

When I next pulled up outside the Pietermaritz Street depot at lunch-time, Ephraim was standing outside waiting for me. He slid into the front seat, commenting critically because the car was dirty and the seatbelt was twisted.

Already events in the townships had moved on. Three days earlier there had been a major battle, outside Thulani's Garage in Macibisa, when a busload of Inkatha members, returning from a rally 30 kilometres away in Mpumalanga, had piled out of the bus and attacked people at the side of the road. The battle had attracted a lot of attention in the press and had become known as the 'Thulani's Garage Incident'. Ephraim was taking the whole thing badly. 'The youth blame us for driving the buses,' he said. 'Inkatha took a Special Hire to take their people to Mpumalanga; our people agreed to drive the buses. The youth were angry when we agreed. They said we were helping Inkatha wage their war and of course they were right.'

At the top of Church Street we turned left, then right, passed a yellow police van and a couple of taxis, and headed off along the Edendale Road. Ephraim pointed out the various stops where buses had been stoned. At the turn off to Caluza he said: 'There, that's a big trouble-spot. They catch you as you turn because it's sharp and you have to take it slow.' I looked across. The road was virtually empty, and in the yard of the corner house an old woman in a yellow doek was feeding grain to some hens. Edendale receded behind us and we began to climb into the hills.

We passed the dirt road along which Phineas Mdluli had met his death.

It was hard to believe that a car, let alone a bus, could make its way along that road, which looked in worse condition than the open veld on either side. 'A good driver takes the rough with the smooth,' Ephraim remarked.

Up in the hills of Vulindlela, in a shallow rural valley dotted with smallholdings, we turned off the main road onto a sandy track which led to the Taylor's Halt bus depot. A number of cars were parked haphazardly outside a corrugated-iron cabin. A long aerial protruded from the roof and chickens ran about distractedly in the mud. A line of buses stood in a row waiting for drivers to begin the afternoon shift, and some early passengers squatted patiently in the shade, hardly talking.

Ephraim ushered me into the cabin where I shook hands with the men on duty. He attended to various matters and then we set off back to Pietermaritzburg. 'You see this farmland, this is Inkatha land,' Ephraim said. 'If you are a good Inkatha member you get privileges from the chief.'

'Such as?' I asked.

'More land, for the first thing. You get the land of the people who have been chased out, you eat their cows which the chief slaughters for a feast for his own people. He gives you beer. Then you also get protection from the youths and there is place for your children in the schools. If you are not Inkatha there is no place for you here at all. The chief won't even allow UDF people to bury their dead here. Once the chief stopped a funeral right on the edge of the grave. The mourners had to take the body to the cemetery at Mpophomeni. It was already beginning to break up – to decompose – you could smell it through the coffin. It was a sad and tragic day.

'Look, as I see it, these people are very, very corrupt. They take money from the poor and people are forced – I'll say forced – to pay protection money. Ntombela gets a new Ford Sierra, R36 000 – the people gave him R600 for petrol straightaway. His bodyguards are all armed, and they get the guns from where? You know what a gun costs these days? R1 000 is cheap, and they're changing them like hats.'

'How do you know these things?'

'I live in the townships, man. To stay alive you learn. I drive the same streets, I have the guns waved in my face. In these areas, if you are not Inkatha you face thuggery. They pour petrol over your head and flick a cigarette-lighter by your eyes.'

'And Inkatha people in UDF areas?'

After a pause Ephraim said, 'It is not safe for them either.'

As we came off the mountain side into residential Edendale, we passed a bus with a starred windscreen. Two panes along the side were also missing. The sight made Ephraim reflective. 'It's a shit job because the hours are too long and the buses are so bad. We work eight-hour shifts with one break of one hour. The first shift starts at 4.00 a.m. so you have to be up at 2.30 to get to the depot. When you finish up you are so tired, you get home, eat and sleep. No time for conversation or family matters. During the day you take every chance you can to sleep, even just for three minutes at a time. And your health suffers.' Ephraim, sitting beside me, exuded strength but the pouches around his eyes were lined with blood, and heavy.

'Most of the drivers at KT have bad eyesight caused by chips of glass,' he said. 'We've asked management several times for thick, shatterproof glass, but they say it's too expensive. They must think it's cheaper for them to buy us a new pair of eyes when the old ones get too bad. Then we suffer from backache because there are no adjustable seats and there are drivers who have kidney ailments because the seats have no shock-absorbers at the back.'

At the Pietermaritz Street depot, Ephraim took me on a tour of the workshops and parking lot. 'I can say that in some ways this is a disgusting job,' he said. He led me over to a 64-seater bus good for rural roads, parked on its own against a concrete kerb. He opened the driver's door and showed me the cabin, a small space separated from the passenger door by a heavy wire grill. The engine block was right inside the cabin at the driver's feet and the air-filter hung in a metal box above his head. In this bus the seat was a wreck. It was split and torn and the old adjustment mechanism was buckled and rusted. Some driver had made a makeshift repair by inserting a series of rocks of different sizes and shapes under the seat to lift and straighten it. The windscreen was missing and there was glass all over the floor. Ephraim leant over and ran his finger along the metal plates around the clutch. There was oil all over the floor. 'This looks bad?' he asked. I nodded. 'It's typical,' he said. 'It's hellish hot in here with the engine, and the airfilter leaks fumes. When you get home your lungs are choked and your face is black. There is oil all over the floor so your feet slip on the pedals and your shoes get filthy. The brakes are weak and defective, the steering locks. You see those stones? Useless. They can easily slip, you fall backwards, you lose control of the steering wheel.'

We walked round the side of the bus. 'No bumpers,' he said, 'and the edges are too square. We need curved windows for turning corners, otherwise visibility is too bad. Just the one wiper in front of the driver – that's terrible in the mist. And look here, retread tyres in the front. They do this to cut costs, but if one of these bursts the bus will overturn. The best buses are the ones I saw when I was in London with the Union some short while ago. The buses there are the answers to our prayers: the engine is at the back, so no heat problems; there's air-conditioning, curved windscreens, shatterproof glass, ventilators, comfortable seats but not like chairs in the theatre so you don't fall asleep. The buses are in good condition; they run smooth and in front it's church quiet.' He pointed

contemptuously to the rows of weak and damaged buses all around. 'Here
there is no job satisfaction for bus drivers. You have too many accidents
because the buses are defective and also from overloading.'

'Is there no way you could prevent that, at least?' I asked.

'I could close the door, you mean,' he replied. 'But that's hard to do
when you're picking up people who live very far out and you know there
will be no other bus for five hours.'

We passed on into the enormous hangar in which broken buses were
overhauled and repaired; there were dozens queuing up for attention.
'Here's a bus which overturned,' he said. It was a sorry sight. The roof had
been squashed down low over the body, bursting the windows from their
frames. The metal was ripped and twisted, and one side was dented and
buckled right along the length of the bus. Inside, some of the seats had
come adrift and there was a jagged gash along the floor where the metal
plates had been forced free of their rivets. 'It's repairable,' Ephraim said,
'but it'll be very shaky.'

'I'll just show you one last thing,' he said, and led me inside to a long
upstairs room in which about thirty drivers were relaxing between shifts.
Three tables of cards and a game of draughts were in full swing and a radio
was playing with the volume up. The noise was remarkable. 'Look at this,'
Ephraim mouthed at me. Behind a row of lockers sixteen low benches
had been pulled together to form a platform. At least twenty men lay along
this, covered in overcoats, asleep in various attitudes. The sound in the
room hung above them like a cushion. 'They'll sleep until the Last
Trump,' Ephraim bellowed. He consulted the shift roster. 'Or 15.00 –
whichever comes first.'

7

Look to the women

At all times the role women have played in this war has been understated. The Thulani's Garage Incident interested me not just because it raised policy problems for bus drivers but because it elicited a swift and unequivocal response from the women of Edendale.

I refreshed my memory on the circumstances of the Thulani's Garage Incident. From the *Natal Witness* I learned that there was no consensus on what had happened. 'Residents', an amorphous grouping meaning whomever the *Witness* reporter had spoken to in the crowd, alleged that the violence occurred at about 6 o' clock in the evening when a crowd of Inkatha supporters alighted from a bus outside Thulani's Garage and began attacking people indiscriminately. One man was shot and killed, and another injured. A crowd of youths from Moscow came quickly on the scene and began stoning the buses and the Inkatha supporters. The police arrived and were allegedly stoned as well. They responded by using shotguns and teargas to disperse the crowd. They injured two men and killed a woman. The police then escorted the Inkatha buses back to town and arrested 24 Edendale residents, some of whom may have been comrades, some of whom may have been stone-throwers.

David Ntombela, Inkatha spokesman and regional chairman for the Maswazini region, had a different version of events. He said that a bus transporting Inkatha members from Mpumuza had been stoned by 500 youths, who kept up their barrage even in the presence of the police. No Inkatha member either alighted from the bus or retaliated in any way.

The police version of events was the most terse. Their report simply stated that a woman had died after an Inkatha attack and had been buried as a pauper.

Despite Ntombela's disclaimer, it seemed fairly sure that the buses had been filled with Inkatha members returning from a ceremony in Mpumalanga at which the police stations were officially transferred from the control of the South African Police into the hands of the KwaZulu Police. The government of KwaZulu and Inkatha had long been pressing for the transfer, so the occasion had called for celebration.

I had a picture in my mind of what had happened, but it was time to speak to someone who had been there, heard the shouts and smelt the cordite from the shotguns.

I made contact with Avril who had been present at the incident. She worked in an office up on the slopes of Town Hill, a northern suburb of Pietermaritzburg. I drove through the shadows of pines and over the humped roots of trees along a sandy drive. Past bowling-green lawns and colonial buildings – red roofs and Victorian trim – I came eventually to a modern building set in a hollow clearing. As I got out of the car the heat slapped me in the face, but the office, like its occupant, was cool and well appointed. Avril was a middle-aged woman, handsome with a streak of grey hair over her ears. She was immaculately dressed and spoke in a soft yet confident voice. She welcomed me, took my jacket, complimented me on the cut, invited me to call her Avril, folded her arms across the blotter on the desk in front of her and said, 'What can I do for you, sir?'

'Tell me what happened at Thulani's Garage as you witnessed it and we'll take it from there,' I said.

Avril's story confirmed that of the comrades. She described the attack and the subsequent events in some detail to ensure that I understood fully the unprovoked nature of the attack and the partisan action taken by the police. 'We were taken quite by surprise as we weren't expecting anything. The Inkatha people caught a man getting off a Kombi. They shot him, several times I think, and stabbed him in the mouth. They cut him right to the ear.

'The police —' she laughed. 'The police came because the Inkatha were in trouble. Some of them escorted the buses back to town. They made sure everyone was safely back on board. Meanwhile their colleagues were dispersing the crowd. They gave us five minutes to disperse but straightaway they began shooting us and spraying teargas. One woman was fatally wounded by the police as she stepped off a bus. They guarded the corpse closely and people were getting worked up as they wanted to know who it was. She was given a pauper's burial; only yesterday we identified the deceased. We were quite upset, I can tell you.

'The police arrested many men but what actually moved us quite a bit was the way they were beaten up and kicked and hurled into the van. It was quite brutal; the men were offering no resistance.

'I spoke to some women that evening and expressed my dissatisfaction with the turn of events,' she said. 'The next morning there was a message going round Edendale that the comrades were telling all the women to stay at home. We gathered at the Advice Office and organised Kombis to take us into town. We went to the offices of the PFP [Progressive Federal Party] and asked the regional director, Mr Keys, to arrange a meeting with the police. We wished to express a number of grievances.' Avril drew a blank sheet of paper towards her and made a tiny mark on the paper for each of the five points. 'No Inkatha rally buses to drive through Edendale; the SAP take the side of Inkatha, they are not fair in their interventions; the brutality displayed was making us most unhappy and very much concerned; the Edendale Hospital is not safe – Inkatha people have been seen roaming around fully armed; we want the Inkatha offices at Marawa House near the Hospital to move, they are a gathering point for armed men.'

She looked directly at me. 'At the PFP offices, Mr Keys tried several times to get hold of the police, but he failed. We waited from 9.00 a.m. until 3.00 p.m. when the Kombis returned to pick us up. Mr Keys phoned again and this time the police denied all knowledge of our delegation or our request. I think I can say honestly that it was a frustrating day.'

Later that day I spoke to a man who had been in the PFP offices when the delegation of women finally gave up their wait. 'You've got to understand,' he said, 'those women had been waiting for hours, first in the offices, then in the Cathedral, and then back at the PFP. They weren't complaining, they just looked strained. Finally Keys called them together to tell them there was no joy to be had from the police that day. They gathered in Harwin's Arcade and he addressed them through an interpreter. They were listening with total concentration, silent and grim. The cops didn't just refuse to see them outright – in some ways that would have been better – instead they prevaricated, wasted time, put them through to one officer after another and finally, at the end of the day, denied everything – denied that they'd been contacted at all.

'Harwin's Arcade is a respectable white shopping precinct, you know, not exactly upmarket, but solid. Shoppers there aren't used to seeing a gathering of 300 black women standing in a group, blocking the entrance and looking immovable. This was at 3 in the afternoon, about the time that mothers pick up their daughters from school and pull them into town to buy things. They would step through the Timber Street entrance into the arcade and do a double-take. I could see the thought go through their heads: "Is this it? Has the war finally arrived in our very own boutiques?"'

In subsequent weeks I discovered that the delegation of women from Edendale were following a precedent first set by the women of Ashdown the previous year. At the end of January 1988, in an incident known as Operation Doom, Inkatha attacked Ashdown with conviction, pouring in from Mpumuza and routing the inhabitants. The following day, on the morning of Monday, 1 February 1988, a group of women went to lay their complaints before the police.

A month later, at the end of February 1988 the police introduced a force of 300 special constables into the townships. These *kitskonstabels* were the cause of much disquiet among the residents of Ashdown and Edendale. Many of the new recruits were known to be Inkatha members and a number were well-known criminals who were subsequently dismissed by the police. On 2 March a group of women from Hammarsdale, Kwa-Dlangezi, KwaMakhutha and Pietermaritzburg went to the Supreme Court building in the city centre to meet the Attorney-General of Natal, Mike Imber. He met five of the women and accepted a memorandum from them in which they spelt out their fears that Inkatha-supporting *kitskonstabels* would use their new position to seek revenge and political advantage. Imber made no comment and seemingly took no action, but the allegations against the *kitskonstabels* mounted and disquiet increased.

On 21 March, the anniversary of the Sharpeville and Langa shootings, the police raided Ashdown and sjambokked and arrested all the men on the streets of the township between the ages of 15 and 35. They were taken away for questioning and most were released several hours later. During the raid a *kitskonstabel* shot a dog which was barking inside its owner's yard. A number of visitors to the township were stopped, searched and questioned before being told to leave and forget what they had seen. This was not a successful public relations exercise on the part of the police.

Later that day a group of women went once again to the PFP offices to complain about police harassment and the behaviour of the *kitskonstabels* in particular. Their complaint was formally relayed to Captain Pieter Kitching, police spokesman in Pietermaritzburg, who responded at once. He said that in terms of the emergency regulations he could not comment on the incidents described to him.

In July of the same year sixteen pupils at Siyahlomula High School in Ashdown were whipped and shot by *kitskonstabels* on the school premises. Again, Ashdown women went into town to see the PFP and on this occasion party officials managed to set up a meeting between them and a number of senior police officials. The women demanded the removal of *kitskonstabels* from Ashdown and yet again called on the police to take action against Inkatha warlords in Mpumuza. The policemen were apparently sympathetic and concerned and promised to take action. The *kitskonstabels* were subsequently removed from Ashdown and the police set up mobile units on the border of Ashdown and Mpumuza ostensibly to monitor and pre-empt attacks by either side.

I was intrigued by the action taken by these women. It seemed to me to be remarkably cohesive and focused in a war in which shifting allegiances and lack of direction were the norm. Their interventions were low key and sporadic and yet they had achieved a number of their objectives. Questions were asked in parliament, their actions received prominent coverage in the press, and even the police eventually gave in to their primary demand for the removal of *kitskonstabels* from Ashdown. There was something elegant and rational about the way the women had behaved, something which commanded respect and attention. By calculating what they could do and doing it, they achieved a rare calmness of action and their responses were subtle and long term. They were not interested in attack or counterattack; they had in mind the benefits of peace rather than continuing war.

In January 1988 a number of COSATU members were interviewed about the war in the townships. The interview appeared in the February 1988 edition of the *South African Labour Bulletin*. They discussed such matters as the cooperation between COSATU and the UDF and the formation of defence committees to ward off Inkatha attacks. The interviewer asked whether women were involved in the defence committees and was told the following by the unionists:

At first women were not involved in the defence committees because their main purpose was defence. But now that the committees are discussing their tasks we are discussing the role of women. Some comrades felt that women are weak, they can easily pass on information. But we pointed out that is not true. Women are an important and integral part of the struggle, and they have particular skills, for example gathering information.

This spuriously generous and patronising attitude to women is common among male activists in Pietermaritzburg. Nhlanhla made some vague comments when I asked him about the role women were playing in the war, and he laughed openly when I asked whether they participated in battles or took part in meetings to discuss strategy. When I pressed him further he became impatient. 'Look, they attend to food, they look after the kids,' he said, and closed the subject. In the townships around Pietermaritzburg, and further afield too, war is a male affair, where issues of personal machismo come to the fore. Young men who kill and risk death along the township boundaries are fighting a personal, egoistical battle as well as a political and ideological one. They see death in the cause of the struggle as poetic and noble and they deprecate women's caution and rationality.

One afternoon Nhlanhla showed me a house in Ashdown which had been occupied by a leading activist, now dead. He listed his qualities of leadership and his political sophistication. 'He tried to educate and politicise the women,' he said. 'He tried to show them that it was wrong to take their grievances to the PFP because as a parliamentary party it is both irrelevant and reactionary. We can solve our problems from within the community through unity and struggle.'

On both sides of the war, the attitude of men to women is sexist. Women are expected to give succour to the fraught and injured, to see that there is food in the house and to provide kitchen and bedroom services. Beyond that, their function appears to be limited. Nonetheless, the women in the townships rise above these insulting and reactionary attitudes and provide stability and continuity in places riven with conflict and set to explode.

I went back to see Avril and asked her whether she thought that the experience of women in the war differed from that of men.

'Life is an activity of constant anxiety,' she replied. 'Death may come in many, many ways. You say to yourself, "Now I'm alive and later I may be dead," and that's all there is to say. I spend far too much time wondering whether I or my family is on someone's list and when they will get round to ticking our names off. As a woman I am under other pressures as well. It is my responsibility specifically to keep the household together, to make sure that we eat, to account for the whereabouts of my children, to try and bring some relief to my husband who suffers badly from ulcer and nervous tension.

'My children are not neutral – I respect that – but it makes it difficult to be a mother these days. Every time I speak to them it may be the last time. I have to be calm, to behave normally, and yet nothing in our lives is normal.'

Avril did not mention that women have unwittingly had to take on the sins, real or imagined, of their husbands and sons. From the first, Inkatha has taken the position that all the members of a family are culpable for the actions and allegiances of any one member. This means theoretically that parents who are Inkatha members become enemies of Inkatha if they have sons or daughters who support the *amaqabane*. Unless they 're-educate', banish or, it is said, allegedly even kill their recalcitrant children, the parents become targets for violence. Velaphi Ndlovu, KwaZulu MP for Imbali, is on record as saying that if a comrade kills an Inkatha member, it is legitimate to retaliate against that comrade's family.

Towards the end of January 1988, a group of men destroyed a crèche in the township of Slangspruit, which lies on the western edge of Pieter-maritzburg. Slangspruit is divided into an Inkatha and a UDF section, and this gang allegedly comprised Inkatha members. They were looking for a comrade, and on failing to locate him, they chose instead to vent their ire on his mother's crèche. They wrecked the place completely. The woman who ran the crèche was non-partisan. She took in the children of both parties, subsidising many of them herself. Several of the men staving in the doors and hurling petrol bombs were the fathers of children in her care. But ironies come so cheap in this war that people can hardly recognise them any more.

I picked up a hitch-hiker one evening on my way from Pietermaritz-burg to Durban. She told me that her name was Emma, that she was a schoolteacher in Sweetwaters and that she was on her way to Umlazi to visit her boyfriend. She was neither patient nor uncomplaining about her lot. She made no sacrifices for men and was not shy to express herself on the subject of sexism as practised by township activists. She was gutsy and the conversation was refreshing. I asked her whether she participated in discussions with them about strategic issues, or whether she was excluded from them. She laughed shortly and cynically. 'The only way those boys talk to women is between their legs,' she said, flipping a new tape into the cassette player.

8
Local geography

Around Pietermaritzburg, urban and rural environments lie adjacent and merge with one another. The whole area is not hard-edged, there is little tar, the roads are sandy and tend not to run straight. Clusters of township houses, four-room cinder-block constructions with corrugated-iron roofs, are separated by a track or donga from rural hillsides speckled with dwellings made of wattle staves, mud and thatch. Between every house the grass grows long and clinging, and mud is endemic. Nothing is flat: roads wind down into the valleys and all movement involves either a climb or a descent. Clumps of trees, tiny spruits, hidden marshland are all characteristics of the region, and the green and brown of soil and mud are infused with flashes of colour from tropical petals. The view is almost always attractive – in fact the contrast between the beauty of the battle-ground and the ugliness of the battles is the most common cliché of the war – but the inhabitants of the region are more concerned with the strategic value of their environment.

Harewood, an Inkatha stronghold now known as Ulundi, and Moscow, a UDF stronghold in Edendale, are separated by a stream. On several occasions Inkatha vigilantes have tried to penetrate Moscow but without success. Now what skirmishes occur take place along the banks of this river. If a comrade is caught in Ulundi he is killed and his body dumped in the stream. His killers stand on their side of the boundary and call over to the comrades on the other side: 'Come and fetch your dog. It is in the river.'

There are frequent battles between residents of the Inkatha-dominated settlement of Mpumuza, and the township of Ashdown, the residents of which were either supporters of the UDF or at least opposed to Inkatha. Originally supporters of both sides lived in Ashdown but even in 1986 there were sporadic clashes between residents as Inkatha members from Imbali tried to organise in Ashdown. By July 1987 Inkatha was making an all-out assault on the political soul of the township: people who refused to join Inkatha were killed and their houses burned. In response, anti-Inkatha residents set up a township-wide defence network, and in December managed to drive Inkatha over the boundary into Mpumuza.

In the past the residents of Ashdown and Mpumuza had shared a number of water points located on the Ashdown side of the boundary. When the boundary became an uncrossable border, people living in Mpumuza lost their easy access to water. They had to make long journeys to Harewood on the other side of the hill to fill their drums and jerrycans. The ensuing battles had as much to do with a desire to regain these taps as with the political and ideological obliteration of the comrades in Ashdown.

For some months after the purging of Inkatha from Ashdown, the defence committee was not able to relax its vigilance for a moment. The attacks came by day and night, three or four times a week, and within a short time the whole township was so attuned to a state of conflict and responded so quickly to general mobilisations, that the defence committee *per se* disbanded. An ex-member said by way of explanation: 'We didn't need it any more. The whole community is the defence com. now.'

Each side can observe the other across the narrow boundary road which dips down into the shallow valley before rising again, and any preparations for an attack are sighted at once. On the Ashdown side there are always people on the look-out, young women or boys of about 12 who are known as the Pioneers. At the first sign that people in Mpumuza are starting to gather, or have begun to cross the hillside towards the border, the Pioneers run through the township giving the alert, shouting, '*Itheleweni*! *Itheleweni*!' People stop what they are doing – even bridegrooms in their tuxedos leave their wedding receptions – and prepare for battle. The sounds of day-to-day living, of township animals and radio voices, are drowned out by the whistling which fills the streets and carries over the hill. Women reach out and grab infants and young children, dragging them inside out of the way. Other children, no more than 7 or 8, go dancing down to the border, singing and taunting, 'Come! Come!' Older youths and men for whom this is not a game try to remove them and send them back, but they return, insinuating themselves into the frontline, getting in the way, throwing themselves open to the maximum danger.

The two armies face up to each other and engage in verbal skirmishing. The residents of Ashdown shout abuse at the *theleweni* who reply shouting, 'Go on, fuck off! Get out! We're coming to turn your houses into fields of sugar-cane.' This is a poetic way of saying, 'We're coming over to lay waste to your houses for the hell of it,' since this is not sugar-cane land.

Houses, too, have a role to play in this kind of urban, residential warfare, beyond the simple provision of cover and shelter. They are places of refuge and concealment and can be used as launching grounds for attack. In Ashdown every house has a fence at the front which contains in its bounds a small garden planted usually with a flowerbed, a tree or an aloe. The backyards, however, are open and flow one into the other. You can cross the township using unmarked paths through the yards of houses. There is an alternative route to everywhere which residents know instinctively, but of which outsiders are both ignorant and fearful. An invading force would be foolish, unless very strong, to try to penetrate deeply into Ashdown. The blank inexpressive façades of houses could conceal a network of defenders, in communication with each other and ready to spring.

Individual houses have become the markers and monuments of famous episodes and acts of heroism or infamy. One deserted house in Ashdown, blank windowed and with a sagging door, has 'Viva UDF, Viva COSATU' scrawled across its front wall. That is the house of an Inkatha member, now dead, who in his time had stalked and killed a number of young men in the township. The house stays empty despite the over-crowded conditions in the township. Another house, badly damaged, belongs to an Inkatha member, a woman, who expressed satisfaction on hearing of the death of a prominent activist. She was attacked and forced to flee, but having displayed appropriate contrition was allowed to return. Later, in an inexplicable reversal of this decision, she was again attacked by a group of comrades, and killed. Next door to her house a dozen refugees from areas throughout the valley have taken refuge. Nearby is the house of a man who says, 'I don't know anything about the war, it doesn't involve me.' Next door to him again is one of a score or more of houses which has been razed by fire. The walls are black and the sheets of corrugated-iron roofing lie on the empty concrete floor, their supports burnt to ash.

The houses in Ashdown standing on the border have no windows intact. Bullet holes pockmark the walls, and people are wary of showing themselves or moving in front of their windows. Stray bullets fired from far off have killed and injured children playing in front of these houses. Even the ubiquitous poultry does not wander here. Across the border, a little way up the hill the shell of a large house stands encircled by tall weeds. The size and design of the bungalow would not be out of place in any white suburb in South Africa. The owner of the house, not a strong Inkatha man, was chased away by his Mpumuza neighbours. Subsequently looters, working in shifts, knocked out and took with them the windows and doors, the window and door frames, all woodwork, all carpets and furnishings, some garden chairs and a seascape which hung above the bed. From a distance the house looks as though once begun, it was abandoned by the builders. In fact it was properly finished and then just as meticulously dismantled.

*   *   *

But despite all this, there are still times when the concerns of war are left behind. On a quiet day, roofs gleaming in the sunshine and the roads steaming after rain, Ashdown exudes a somnolent peacefulness. The hens peck among the puddles, small children squat to prod frogs, the soccer balls emerge and the inevitable police patrol vans pass slowly and infrequently. On days like this even the roofs of houses have a particular character. Every roof is adorned with a car tyre as the householders believe they serve as effective lightning-conductors. Placed next to the tyre, often propped up against it, there are pumpkins, marrows and squashes, raised aloft to ripen in the sun. Carpets are washed and spread across the corrugated iron to dry, and on a hot day men and women sunbathe on their roofs.

On one such morning we drove past a man standing on top of his house, training his hose on some hidden object. 'His car,' said Nhlanhla. The woman lying beside him looked up from her book and waved lazily. Then she adjusted her sunvisor and continued reading.

9

The nuts and bolts of war

In the first few months of the war, it was not uncommon for there to be clashes between armies of between 200 and 300 men. There were various ways of raising a force of men this size. On the Inkatha side the initial recruitment programme carried out from September 1987 onwards was intended not merely to swell the membership of Inkatha and bring in registration funds, but also to add to its military strength. New recruits were not allowed to sign the book, pay their money, and then go back inside and close the door. It is said that they were threatened with serious injury unless they reached behind them for a weapon and stepped outside to join the ever-growing army of vigilantes. A small force of ten people could grow five-fold in the course of a night's recruiting.

Out in the rural areas, chiefs and indunas – almost all of whom gave their allegiance to Inkatha – could exact their traditional rights from farmers and homesteaders in the form of military duty. In return for favours ranging from land allocation to the issuing of licences, these rural potentates could call on the inhabitants of their fiefdoms to fight when necessary. This was not a legal obligation, but a difficult summons to resist nonetheless. Those families who did resist were given an ultimatum – usually a day – to leave the area. If they failed to comply they were wiped out.

Another source of soldiers was the great crowds of men who came bussing in to attend Inkatha rallies. They would be grafted onto the local army, thereby creating a force of formidable numbers. These armies were led by local warlords or their second-in-commands. In the main, the leaders were drawn from the ranks of the chiefs, indunas and local Inkatha branch chairmen. The warlords provide food, transport and bellicose incitements to action; and what guns there are, they distribute.

Inkatha vigilantes use a variety of weapons. The most common are the knobkerrie – a wooden stave with a heavy bulb at one end – and the assegai – a short stabbing spear used in hand-to-hand combat. Also popular is the panga or bush-knife, a slightly curved broad-bladed knife used equally effectively for cutting back weeds, harvesting crops and hacking people to pieces. Soldiers often come equipped with pockets of stones and cans of petrol to start and finish the job. Finally there are a number of handguns, a few rifles and shotguns available. Many of these are purchased by warlords and Inkatha leaders who have been granted firearm licences. Others have a more murky provenance – no one knows quite where they come from. They are obviously provided by someone or something with access to firearms and a political preference for Inkatha. In the townships there is a widespread belief that warmongers in the security police are running guns to vigilantes and that other guns come in from Ulundi through the KwaZulu Police. But there is no solid proof that this is the case.

The comrades for their part put together armies from a reserve of refugees, members of local UDF-affiliated youth organisations, and residents of non-Inkatha areas who are politically non-aligned but want to defend themselves from Inkatha attacks. There seems to be little evidence of men being pressganged into joining UDF forces, although residents sympathetic to Inkatha have certainly been chased out of UDF areas and occasionally killed. The *amaqabane* arm themselves with stones, sticks, pangas and smaller knives. They too are expert in the uses of petrol although it is interesting to note that at no stage during this war has either side made use of the infamous necklace method of killing, although many people have been burnt to death. The comrades also favour two other deadly weapons: the first is a club made from a solid metal rod with a heavy bolt welded across the bottom. The weapon is wielded like a mace, and one blow would disintegrate a skull of iron. The second weapon looks like a walking-stick except that a long metal spike protrudes out of the end. This can be concealed in the ground like the point of a shooting-stick.

When it comes to weapons the comrades have need to be inventive as they have practically no guns. Whenever one surfaces it is confiscated at once by the police, and its owner detained and charged with unlawful possession of firearms. To overcome this disadvantage, a variety of home-made guns have been manufactured, but these are rare and unreliable and there remains the problem of obtaining suitable ammunition.

The fact that Inkatha completely outguns its enemies has unquestionably kept the death rate in the war lower than would otherwise have been the case, but this objective consideration provides small comfort to the comrades.

The UDF forces are led by committee members of the youth organisations, sometimes boys no older than 15. Leadership is often split between those with an aptitude for political and military strategy, and those with an aptitude for fighting. The leaders of comrade armies do not have it easy. They are the first to be detained by the police or assassinated by their enemies. In addition, although it may be possible to gather an army together, it is not a simple matter to maintain it. Food and shelter are necessary, as are victory and hope, and these resources are not easily come by. More than that, a large body of young men suffers from a crucial problem – they are too visible. Any gathering over a certain size is immediately spotted by the police who arrive in copious numbers of yellow vans to break things up through the employment of teargas, quirts and mass detentions.

The Inkatha forces do not seem to share this handicap. Huge bands of armed vigilantes range over wide areas of the landscape, chanting, singing, threatening and even attacking people, and yet they are neither stopped nor challenged by the police. Velaphi Ndlovu, KwaZulu MP for Imbali and a senior Inkatha member, ascribes this unusual *laissez faire* attitude of the police to the essential 'Zuluness' of the Inkatha bands. 'It's the necessary cultural thing,' he says. By this he means that marches of armed Inkatha warriors are merely a harmless, cathartic cultural expression of tribal identity. Many Zulus living in the Pietermaritzburg area who have fallen victim to the cultural fervour with which the vigilantes play out their traditional role would disagree with Ndlovu's characterisation.

In the early stages of the fighting, members of the various youth organisations appealed to the township youth to set about establishing defence committees to defend those non-Inkatha areas under attack from Inkatha vigilantes. Committee members would be constantly on the alert: at the height of the fighting sentries would be posted throughout each area, awake and on watch all night waiting for the first whispering approach of a hostile force – with contingents of back-up fighters, asleep but able to be roused and mobilised immediately. Following biblical precedent they slept with their weapons in their hands.

Defence committees from different areas established codes of communication. In the event of an attack, whistles from one defence committee would be heard and 'read' by another, which in turn would issue a call for all men to go to the assistance of the section under attack. Armed, and following the direction of the whistling, this auxiliary force would arrive to reinforce its comrades.

The pace of the fighting has fluctuated over the months. With the exception of certain spectacular clashes between large armies – such as the invasion of parts of Ashdown and Vulindlela by Inkatha in March 1990 – there is a shortage of the stuff that newspaper headlines are made of. The sweeping mobilisations are always necessarily short-lived, limited by a lack of resources – how much livestock does one need to feed 300 or more men every week? – and through sheer exhaustion caused less by the fighting than the waiting.

With each new downswing in the intensity of the war, people hope that the war has run out of steam; but this hope is so strong they forget that the grand battles have never been the major contributor to the casualty figures. Most of the deaths are caused by small bands of men moving and striking swiftly at easy targets, and these killer bands have not stopped operating.

If anything, they have stepped up their strike rate. The nocturnal calls, the bullet-spewing passing car, these continue to haunt the townships and rob the inhabitants of their sleep. Spirals of revenge, feuds in which the personal and political elements have become inextricably linked, flare up like matches in the night. The hatreds are more bitter now than they were two years ago and the polarities more entrenched.

10
Operation Doom

Of all the battles fought in the course of the war, the invasion of Ashdown by Inkatha supporters coming in from Mpumuza was pivotal as it established the form in which the war was fought subsequently. With one notable exception – the massive Inkatha attack on UDF territories in March 1990 – this form has endured ever since. After January 1988, the war shifted from being a series of encounters by which territory was won or lost, and became instead a dirty stalemate in which each side gave up attempting to overrun the other, and concentrated on consolidating its own territory, using spoiling tactics whenever an occasion was presented.

In the four months to the end of January 1988, Inkatha suffered remarkable setbacks. Its attempts to win ground in the urban areas failed and it lost support in rural strongholds. In January, with police support, these rural areas were recaptured, producing an impasse in which Inkatha controlled much of the outlying region on the further outskirts of the Greater Pietermaritzburg area while the UDF and its supporters controlled the urban townships of Ashdown and Edendale.

As the Inkatha fight-back gained momentum, in non-Inkatha areas people went on the alert for a grand offensive, nicknamed Operation Doom, to be launched against urban UDF strongholds on 19 January. In the event, the operation was delayed until 31 January, on which day an Inkatha rally in Mpumuza was used as the springboard for a powerful attack on Ashdown. The events of this day formed the substance of the largest of the interdict applications launched by COSATU against Inkatha, namely *Zondo, COSATU & Others* v *Inkatha, Mvelase & Others*.

I use the affidavits of some of the applicants, as well as those of two well-known Inkatha personalities cited as respondents, to reconstruct, through a montage of witnesses, the applicants' version of the events of Operation Doom.

CHRISTOPHER MADLALA, 34

On Saturday, 30 January 1988, at approximately 13h00, I was travelling by bus from work towards Sweetwaters. As I got off the bus at the bus stop near home, I saw three cars parked in front of the bus. Chief Zondi and Induna Ntombela alighted from the cars together with other people including a Zulu policeman dressed in green overalls. A shot was fired into the air by Chief Zondi. He had a pistol in his hand.

Chief Zondi said in a very loud voice to those that alighted from the bus that there was to be a meeting on Sunday at KwaMkhulu. He said it was arranged by Inkatha and anyone who did not attend the meeting should pack their belongings now and leave the area. This was Zulu soil and belonged to Zulus. Those who would not join Inkatha should leave now and go to their 'Coolies' and find a place to stay. Inkatha would send people out to comb the area for those who refused or failed to attend the meeting. It did not matter whether it was an old man or woman or even chicken, those that did not attend the meeting would have to face the consequences.

ANDREAS MPANGASE, 45

On Wednesday, 27 January 1988, in the late afternoon, I was at home when Philip Zondi, brother of Inkatha Chief Nsikayezwi Zondi, drove into my community. He announced over a loud-hailer mounted to his car that everyone would be expected to attend a prayer meeting organised by Inkatha at 10h00 on Sunday at KwaMkhulu, the name given to the property of Chief Zondi in Mpumuza. Residents were warned that if they did not attend they should pack their belongings and leave the Chief's area. He threatened that after the meeting concluded, all those who did not attend would be attacked and their houses burnt.

I thought it wiser to attend the meeting rather than run the risk of having my family harmed or my property damaged. When I arrived a large number of people were there, many with Inkatha uniforms wearing Inkatha colours and badges. Most of the men were armed with sticks, stabbing spears and shields. There were several police vans parked in the vicinity and a number of white and black policemen were in attendance.

In front of the crowd and on slightly elevated ground, the speakers and various Inkatha officials sat on benches.

One of the early speakers at the meeting was V V Mvelase, the Urban Representative of the KwaZulu government. The substance of what he said was that the only way to end violence in the area was to drive the UDF and COSATU from KwaZulu to Xhosa areas. The UDF and COSATU were 'Indian' organisations and all those who belonged to them should go and live with the 'Indians'. Any 'Indian' who does not move or who does not repent and apologise will be killed. He advised parents whose children had joined the 'other camp' to kill their children.

Velaphi Ndlovu [KwaZulu MP for Imbali, who spoke next] began his address by instructing us to remain loyal to the chiefs and to be certain that if we live in a Chief's area to be members of Inkatha. He stated that our children must also be members of Inkatha and if they were not they must be brought to the Chief's house where a formal apology was expected. Failing that, we would have to leave the area. He threatened that refusal to join and refusal to leave would be reason for being killed.

A chief from Ladysmith also addressed the crowd. He said COSATU was controlled by Slovo who was receiving instructions from Russia. He became emotional and started chanting. He rhythmically punctuated his chant with the Zulu word 'abajojwe' (stab them) while simultaneously stabbing into the air with his spear: 'What should we do about them? Abajojwe! Let's stop them! Abajojwe! Finish them off! Abajojwe! Kill them!' At each stabbing of the spear the women would ululate and the men would stab into the air with their spears or sticks.

It was at this point that a woman, very agitated and hysterical, screamed, 'Houses are burning at ePhayephini'. The people rose and many stormed off in the direction of ePhayephini.

The final speaker was David Ntombela. He said that anyone who did not want to belong to Inkatha should be killed. He said that he is prepared to go anywhere and kill all those who are not Inkatha.

Andreas Mpangase was later forced to take part in the attack on Ashdown as part of a large vigilante raiding party. However, the other members of the party suddenly challenged him to explain why his sons had not been at the meeting. Mpangase ignored the challenge and was shot in the back by a vigilante. Despite his injury he managed to evade his attackers and eventually reached Edendale Hospital where the wound was treated and the bullet removed.

According to the applicants, after the meeting hundreds of Inkatha supporters, accompanied by the police and the SADF, poured into Ashdown as Inkatha tried to erase the memory of past defeats and to regain ground lost over the past few months.

SIPHIWE ABMAEL KHOZA

On Sunday, 31 January 1988, I was visiting friends of mine in Ashdown. At approximately 13h30 I noticed certain police vehicles and an army Buffel parked near Ashdown dam. These vehicles were later joined by a brown Toyota bakkie, a light blue Toyota bakkie and a red Toyota Hi-Ace combi.

The combi, which was overloaded, passed the house I was in. We, that is my friends and I, were sitting outside. Someone from the red combi shouted that we, comrades of Ashdown, were going to be dealt with by Inkatha. The combi stopped. People piled out of it. Some were dressed in the uniform and colours of Inkatha, some were armed with spears and shields. As they moved towards us, I immediately ran away. In my flight I had to avoid other groups of Inkatha youths and I found refuge near Siyahlomula High School and remained there until it was safe. From that vantage point I saw groups of people dressed in Inkatha colours chasing individuals and stoning houses.

EUNICE NTOMBI CHAMANE, 26

In the early afternoon of 31 January 1988, I was asleep at home and was woken up by a commotion. I looked outside and observed a crowd moving down the hill from Mpumuza from the direction of Ashdown dam.

The Inkatha mob entered Bekuzulu Road and the soldiers continued to follow behind. I assumed that the soldiers would prevent matters getting out of hand. However, as they approached, the Inkatha group began to throw stones. I saw the windows of the Shange house being broken. I ran for cover. When I thought it was safe, I returned home. On my way back, I happened upon several white soldiers sitting on top of a brown Hippo.

I asked them why they participated in the Inkatha attack and did not protect the residents as they should have done. The soldiers explained that it was not their fault but the fault of the SAP. Whenever they tried to prevent violence, the SAP criticised them for interfering.

JABULISILE MAUREEN ZONDI

On Sunday, 31 January 1988, at approximately 13h30, I was at my store. I observed a few people running down the road past my shop. They were shouting that the 'theleweni' were coming in large numbers accompanied by the police.

I then went outside to see what was happening. I noticed a large crowd as well as a convoy of motor vehicles coming down the road from Mpumuza. As the crowd and convoy got closer, I decided to go into the shop and lock up. I watched what took place from the window.

Some people in these groups were dressed in Inkatha uniform and others sported Inkatha colours. They were shouting challenges to the 'Amaqabane dogs' to come out so that they could kill them. I noticed Ami Mkhize specifically because he was continuously shouting, 'Here we are, we are going to kill you!' He was saying that in the Zulu language: 'Sesil lapho sizonibulala!'

I did not witness any acts of violence, but when the convoy of vehicles moved on and it appeared safe, I went outside to find a man lying on the ground with his feet on the seat of the bus shelter nearby. I learnt later that the young man was Michael Mandla nicknamed 'Magic'. I did not see who the perpetrators of this murder were.

I am concerned that nothing was done to stop the attacks by the armed group of Inkatha supporters. The police were present during the attacks; nothing was done to disarm, and to the best of my knowledge, nothing has been done to follow up on Magic's death.

MALUSI SHABANE, 22

On Sunday, 31 January 1988, at approximately 13h30 I was at the soccer field watching soccer. From the playing field I noticed a large crowd coming down the hill from Mpumuza towards Ashdown. The crowd was large and armed with spears, shields and assegais. I noticed a number of soldiers dressed in brown uniforms walking alongside the crowd.

I decided it was best to leave and go home. On my way home I noticed a yellow police van with two white policemen inside coming down Mngadi Road towards a circle to which Mngadi Road leads. There is a bus stop which is situated at the circle. I was about twenty yards away from the police van. It was followed by a red combi which had people inside. Behind the combi was a blue Toyota van without a canopy. There were armed people at the back.

The vehicles came to a halt. People armed with spears and bushknives alighted – some of them dressed in Inkatha uniforms or UWUSA T-shirts. I think some of the vehicles proceeded elsewhere, but I am certain one of the police vehicles stopped and remained there during the incident I am about to describe. Before the vehicles arrived I noticed Michael 'Magic' Mandla, sleeping at the bus stop.

The Inkatha group split off into smaller groups, which went off in different directions. One of these smaller groups attacked Magic at the bus stop, hitting him with their weapons.

After the attack on Magic they stoned a motor car belonging to Mr Mhlongo. He does not live far from the bus stop. He had just driven up and parked outside his house when they started stoning it. He got out and ran into the house. The group smashed the back and the driver's right-hand side windows. They tried to set the car alight but were unsuccessful. They then got into their vehicles and drove away. The police vehicle followed them.

I went to the bus stop where Magic was. There was a large crowd of about forty people around the bus stop. Magic's feet were on the bench of the bus shelter, his body sprawled on the ground, face up. There was a deep horizontal bushknife gash on his forehead. There were stab wounds in his throat.

The police arrived in yellow police vans. There were about ten policemen, black and white, dressed in uniform. They were all wearing light blue shirts and blue pants. I heard someone from the crowd complaining to the police saying, 'Look what Inkatha has done.' One white policeman replied in English, 'Shut up!' and then fired teargas. The crowd dispersed and I ran home.

Later in the day, Johannes Nkomo, a 70-year-old Inkatha member living in Sweetwaters, was visited by a group of vigilantes who demanded to know why he and his family had not attended the meeting. He and his wife were beaten up and later the outer huts of their homestead were burnt down. When Nkomo approached the induna of the area, Mfana Mtha-lane, to complain about this treatment, he was told it was his own fault for not cooperating in reporting his children's misbehaviour. Nkomo there-fore decided to join the Zondo interdict application as the sixteenth applicant to seek relief from the court in the form of an order restraining Inkatha members from killing or otherwise assaulting local residents.

However, on the day before the application was due to be heard, when papers had already been served on the respondents and the identities of the applicants were known, Nkomo was killed in his house by vigilantes. His wife was also attacked and later died of her injuries.

After the main assault on Ashdown on 31 January, Inkatha vigilantes from Mpumuza, under the leadership of Mamfana Majola, launched two further attacks on Monday afternoon, 1 February and the early morning of Tuesday, 2 February.

SBUSISO MADONDO, 17

During the afternoon of Monday, 1 February 1988, Mamfana Majola, who is in the Mpumuza leadership of Inkatha, stood next to a shop on the hill and shouted threats into the township of Ashdown. He warned that Inkatha will, by 01h00 on Tuesday 2 February, start killing the people of Ashdown, and after killing all the residents Inkatha would occupy the township. There were well over a hundred Inkatha people standing in a group with Majola, performing some ritual, dancing around a fire and burning muti.

Suddenly the whole group of Inkatha people began running down into the valley. They stopped at the river separating the townships of Mpumuza and Ashdown. Several residents of Ashdown came out of their homes, grouped together and went towards the river to defend against the ensuing Inkatha attack.

Immediately the police arrived in two yellow Landrover vans. They jumped out of the vehicles and began sjambokking the group from the Ashdown community. As we fled back to our homes, the police shot teargas cannisters over our heads, forcing us to run through the burning smoke to escape being sjambokked, with the police following in pursuit. The police paid virtually no attention to the Inkatha group standing across the river. They certainly did not chase the group away nor did they fire teargas at them.

I stopped to wash my face at a tap to relieve the burning of the teargas in my eyes and on my skin. While I was doing so, two uniformed white policemen approached me carrying sjamboks and shotguns in their hands. One of them handed his shotgun over to the other, took me to the wall of the house and banged my head against the wall. The other policeman then hit me with his rifle butt on my left arm. The rifle butt caused an open wound a few inches above the elbow. They departed and I went home where my sister bandaged my arm.

Later that night, my friend Siphiwe Khoza came to fetch me and together we joined several neighbours to guard our homes against further attacks as Majola had promised. At approximately midnight, we saw a large Inkatha mob coming down the hill from the Mpumuza township towards Ashdown. They were armed with shields, assegais, knives and pangas. As we saw them approaching our homes we immediately started to gather stones. As some of them entered the gate of the home where we were stationed we began throwing stones at them. They stopped the stones with their shields and started shooting at us. My friend Siphiwe Khoza was struck by a bullet. The rest of us fled.

A large group of residents converged on the scene and a shot was fired at the Inkatha mob, causing them to run back in the direction of Mpumuza.

Inkatha, the organisation, and the various other respondents issued replying affidavits in which they denied the allegations set out in the affidavits of the applicants, or alternatively denied responsibility for them, or alternatively claimed that Inkatha members were merely retaliating against earlier attacks by Ashdown residents on Phayephini, although there was no evidence to link the former with the latter.

Both Mangosuthu Buthelezi, submitting on behalf of Inkatha, and Vitus Mvelase claimed that even had there been unlawful behaviour on the part of individual Inkatha members, the organisation as a whole was powerless to take action against them. In addition to these disclaimers, Mvelase even went so far as to suggest that the attackers were not Inkatha men at all, but UDF supporters cunningly disguised as Inkatha vigilantes.

MANGOSUTHU GATSHA BUTHELEZI

The applicants make allegations against various Chiefs in their papers. I point out that there is no nexus whatsoever between those Chiefs and myself as President of Inkatha or between them and Inkatha as an organisation. If they are members of Inkatha, that is incidental in my submission. I am unable to control the manner in which they act in their capacity as Chiefs. To criticise me, Inkatha or the other Officials of Inkatha for the alleged unlawful acts of such Chiefs is unjustified.

VITUS VUSIMELA MVELASE

If the Inkatha members of a certain branch were to act in self-defence against an attack by the *radicals*, no punishment would be called for. Even if members of a certain branch of Inkatha had actually gone on the rampage, there is very little that the Disciplinary Committee can do in terms of the Constitution: firstly it does not have the capacity to police these events and to bring the culprits to justice, and secondly it does not have the deterrent force to have any such effect. It stands to reason that the Disciplinary Committee of the Constituency that might well become aware of the transgression would have greater difficulty in establishing what had transpired and to deal with the matter. To the higher echelons of authority in the Inkatha structure, it is totally impossible to take any effective steps whatsoever…

Both Inkatha and the ANC share the same uniforms and colours. The ANC and Inkatha's uniform consistss of khaki clothing with green, gold and black epaulets and a tie of similar colours. It is impossible to distinguish between a supporter of Inkatha and the ANC and the *radicals* often wear ANC uniforms.

The *radicals* often deliberately wear clothes with Inkatha colours to commit atrocities for which Inkatha would ultimately be blamed because they would ultimately receive publicity. Identification based upon the so-called uniform and colours of Inkatha could be, and often is, misleading.

Neither the abnegation of responsibility for the actions of members of the organisation, nor the bizarre and far-fetched interpretation of Vitus Mvelase, succeeded in altering the fact that on 31 January 1988, and over the following two days, Inkatha supporters launched what was intended to be a full-scale invasion of Ashdown.

In the event, Majola and his men did not manage to conquer and occupy the township. It proved impossible to drive the UDF out of Ashdown in the way Inkatha had been expelled over previous months, partly because the Inkatha force was not strong enough, but mainly because the whole community was united against Inkatha. The invading force learnt, to their cost, that it was no longer possible to distinguish between UDF and non–UDF residents – this division had been elided into a single political position: non-Inkatha.

11

The guardians

Slanting mid-afternoon sun coming through the slats of the blinds cut stripes across my notebook. The room was stuffy and Nhlanhla was moving about like a caged bird, long-legged and jerky, talking. I was listening but not writing much. At times the effort of transcribing the flowing words from his mouth to the discrete silent signs on the page seemed futile. I understood what he was talking about, could even visualise it to some extent, but only the occasional unexpected verbal inflection, or laugh which meant anything-but-funny, gave me any real insight into his story.

Eventually I shifted my notebook out of the sun so that I could see the lines, and wrote a heading, 'CV of a Maritzburg Activist', underlined it three times, and set out Nhlanhla's personal account of himself in point form:

1984 (14 years):
— August: Joined Edendale Youth Organisation (EYO) to protest against the visit to Imbali by Minister of Co-operation and Development, Piet Koornhof.
— September: Active in bus boycott organised to protest against fare increases.
— December: Detained for 48 hours as a 'stone-thrower'.
1985:
— February: Participated in massive schools boycott called nation-wide by members of the Congress of South African Students (COSAS).
— March: Detained for three days as an 'activist'.
— September: First clashes with Inkatha. Protests against gathering of vigilantes at the gates of Sebukuzulu High School, followed by clashes with them during exams. Students injured by spears, some run over. Even the teaching staff intimidated. Some labelled as 'agitators'. (Nhlanhla came over to look over my shoulder. 'You should have heard these people,' he said. 'They were shouting, mocking. They came with spears and bush-knives and they were enjoying themselves. They wanted anxiously to fight. Shouting things like, "You wanted to play, we also. You have been provoking us so now you must fight. Why are you running away?"')

1986:

— Students and staff had to sign loyalty forms to the Department of Education and Culture (DEC). Vigilante harassment so intense had to leave school. One of a list of eighteen student leaders marked down for killing by vigilantes. Decided to leave Pietermaritzburg to stay with relatives in rural areas. Sought for by security police.

— June–December: In hiding during the worst of the state of emergency crackdown.

1987:

— Returned to Pietermaritzburg to begin matric.

— June: Detained in raid on refugee hostel in Lusaka (Macibisa).

— August: Released, redetained and charged with nine counts of murder. Charges dropped. Released. Attacked by police in Sobantu. Shot through the trouser-cuff diving over a wall to escape.

— November: Redetained as 'politician' with other UDF leaders as peace talks were getting under way.

1988:

— July: Released and restricted. Subsequent jobs as a township field-worker for academics and researchers.

All this by the age of 19. Nhlanhla was unperturbed by the round of outrageous and pernicious circumstances served up to him each year with seasonal regularity. He met and overcame these obstacles by adopting a calm and philosophical approach and refused the entrapments of self-pity and wishful thinking. He was optimistic about the long-term future, on behalf of which he was prepared to endure the present. Whenever I asked him whether he felt weary or depressed, he would brush the question aside with his favourite slogan. 'You should know this – there's no easy walk to freedom,' he would say.

To be an activist in the Maritzburg townships is to take on a tough job. The rate of turnover is high among these 'radical elements', as the Minister of Law and Order chooses to label them, as the cycle of detention, restriction and death exacts its toll. Activists have to operate underground, expending the energy they need to be effective leaders on eluding capture or assassination. Organising a meeting becomes a difficult and hazardous undertaking, and it is almost impossible to maintain regular programmes of training and discussion among the comrades. The organisational structures needed for this kind of work are lacking – banned for long by the state or smashed by the war – and the leaders capable of inspiring trust and commitment were either until recently in detention, or in a caged limbo outside the prison walls, their voices stapled up with restriction orders.

The activists who remain devote themselves to a programme of damage limitation, trying to control and ameliorate the disruptions to community life caused by the war. In Ashdown and Edendale advice offices were established in September 1988 to deal with the complaints and problems of the local residents. The offices are staffed by members of the Ashdown and Edendale Youth Organisations, and are sponsored by donations from residents and from aid organisations such as the Red Cross and the Pietermaritzburg Agency for Christian Social Awareness (PACSA).

I drove back into Edendale past the now familiar pile of bricks which together constitute the Edendale Hospital. Just before the Caluza turn-off I steered right onto a dirt road which went past a couple of old-fashioned petrol pumps. The road threatened to disappear into a ditch, caught on again, turned two more corners and brought me into a small compound in which a long, low brick building stood surrounded by beds of dusty roses. I went inside, stepping into the second of the three large rooms into which the building had been divided. The room was empty and served as an entrance hall to the other two that flanked it to the left and right. On my right was a small store from which good smells of lunch-time cooking were seeping. A small girl came through and went inside.

I turned left, through a door bearing a printed sign which said 'Edendale Advice Office'. There were three people in the room: a young man in a flak jacket sitting behind a desk and two other men sitting on plastic chairs placed along the wall opposite the desk. From the door the first man was partially obscured by an ancient manual typewriter from which a thin curl of carbon paper protruded. Behind the desk there was a row of bookshelves on which stacks of correspondence-course booklets had been placed. The other furniture consisted of filing cabinets, a Roneo machine, a Xerox copier and a few posters on the pink plastered walls. The linoleum was cut and scarred and thin, wire burglar bars afforded the windows flimsy protection.

I approached the desk. The occupant rose up from behind the typewriter and greeted me – 'Aaron,' he said. We fell into conversation about the Advice Office. 'We deal with all the community grievances we can – things like unemployment insurance benefit, workmen's compensation, pension. Such-like things. We show people how to fill in the forms and tell them where to go. When there are old women who are too sick and tired to stand in the pension queue we go along as well to help them. Sometimes a person has to go and collect the pension in a wheelbarrow.

'Of course other people come to demand a pension and we have to tell them, "You are too young still. Wait some years," but at all times we are giving advice. If people are injured or attacked by Inkatha or the police – or even if they do not know who it was – we help them make a statement of what happened and send them to a lawyer in town. Sometimes we send them to the Legal Resources Centre in Durban but that's quite far away and we haven't got the money to help them with transport. We advise people with grievances to lay a charge at the police station even though we know that nothing will be done.'

Aaron sat very straight in his swivel-chair. He had one long fingernail which he occasionally tapped on the space-bar of the typewriter to emphasise a word or phrase, but otherwise he seemed very still. His face and body hardly moved as he spoke. Both his eyes and tone expressed a wary friendliness; he knew he could speak to me as I had been vouched for by other activists, but he was not sure how much to say. 'But we really only started up because of the war,' he said. 'People lost their loved ones; their property was destroyed so they came to the youth organisations for help. But more than that there was the problem of refugees. Hundreds of people kept coming into Edendale from Vulindlela and other Inkatha places. They had nowhere to stay, nothing to eat, no jobs. We sent them at first to PACSA and they provided some money but not enough. Instead they sponsored us to set up this Advice Office, and gave out food parcels and money for rent for some refugees. We raised money with plays and poetry performances as well and the community donates, but it is never enough. Refugees are living twenty to a room in some places. They do not eat much food, the infants get sick and die easily. What we do is to keep a list of all the refugees who come in so we know how many people there are, what the size of the problem is. This way people can't just become invisible like before. Before, the war was like a sink, you could just get washed down it and away. But now we are like a sieve, and we can catch them before they disappear.'

A woman came into the office. Her left calf was heavily bandaged and she was limping. She had just been to the store and was eating a packet of fried giblets and chips. She greeted everyone in a soft voice and chose a seat. Aaron told me her story. She had been sitting outside her house in Caluza when a busload of Inkatha supporters drove past, firing indiscriminately out of the windows at the passing world. She was hit in the calf and taken to Edendale Hospital where she was given ten stitches. Today she was due to have her stitches removed and had come to the Advice Office to meet a group of women who had promised to accompany her to the hospital. 'What for?' I asked.

'It's an Inkatha place,' said Aaron. 'She is very frightened and nervous to go there on her own. Some of the Inkatha people walk around the corridors. She feels it is dangerous to be there alone. She feels—' he searched for the word, 'exposed.' The woman nodded, still eating.

I had been wanting to find out more about an amorphous grouping which had sprung up in the course of the war and I thought that Hadebe was the man to ask. For some time people had been talking about groups of youths who engaged in various criminal activities while claiming to be comrades. They had been named the *comtsotsis* and their existence posed new problems for genuine activists. The *comtsotsis* assaulted and robbed people and shops; they preyed on commuters and mugged workers on pay-day much like *tsotsis* (gangsters) in other parts of the country. The difference was that they explained that their actions formed part of a political strategy. If they robbed a taxi-driver or a store they would justify the crime on the grounds that the driver or store-keeper was either a member of Inkatha or served Inkatha members.

The comrades were very unhappy about these developments which they felt were giving them a bad name. The existence of the *comtsotsis*, moreover, provided ammunition for those analysts who denied that there was a political aspect to the conflict in the Maritzburg townships. They could point to the activities of the *comtsotsis* to support their claim that what was going on was only widespread criminal gang warfare. Political opponents of the comrades, such as Inkatha and the police, have also derived propaganda value from the deeds of these pseudo-comrades, using them to support their argument that the comrades in fact work against the communities they claim to be serving.

'Some of them were always *tsotsis*,' Aaron said, when I raised the subject. 'They fought in gangs before the war started, but they were quite small. Then later some went to Inkatha, some came to us. They said that Inkatha was very bad and violent and they wanted to help the community. And they are good fighters when the violence starts, but when you are only a fighter a war is good business. You can commit crimes and pretend you are still fighting the war. Some of them are genuinely believing in the UDF, but they get – how should I put this? – a taste for fighting. They can satisfy this appetite when violence escalates, but when it diminishes they have fewer targets and they get restless. What we need are proper structures to channel such energies of theirs, but the state has tampered with our structures and it becomes hard for us to teach them political discipline and responsibility.'

'I've heard', I said, 'that people are blaming the refugees for a lot of the assaults and robberies that have taken place.'

Before Aaron could reply, one of the other men in the room broke in. He wore a light beard and a blue cardigan and had introduced himself at the outset as Exodus, and then lapsed into silent concentration, following our conversation closely. Now he pulled his chair forward, catching its legs in the tears in the linoleum, leaned over and tapped me on the knee. 'That is almost quite wrong,' he said in a passionate, breathless voice. 'In fact, you have to understand the dynamics, I can say this, of the life of a refugee. Sometimes they do wrong things, but they are not *tsotsis*, they are, let me say it this way, desperate people, sometimes. Some of these youth have a problem with their parents. They get chased out of their home area by Inkatha but their parents won't help them. They say it's your fault for getting involved in politics. So they have to look elsewhere –

maybe PACSA – but there is not much to go round: you have to eat; you steal.

'Maybe at home they were doing my washing; now I'm alone, I don't know how to look after myself so I get a girlfriend to do my washing for me. She's out of home too so I can easily manipulate her, but I have to get money or she'll find someone else. So I attack a bakery, and when I have to be disciplined I'll pretend it was a KwaZulu bakery. It is hard for the leaders to control all of this. People come to them and say, "I am disciplined but I must eat. Give me food, otherwise I must steal it." How can you blame them? These are youth who have a genuine desire for their education, but the schools are full and they spend so much time looking for food and shelter, how can they study? You can also find that these refugees stone buses which carry Inkatha people back to the places where they themselves were chased out. We don't like this behaviour, but we can surely understand it.'

The other people in the room nodded their endorsement of Exodus's comments. Some cats crossed the floor and Aaron fiddled with the stiff keys of the typewriter. In the temporary silence flies buzzed loudly in and out through the wire mesh across the windows. 'I would not, at this point in time, say that the *comtsotsis* are the greatest problem,' Aaron said eventually. 'They are not such a big phenomenon, there are not so very many. If the state was serious about peace they would release our leaders who can speak seriously to these youths. We need to use our structures for peaceful activities, not just defence. We need money for projects, like building construction, or typing, something to keep them busy and occupied. We need someone they can respect to teach these *comtsotsis* how to behave themselves, how to make their communities proud. In the meantime we have to watch them, and discipline them when necessary.'

'And what form does this discipline take?' I asked, pen poised. Aaron shrugged but did not reply. There were some things he was not prepared to divulge, no matter how good my credentials.

In fact I had been told by various people how the comrades disciplined unruly elements within their ranks. The offender was brought before a committee which recounted the infringement and then pronounced and carried out sentence. At the least, the guilty party could expect a severe beating, and on occasion, the beating resulted in death. The comrades justified these summary and brutal methods on the grounds that they were honouring their undertaking to discipline any within their ranks who promoted or provoked violence.

These harsh forms of internal control have not always achieved their objectives. Not surprisingly, any person ordered to report for discipline tends to take flight, and once flown, seeks out and joins forces with others hostile to the comrades. In Dambuza, for example, there are groups of *comtsotsis* who regard both the comrades of Ashdown and Inkatha as their enemy. A prominent Ashdown activist, Sipho Maloko, who visited Dambuza in order to discuss a rapprochement between the two areas, was ambushed and murdered by *comtsotsis*. They stabbed him, looted and then burnt his car, and stole the R240 rent money he was carrying on him. By the time the police arrived soon afterwards the vehicle was already a shell. The police then drove down to the Ashdown Advice Office and arrested four of Maloko's colleagues on a charge of attempted murder. Maloko's actual killers were not arrested but instead celebrated a profitable day's work. The *comstotsis* killed Maloko to avenge the beating sustained by one of their number who had been disciplined for robbing a store in Ashdown.

I heard about this sorry chain of circumstances shortly after visiting Aaron and thought that perhaps both the *comtsotsis* and the preferred methods for dealing with them were more of a problem than he was prepared to acknowledge.

The comrades do not confine their disciplinary activities to their own ranks, however. Township residents are also punished if they infringe some newly imposed standard of decency and good behaviour. Khaba Mkhize, characteristically attuned to new developments in township life, writes about crime and punishment in his *Frontline* article, 'Blood River at Sleepy Hollow':

Mr Average Smoker no longer puffs in peace on his way to work. Comrades have banned smoking in buses…

The comrades have argued that 'polluting the air of our parents is disrespectful'. The disciplinary campaign includes meting out punishment to all those who are disrespectful towards their elders, as well as to thieves and other 'wrongdoers'.

The new system of punishment is 'modelling'. This is where a person is stripped naked and forced to parade, confessing his or her offence. There are heated arguments about 'modelling'. Some elders are strongly for it. They say it has helped clean up crime…

Defenders of modelling admit it is humiliating but say it is better than the necklace. A comrade argues: 'Modelling the offender acts as a rehabilitating exercise to deter crime.'

Inkatha officials have told me that modelling is bringing them new supporters. They say Inkatha is being asked to stop the *amaqabane*'s immoral punishment.

There is no doubt that township residents dread and abhor modelling. Of course it is a preferable punishment to the necklace, but this is hardly an argument for its usage. The comrades' desire to prove their responsibility to their communities is genuine enough; they want to clean up their environment and they want to stamp out crime, which acts as a further burden on violence-weary township residents. However, in their puritanical zeal to purge and cleanse, youthful comrades are humiliating those very elders on whose behalf they claim to be acting. Moreover, they may end up alienating their own communities, losing the goodwill and support won with blood in their fight against Inkatha.

12

'Preventive' detention

At the seminar on Political Violence in the Pietermaritzburg Area held at UNP in April 1988, Christopher Merrett presented a paper on the pattern of detentions in the area. He showed that between June 1987 and April 1988, some 1076 people were detained, the majority in November and December 1987 and January 1988. In fact, in December at least 10 people were detained per day. Most of the detainees were held at New Prison in Pietermaritzburg, but a number were farmed out to distant police stations like Thornville, Boston, and New Hanover in the rural areas, or to more urban cells in the Plessislaer, Hilton, Town Hill and Mountain Rise police stations.

Merrett came up with a portrait of the average detainee during the period October 1987 to March 1988: '[He] was male, between 18 and 25 years old, had not been detained before, probably did not belong to a formal grouping in the political spectrum, but could be described as anti-Inkatha.'

This formulation is in accord with Merrett's assessment of police motive in detaining over a thousand people in nine months. First of all, he says, the number of detentions only escalated dramatically when Inkatha was suffering serious military defeats at the hands of the comrades. The police tried to restore the balance of power in Inkatha's favour by detaining hundreds of young comrades, members of township defence committees. They also disrupted the peace talks between UDF–COSATU and Inkatha by detaining key UDF representatives, not once, but twice – first in November and then in February. Certainly the police approach could not be described as light-handed. In March they conducted swoops in the townships of Sobantu and Ashdown, both UDF strongholds, arresting any male over the age of 15 who happened to be on the streets as the yellow vans rolled past. These hapless residents were simply plucked up, photographed and released the next day. They returned home, some with new bruises and all a day of life the less.

To add insult to injury, of the more than one thousand detainees listed by Merrett, probably one per cent or less comprised Inkatha members or sympathisers. And furthermore the police attitude towards the warlords was particularly baffling. Despite the fact that numerous allegations of murder and other crimes were being made against senior Inkatha officials, the police appeared uninterested in investigating the claims at all. Instead they channelled their energies into chasing and detaining township youths for reasons incomprehensible to the lay person, and which the police were not inclined to divulge.

Brigadier Leon Mellet, chief spokesman for the SAP, attempted to clarify the matter. He said in January 1988: 'If people are being arrested it is in connection with crimes that have been committed and not because of their membership of any political organisation.' Brigadier Mellet failed to explain why, if this was the case, only a tiny fraction of those detained were ever charged with any specific crime. Most of the detainees were incarcerated for months – some for more than a year – only to be released without either explanation or apology.

People are in fact detained for three reasons: to soften them up before being charged and tried; to interrogate them for the purposes of trying other people; and to withdraw them from ordinary life, to put them on ice and curtail their activities. Merrett concludes that in the case of the Pietermaritzburg detainees, the third reason is primary. He points out that few of the detainees were interrogated and that the chief effect of the detentions was to disrupt both extant and nascent UDF organisations and to remove responsible leaders from among the comrades. In fact, the detentions could be viewed as a punishment not for any specific acts, but for having the temerity to be involved in political activity at all. Not content merely with punishing the detainee, the authorities also appeared to draw the families into the punishment as well. Sometimes families arrived at the prison only to be told that the visit had been cancelled because of some ostensible misbehaviour on the part of the detainee. When they were allowed in, no physical contact was permitted and all conversation had to be in English or Afrikaans or else conducted through an interpreter.

Prison conditions were poor, to say the least. This was largely an inevitable consequence of the tremendous overcrowding in New Prison – somewhat relieved when detainees were moved to Westville Prison outside Durban – and had the effect of further penalising the detainees. In January 1988, R Thakurdin, an attorney practising in Pietermaritzburg, submitted a memorandum to the head of New Prison, in which he set out a number of complaints about the treatment of detainees. In point form, these amounted to the following:

(1) Overcrowding. Up to 50 people in a 5 by 12 metre cell.
(2) Bad food. Cold and covered with flies. Sometimes pieces of hair, glass and wire found in it.

(3) Prisoners not always informed when money is paid into their accounts.
(4) Insufficient exercise.
(5) Detainees punished when they request medical treatment.
(6) Detainees denied study facilities, although such facilities are provided for in the regulations.
(7) Warders are abusive and aggressive towards detainees.
(8) Detainees are summarily punished without inquiry by deprivation of meals or visits.
(9) Detainees assaulted and teargassed.

Prison conditions improved after this memorandum was sent out and in July the overcrowding was alleviated when Brigadier Jacques Büchner, head of the security police in the region, signed the release papers for a large number of detainees. Then in February and March 1989, more detainees were released after a successful hunger-strike campaign in which detainees nation-wide refused to eat until they were either charged or released. Clearly unable to find any grounds on which to charge them, the Minister of Law and Order, Adriaan Vlok, released hundreds of detainees, many of whom had been held for more than eighteen months.

By the end of 1989, however, there was a discernible change in police attitudes towards detention. People detained were no longer held for long periods, but hauled in for short, intensive interrogation sessions, threatened, and then released.

Nhlanhla, a veteran ex-detainee, had much to say on the subject. 'Going into detention is like going to school. Each time you go in you are in a new class. The first class is for the stone-throwers. The police bring you in and beat you up. They can be very harsh and they say you are less than rubbish. The white policemen call you a "stupid kaffir" and the black policemen find Zulu swear-words. They ask questions and then hit you before you can answer. Eventually you answer before they even ask. They ask you things like: "Who is instructing you? With who have you stoned buses? Who killed so and so?" They keep you for a few days until you are really soft, and then just before they let you go it's all smiles. They want to be your friend; they bring you things to eat (but you can't eat because you still feel too sick); and they try to make an arrangement with you. They catch lots of people this way.'

The room we were in was stifling and Nhlanhla shifted his position and fanned himself with his jiggling fingers. 'OK, you work some time more in the structures – say you go on the school SRC. Now the next time they bring you in, it's as activist. This time they don't always assault you. Instead they try to talk to you like your father, or the priest. They say, "Why are you doing these bad things? Who is advising you? Don't you know there are whites and Indians who want to corrupt black youth?" They keep you for longer this time, although even then they don't ask too many questions. They are trying to punish you, you see. If you try to explain what you are doing, why SRCs are good things for the people, they say: "Fogoff, man, that's rubbish. You kaffirs can't even speak English, how can you do this by yourself?" If you talk back too much they hit you for being cheeky, although some of the interrogators are more moderate.

'Once, they arrested me as a stone-thrower when they were really looking to detain me as an activist. The interrogators asked me if I knew Nhlanhla. They said they had been looking for a long time and that he was a very bad *tsotsi* and that if I saw him I should tell them straightaway. I said that I didn't know him, just his face and that I would tell them for sure if I could meet him. Then they let me go.

'If you are really active they pull you in again. This time you are a politician and they treat you like a dangerous enemy. This time they blame you for everything and say, "Why do you tell people to kill each other?" Or they say, "We know you're being instructed by the ANC and the SACP. You're telling people to make sacrifices for Tambo who can't be detained." When you're a politician, [Special] Branch treat you more carefully. They don't assault unless you have a provocative conversation. The trick is to beat them with logic. So for example if they say, "Do you know the UDF is ANC?", you say, "I don't know that, but I know what the UDF is. It consists of progressive organisations striving for a non-racial, democratic South Africa. If the ANC is that, then UDF is ANC, but only if those conditions are fulfilled." Or they say, "Do you know the Freedom Charter is SACP?" and you say, "I don't know that, but I know the Freedom Charter says such and such. If the SACP say the same things, then the Charter is SACP, but only under those circumstances." Then they leave the room and go out to discuss a new tactic. They always caucus their questions, then they come in again. And they can keep you this time for months, even years, just to keep you out of the way because they fright our political organisation."

When Nhlanhla left I went across to speak to David who was working in his office across the passage at the University. He was detained on 10 February 1988, together with other senior UDF officials and held until mid-July. As I came in, David leaned back and touched the sparse beard which ringed his wide face. Whenever I saw him he seemed to be smiling, and he smiled throughout our impromptu interview, despite the fact that his day was already more than packed with a diary full of appointments. I asked him about his experiences in detention, and he smiled again. 'I was held in Boston for four months before they moved me to New Prison. I think they must have a policy of splitting people in leadership positions from the rest, because I was out there on my own, and some of the other comrades were on their own at other police stations too, while at the same time there was overcrowding at New Prison.

'To tell you the truth, things weren't too bad at Boston, just very slow. Most of the police from the Upper Areas, you know, Vulindlela, acknowledge that the violence was caused by Inkatha's forced recruitment campaign, but there's nothing they can do about it. You find ordinary police frustrated from doing their police duties: you arrest someone for murder, but then an order comes down from above to release him, or you hear about a crime but an order comes down not to investigate.

'You have to realise that the police are not all the same. The security police – Branch – they're clearly anti-comrade, even the black cops; there's nothing to be done about that. Then the riot squad is made up of people moved from one area to another around the country so they can't develop any sympathy with the locals. They're pretty vicious. After that you get the *kitskonstabels*, the new boys. There are so many who are just criminals and Inkatha vigilantes,' he laughed, 'I should say, criminals–Inkatha vigilantes, that no one likes them or trusts them. Of course, a few may be all right; there are always a few good people in the worst crowd.

'But among the ordinary black SAP it is different. They are just as much under threat from Inkatha as we are. They are the ones who can see most clearly what is going on, and as I just said, if they don't like it there is nothing they can do about it. But at least for me to be held at Boston wasn't so bad. It's a small place, there's nothing to do, so contact is inevitable. The police get bored too so they would let me out to sit in the yard while they cleaned their uniforms or listened to the radio. We would chat about small things like sport or music, but sometimes they might ask why I supported the UDF – "It's a communist organisation," they'd say. So then I would try to explain a few things.

'While I was there I was not interrogated at all. Branch came four times, but only for five minutes. That was in the first month. The food improved after Vlok instructed the police to cook for the detainees and feed them the same food they were eating. So the food at Boston was much better than the food at New Prison. After 30 days they allowed me to have books, and sometimes one of the sympathetic ones would bring me the *Witness* or *New Nation* or *Weekly Mail*.

'In June, in detention, I was redetained at the start of the new emergency, and taken to New Prison. There were about 70 detainees there, 15 to a large cell. Conditions were different in prison. The warders were very hostile and aggressive, you could see it in their eyes. They held on to their sjamboks tightly and watched us closely just hoping for a chance. Once the food was so bad that the detainees refused to eat. After lunch, as we left the food-hall, we smashed our metal plates into the metal bin where you scrape off any scraps. It made a hell of a noise. At the next meal the warders were lined up along the walls, holding their sjamboks, waiting. It didn't improve the food.'

David was released in July, but release did not mean a return to normal life. Many of the ex-detainees found themselves still bound to the police, only on a longer leash. Activists were allowed out on condition that they adhered to all or a combination of the following restrictions: that they did not take part in any political activity, did not address groups of more than five people, did not give interviews or speak to journalists, reported to the police every day, stayed at home between 6 p.m. and 5 a.m. every night, and did not leave the Pietermaritzburg magisterial district without obtaining police permission.

David said, 'When we were released, all of us who were restricted were taken up to see Brigadier Büchner. We went in one by one, it was very formal. Inside the office, Büchner was sitting behind his desk in full uniform. He was even wearing his cap and his face was very bright, you know, shiny. I wasn't sure if it was cream, or if he was just sweating because it was hot in there. The police were making a videotape of each interview and they had a lot of heavy lights around the desk. At first I thought it was just Büchner trying to get into films, making sure that his face also was safely in the police video archives, but then I saw that the camera was pointing at me. He said, "Are you aware that you're on video. Just so you can't say you weren't told." I said Yes. After that he took me through the terms of my restriction order, point by point, and asked me after each one if I understood. There was an interpreter there who translated everything even though I didn't need him. After each point I said Yes, and then he asked if I understood the order in its entirety. I said Yes. Then he made me sign the form to show that I understood. All the time the camera was on me. Then Büchner said, "My Minister, against my better judgement, has instructed me to release you." Even though in some ways it was funny – ridiculous – by then I was sweating too.'

David paused to muse and even stopped smiling briefly. He continued, 'These days in the evening I just read books – but I read all day at work, and eventually it can get tiresome – or I sit on the phone speaking to my friends for hours, running up tremendous bills. I have to be at home every day from 6 o'clock onwards, so what can I do? I can't visit friends, I can't go to meetings. These restrictions are particularly hard on academics. Say I'm invited to a conference or a seminar in Jo'burg, even Durban, I have to apply to the police two weeks ahead for permission. Sometimes I get a call saying, "We're having a discussion next week, we'd like your input." I have to refuse. I can't publish anything without permission, and when you do ask permission they sit and sit and sit on it before they decide. Look, I could take the car to Durban this afternoon and they'd probably never know, but if they did catch me, I'd be in big trouble, so it's not worth it. Not for my own sake, but because the System could use it for propaganda value....'

His appointments were mounting up so I left. He called after me, 'It's bad, but at least I don't have to report to the police twice a day like some of the others.'

This last comment was a reference to a spate of incidents surrounding activists recently released and restricted to the Durban area. There had been reports of people who spent all day travelling to and from distant police stations to check in. The police compassionately offered to let them sleep on the veranda of the police station, 'to save them the long journey.' A more sinister consequence of police restriction, however, was the fact that once the activists were held to a set daily routine it became child's play for their enemies to monitor and predict their movements. This convenient information could be used for harassment or even assassination. The first death had already occurred. Chris Ntuli, a Durban detainee released and restricted after a long hunger-strike in detention, was killed in April 1989 on his way back from his daily encounter with the police.

Activists and their sympathisers in Maritzburg were understandably nervous about the spread of such practices to their townships. So far this has not happened, but the restrictions, as the police must be well aware, serve to strip away yet another layer of protection from people already vulnerable and exposed.

Some days after my interview with David I was in Edendale when I ran into Exodus again. This was a stroke of fortune as he had mentioned several times at our first meeting that he was a restricted person, and I looked forward to hearing his views on the restrictions. He squeezed the last few drops out of a box of Liquifruit and chewed the straw noisily before launching into a diatribe, much of which I did not catch. Finally he said, 'We just hang around and hope that on 11 June – when this emergency runs out – miracles will happen and they'll lift the restrictions. I personally am not afraid of speaking to the youth but they ask me questions I can't answer. I'm a restricted person and so I am limited. I have dreams of working, but I'm not. I'm just sitting in my possie, my place, waiting for something to happen. Maybe I could get a job, make some money, buy a cassette, put some of my knowledge and advice to young comrades on this tape. Maybe I can leave it in the back of a taxi on my way home if the driver is right. The youth could find it and listen to it. But perhaps I'm just dreaming.'

He swivelled and launched the empty carton into a rusty metal drum like a pitcher throwing a curve ball. 'You wouldn't know this,' he said, 'but to be restricted is like living in a fish-bowl. You can see everything but you can do nothing.'

PART III
Places

13
Shongweni

We came over the brow fast. The road dropped steeply and the car smacked down into a crater with an axle-crunching thud. Before us the Shongweni valley lay spread open in a great bowl. The familiar patterns of settlement were visible: cubic houses with coloured doors set off against the spinach-green hillside. We had just driven through Mpumalanga, and we could still smell the woodsmoke and bus fumes. Mpumalanga has had more than its fair share of the war but the township was peaceful on this Wednesday afternoon. Crowds of people lined the roads, stepping in and out of shops and houses. Buses shuttled back and forth, and in the road feathers fluttered from a chicken that had just been run over. From the top of the hill we could see the scores of blackened houses, torched by arsonists over the months of the war. They stood out like rotten teeth in a giant mouth.

It is possible to live in Natal and never see beyond the borders of the N3 as it winds its way down from Pietermaritzburg to Durban. The exit signs point to places which become familiar over dozens of journeys, but which one never visits. When I first became interested in Mpumalanga and Shongweni the names were already well known to me. I could say at exactly which point of the journey to Durban the signposts would loom up before disappearing in the rear-view mirror, but I could not tell whether the places they referred to were close to the highway or whether a long journey along a rural road was necessary before the townships themselves swung into view.

Now I was finding out. We drove downhill, swinging from side to side to avoid craters, and negotiating the narrow traffic circles which were an inexplicable feature of the roads in this region. In the car with me was Wendy Leeb, a researcher at the Centre for Adult Education at UNP, and Brian Pearson, a reporter on the *Natal Witness*. Some weeks before, they had visited Shongweni and discovered a town in the process of dissolution. They found people packing up, abandoning their houses and relocating to Pinetown on the outskirts of Durban. 'Where is everyone?' they asked.

'Fled, or dead,' they were told. Families stood at the side of the road surrounded by boxes and suitcases, waiting for the truck that would take them away. They left their houses unlocked in the hope that an enemy would destroy a locked house, but might spare one to which he had access.

KwaMbiza had been virtually untouched by the war. Supporters of the rival political forces lived together without much tension. The local Inkatha leader seemed relaxed and disinclined towards conflict, and the youth likewise. In January 1989, however, a new Inkatha man arrived, a warlord of the old school, determined to bring the town into line behind Inkatha at all costs. According to local residents, people disappeared or were killed openly and property went up in smoke. The warlord and his men retired to a distant part of the valley to regroup and take stock before making their next move. The residents of KwaMbiza did not wait to find out what that would be. The town emptied itself and by the time Leeb and Pearson arrived only the stragglers were left. A butcher closed up shop, lowered the shutters and, without a backward glance, walked away.

I was returning with Wendy Leeb and Brian Pearson to see whether the town had revived in the months that had elapsed. We turned into KwaMbiza along Mkhize Street and stopped at the Mkhize store. Inside we met Reginald Mkhize, a local entrepreneur who owned the shop and other property in the area. He was listening to a tape-recording of speeches delivered at the funeral of Samora Machel and popping cigarettes into his mouth, one after another. He chatted amiably and in return we bought things we did not need. Mkhize confirmed that the town was a shadow of its former self. 'But I'm not planning to pack up myself, just yet,' he said. 'I have too many assets sunk in this place. We're looking at a temporary political aberration which admits of a political solution.' He said that a band of comrades had returned recently and destroyed a whole contingent of the warlord's vigilantes. 'That's not been reported,' said Pearson.

Mkhize sighed. 'But that doesn't mean it didn't happen,' he said, lighting up a third Kent. 'This place has become a battleground. Both sides come into the town to fight it out and then retreat. This shop, these houses nearby,' he gestured vaguely, 'they're the only inhabited places left.' Without looking at us he tossed a couple of sweets to a child standing in the doorway.

We drove deeper into KwaMbiza. The silence increased and became uncanny. The roads were deserted and when we stopped to look around we could hear nothing at all, not even the cries of animals. All rural settlements in Natal hum with noise: bouncing around the valleys can be heard the sounds of crying babies, radios, the distant rumble of heavy vehicles and the barking of dogs. Voices float on the air, clear and disembodied; chickens cluck. These sounds are to be found everywhere in Natal except KwaMbiza. In such emptiness the houses themselves assumed a peculiar blankness, at once open and repelling.

To our left, three donkeys had taken over an abandoned house. Two were inside and stared dimly out through the front windows. The third stood on the porch swatting flies with its tail. Brian Pearson whipped out his camera and began shooting film with desperate haste. 'It's such a relief to find a newsworthy shot of the townships we can actually use,' he said over his shoulder. 'Almost any other picture would contravene the emergency regulations.' The donkeys found the snap of the shutter disturbing and cantered off to join another group clustered on the stoep of the next house. It was soon overcrowded, the donkeys became visibly upset, so we left them.

Further along we came to the remains of a general store. Arsonists had completely destroyed the building, creating a conflagration so intense that the glass in the windows had melted. Three weeks earlier the store had sold sweets, newspapers, bread and charcoal in five-kilogram bags; now you could pick all the charcoal you wanted out of the eaves which had fallen through inside the building, bringing down the corrugated-iron roof. The cement blocks in the wall had crumbled and iron piping lay twisted all around. We wandered through the store-rooms, coming across the ashen remains of sacks and boxes. Hungry mongrels circled us warily. Some puppies in an iron pipe shivered as we passed. They were starving to death.

The building was eerie with ruin. We left before the walls tumbled in on us. Outside in the road a sparkling billboard pointed to the shop. A woman with unnaturally brilliant teeth held aloft a bar of soap, also shining, and said, 'You can trust the fresh, clean, mild purity of Sunlight every time!'

There was nothing more to see. We pulled out of KwaMbiza and set off up the hill to the Albini Mission where Wendy Leeb wanted to check on some refugees she had met previously. The drive was more perilous than ever. The floods of October 1987 had scrambled the road which led to the gates of the mission. Access was ludicrously difficult in a car; on foot, which is how most people approached, it was merely awkward.

I parked outside the church, which overlooked a series of valleys stretching into the middle distance. It seemed an appropriate place for the practice of religion. Behind the school the nuns had turned a few rooms into dormitories for the refugees from KwaMbiza and other nearby areas. During the day these people set off from the mission to find work, or to return to their homes if that was possible, but they returned predictably every evening, the time of attacks. It was late afternoon when we arrived and already a large crowd of women and children were milling around. The children approached us saying, 'Good-day. How are you? I am very well. Good-day.'

Brian Pearson stepped into one of the rooms and congregated the refugees around him to take photographs. He arranged them carefully, taller people at the back, others kneeling, and children and wandering infants on the floor. It looked as though he was about to take a team photograph. The good humour in the room was palpable. Everyone was smiling and the children were laughing. Pearson wanted them to compose themselves more appropriately; he wanted their expressions to reflect their circumstances but they could not comply. Their circumstances were dire, but they could not help smiling because they hoped that our presence might bring them some relief and because they liked to smile for photographers. An old women, bedridden in the next room, raised herself on an elbow to see what was going on. Eventually Pearson was satisfied. He snapped the shutter and found he had used up all his film on the donkeys.

One of the nuns took me aside. She was ancient, with a wrinkled face and grizzled hair which escaped the sides of her wimple. 'They come at night to attack and kill,' she said. 'They frighten and terrorise these people. They have no common human decency, they wish only ill on their fellow man. The scoundrels!' she exclaimed. 'The dirty rascals! The rotten scoundrels!'

Back at the car we found that more fingers had been at work drawing patterns in the dust. Chassis groaning, we set off for the highway, getting lost and retracing our route several times before we found the homeward road.

14

Trust Feed

The rural township of Trust Feed is situated near New Hanover, about 30 kilometres from Pietermaritzburg. In October 1988 it had a population of about 5 000 people. The present population is now less by about a third. At 3 a.m. on Saturday, 3 December 1988, a group of gunmen opened fire on a house, killing eleven people and wounding two others. The youngest victim was 4 and the oldest 66. Coverage was swift and extensive – the *Natal Witness* carried the story and related articles almost every day for more than a week. The *Natal Mercury* weighed in with a report, as did the *Sunday Tribune*. This act of violence was neither senseless nor aberrant. It was not a once-off expression of madness, but the culmination of a systematic political process of terror and coercion which had steadily crushed and sapped the resilience of the residents of Trust Feed over a period of many weeks.

The roots of the problem, however, went back considerably further in time. Trust Feed is a township occupied in freehold by about fifty landowning families who let their land to tenants and squatters. In the language of apartheid, it is a black spot on the green face of white Natal. For years the community lived under the continuous threat of removal, but in 1982 the Trust Feed Crisis Committee (TFCC) was established by residents of the township to combat this peril. The TFCC enjoyed remarkable success. The prospect of removal receded and Trust Feed was transferred to the authority of the Development and Services Board, which began improving conditions in the township.

In 1982 there was one school and three taps to be shared among the entire population. By October 1988, a clinic costing R59 000 was nearing completion, the water supply had been improved, plans were afoot to build a community hall with money raised within the community, and the roads had been upgraded at a cost of R65 000, a project which provided 103 local residents with employment. In short, most residents supported the TFCC, endorsed its activities and elected its office-bearers.

At the beginning of January 1988 the wife of a COSATU member living in Trust Feed was killed and his house burnt. In March, Trust Feed was proclaimed a black development area. This laid the ghost of forced removals once and for all as black development areas are rural settlements in which blacks have the rights of permanent settlement and freehold. At the same time, Inkatha activity in the area increased rapidly. A committee comprised of local Inkatha members was formed in opposition to the TFCC. The committee lobbied for the inclusion of Trust Feed into KwaZulu, but the community strongly resisted this plan. After this setback Inkatha supporters apparently decided that committee politics was a hopeless strategy and that it was time to launch a campaign of active recruitment.

In August a prominent Inkatha member from Pietermaritzburg visited Trust Feed and addressed a public meeting there. He lambasted the TFCC, calling them a bunch of thugs, and he made other comments in threatening language. The TFCC was alarmed and wrote letters about the incident to the South African Police (SAP), the Inkatha leadership at Ulundi, and the Natal Provincial Administration, but to no effect. In October, Philip Shange, the chairman of the TFCC, was shot with a home-made gun. His assistant was also shot and wounded but both survived. In late October and early November a battalion of vigilantes began knocking on doors late at night, demanding allegiance to Inkatha from the occupants and threatening those who refused it. Inkatha gained members rapidly as well as a few supporters. The township was divided between supporters of Inkatha who lived on the lower slopes, and supporters of the TFCC who occupied houses further up the hill. On 18 November, the house of Mr B M Nyoka, a TFCC supporter, was burnt down. His possessions were destroyed and his family was scattered.

An official with the Development and Services Board drafted a letter to the Natal Provincial Administration in November 1988, in which he expressed real unease at new developments in Trust Feed. He wrote that the black landowners, in conjunction with Inkatha, wanted to be put in administrative control of Trust Feed. Inkatha in particular had appealed for tribal structures to be imposed and demanded that the community accede to control of the area by indunas under the headship of a chief. The SAP, while claiming neutrality in the matter, gave implicit support to Inkatha – they made it clear, quite separately, that they wanted to work through a tribal authority. Moreover, the landowners objected to the initiatives of the TFCC, saying that tenants had no right to decide what should be done on land they did not own.

The official at the Development and Services Board was not swayed by these considerations. He wrote that there was no evidence that either Inkatha or the landowners enjoyed any support in the community, in contrast to the TFCC, which had been elected democratically and had widespread, evident support. He wrote, too, that he had perceived no interest on the part of the landowners in improving the quality of life in

Trust Feed; they were all in violation of the law because they allowed uncontrolled squatting on their land; and of the rates due from them, two-thirds were outstanding.

The report notwithstanding, trouble for the residents of Trust Feed really began on 23 November when a large number of Inkatha supporters were bussed in from Msinga and Edendale to launch a massive recruitment drive. Many residents fled the area; others were forced to join Inkatha. Over the next week, cars and houses were stoned and burnt and many people were assaulted and stabbed. At 11 a.m. on 30 November, four youths were killed. They were all supporters of the UDF and were killed by Inkatha vigilantes as they tried to return to their homes after a meeting, having been turned back earlier. Thus by Thursday, 1 December, Trust Feed was virtually deserted.

A reporter on the *Natal Witness* who visited the township found only a group of Inkatha men sitting around drinking sorghum beer. They were armed with sticks and knobkerries and they abused him, calling him a 'terrorist' and accusing him of having been sent by the *amaqabane* to spy on them. The police ordered him out of the area to the hoots and applause of the men. The police also confiscated a roll of film in his camera which contained pictures of a family leaving Trust Feed to become refugees. They were departing because they feared a massive confrontation was looming and they reported that hundreds of people had already fled, many of whom were now sleeping in the veld near New Hanover.

The following day, Friday, the police detained twenty youths, among them four members of the TFCC. Residents claimed that the police had divided the detainees into Inkatha and non-Inkatha groups, and sjambokked the latter. The police denied these allegations. On the same day, Pierre Cronjé, MP for Greytown for the now defunct National Democratic Party, warned the police that residents feared and expected attacks by Inkatha vigilantes at any time. The police gave some verbal assurances that the area was under control.

That night, a wake attended by about twenty people was held at the house of a person who had, somewhat surprisingly, recently died of natural causes. At 3 a.m. there was a knock on the door. The door was opened by one of the mourners who found herself confronted by a crowd of men armed with rifles, revolvers and shotguns. They began firing immediately, through the door, the windows and the walls. Eleven people were killed, literally shot to pieces, and two were wounded. Later in hospital one of the survivors said: 'They just kept on firing brutally. All around me people were crying and screaming. They were running around the house not knowing where to hide. The shooting carried on until all the screaming stopped.'

A further perspective on the events of the night was provided by Lephat

Nyoka, aged 73. His sister-in-law was one of the women murdered that night. Nyoka declared that he had been at home on Friday evening when he heard shooting coming from the direction of the store owned by Philip Shange. He fled into the canefields where he spent the night. He heard the sound of shots throughout the night but saw no evidence of the police. He watched as fire destroyed the store and the houses of three other families prominent in the TFCC. At dawn he returned home. He stepped outside to draw water for tea and found himself surrounded by seven armed men, two of whom he identified as sons of the local Inkatha leader. The men asked him who was home and when he replied that he was alone, they brandished a gun in his face, ordered him back into the house and struck him on the back of the neck as he turned to go. He went inside and locked the door, at which point the men moved across to the other house on his property which they looted, destroying whatever they could not carry.

Over the next few days, the local Inkatha leader refused to speak to journalists. A CBS news team was chased out of Trust Feed by a crowd of men armed with stones and knobkerries, and shortly afterwards a *Natal Witness* reporter was threatened by a crowd in the presence of the police when he attempted to interview a prominent Inkatha member. The police advised him to leave the area, saying they could not guarantee his safety.

The police thereafter swung into action but made no arrests. They refused to allow reporters to visit the scene, claiming again that the situation was under control. Captain Kitching, a police spokesman announced: 'Extra policemen have been deployed in the area and extra patrols are being conducted. We are doing our utmost to keep the area calm.' They said they could not disclose the political affiliation of the people killed as the matter was still being investigated. Despite police assurances, the more than one thousand people who had fled the area were too frightened to return to collect their belongings.

Pierre Cronjé arrived in Trust Feed the day after the killings and saw the blood-stained house and the smouldering ruins of other houses which had been razed during the night. He said later that the violence could be traced directly to attempts by Inkatha to gain control of the area. Cronjé pointed out that the TFCC had sent letters to the Minister of Police, the Administrator of Natal as well as to various newspapers and members of parliament, warning that a slaughter like this might happen. 'The irony of it all', he said, 'is that the people representing the community have been driven out of the area.'

This was true. The TFCC had dissolved completely with members scattered all over Natal, many of them untraceable. Philip Shange, when asked about his future plans, displayed weariness and uncertainty. A newspaper report which appeared on 8 December mentioned that Inkatha landowners had taken full control of Trust Feed and that residents were being forced to join Inkatha. People still living in Trust Feed were flocking to the Inkatha office at the house of the local Inkatha leader, Jerome Gabella, saying that they were afraid of the consequences of not joining. A local clergyman reported that he had joined up on 3 December because he was forced to. 'If I had not joined my house would be burned. It's the same thing the UDF are doing in other areas. During the week my sister called me at work to tell me to return home immediately because people were threatening to burn down my house. They found it empty, you see, so they assumed I had fled, which would mean I was UDF.'

After the carnage, the reckoning. Inkatha at once denied all responsibility for the killing. Zakhele Nkheli, the Inkatha Central Committee member under whose authority Trust Feed fell, denied that any vigilantes had been bussed into the area. He blamed the UDF for everything that had happened in Trust Feed, saying, 'Now that they have been thwarted in Mpumalanga they have moved into Trust Feed. Hopewell and Mpolweni are next on their list.'

Velaphi Ndlovu joined in the argument as well. He dismissed claims of forced recruitment as nonsense. Chief M G Buthelezi issued a statement on 6 December in which he denied that Inkatha was responsible and said that he would sue any newspapers which irresponsibly blamed his organisation for the violence. Later that week he issued a further statement in which he claimed his lawyers had established that the victims were in fact all Inkatha members.

This claim contradicted a statement made by the survivors in which they said that they and the eleven people killed were not members of Inkatha. At the funeral of Mrs Nyoka, relatives of the deceased woman and other local people denied emphatically they were members of Inkatha. They wanted the fact to be made public. As far as they were concerned they were politically non-aligned. They supported the TFCC, which was a non-aligned body. One resident said, 'Look, I have personally, with my own eyes, seen the sons of the Inkatha leader going around looting the houses.'

On 6 December the *Natal Witness* published an editorial in which the following was written:

At the root of the problem lies the growing disenchantment of a rapidly urbanising population with tribal structures which are perceived to have been used by the state to enforce its policies. Since these structures underpin its power, Inkatha finds itself locked in a battle against people attempting to erect alternatives. At Trust Feed these people are a community-elected 'crisis committee' and its supporters.... Seen from this perspective, the atrocities shed a bleak light on ideologically-inspired political structures which are neither democratic nor acceptable to growing numbers of black Natalians.

The battle for control of Trust Feed was won decisively by the vigilantes. They put into practice the principle that in politics might means power – even if there is no one left over whom to exercise that power.

A year later, the inquest into the killings found that three policemen, two of whom subsequently disappeared, may have been involved in the slaughter. The matter was referred to the Attorney-General of Natal for consideration. The Inkatha connection was not touched upon at all.

15
Retief Street

In January 1988, the mayor of Pietermaritzburg, Mark Cornell, issued a misconceived appeal to the police, requesting them to stop associating the township violence with the city of Pietermaritzburg. 'Several of the townships are far away from the city itself but the impression is given that the whole place, including Pietermaritzburg, is burning. This can't be good for our image,' he complained.

As if to oblige his desire for accuracy, the war arrived in down-town Pietermaritzburg and settled in around the bus terminus at the bottom of Retief Street. The white population observed this development nervously. The street is one which is only frequented by blacks who do their shopping, catch their buses, and visit their doctors and lawyers along its length. Nonetheless Retief Street is still close to the manicured parks, glossy arcades and plate-glass windows of the city centre. White shopkeepers and their customers cast a glance over their shoulders now and then; they fear the war may spread and come marching up the road to invade their special places. As long as it remains in Retief Street they are content: while they cannot exactly disown the violence – despite its effect on the city's image – they can at least draw a veil over its more unsavoury features.

Retief Street is a street of small shops and small professional practices. The shopkeepers occupy the ground floor of the low buildings while the professionals take the rooms above. Black workers tread the pavements, going into food shops, visiting doctors, and buying clothing and domestic appliances on hire purchase. Along Retief Street you can have your teeth pulled, buy a bedroom suite on hire purchase, or pick up a good cheap suit and choose from a wide selection of hats. The hawkers do well too, selling their mealies and fried chicken pieces to passengers congregating at bus stops and taxi stands. A black person who lives in the townships near Pietermaritzburg cannot avoid Retief Street; it is a hub, a point of entry and access to the city. It is also a danger, a point of vulnerability, a place where people trying to hide can be found.

Refugees from rural areas like Vulindlela and Sweetwaters who fled their homes under threat of death from vigilantes, found temporary places to stay and moved frequently from one residence to another. They came into town and alighted from buses and taxis at the terminus in Retief Street. And it was here that their enemies came to track them down. In November 1987 the first fights occurred at the terminus; a man was stabbed and another abducted. Then in February 1988, a large group of Inkatha members gathered outside the Retief Street beer hall. They injured one man and stabbed a 14-year-old boy to death. The boy was drunk and tried unsuccessfully to hide under a Kombi. His attackers hauled him out and sliced him up. The boy had cursed the men, calling them *Theleweni!*, but later, when the body lay draining in the street, it was hard to tell whether he delivered the insult before or after the men reached out to grab him.

Soon afterwards, 43 Inkatha members who had attacked commuters at the terminus, and flicked the cheeks and noses of men with their knives, were arrested and pleaded guilty to charges of forming an illegal gathering. Their sentences were more entertaining than sobering, and the men came out of court laughing and defiant.

From July onwards, Retief Street battles became more and more frequent. The number of stabbings increased, as did the number of abductions. The method is always the same. The target is sighted, either walking alone or with one other person – more than that makes the operation too difficult – and the car glides up alongside. Four men spring out and grab the victim, fending off his or her companion and threatening any onlookers. They bundle back into the car which has already started to move. Once out of the city they remove to some quiet location where the victim is tortured and then slaughtered. Occasionally an abductee is found or returns alive, but not often.

The case of Richard Nkomo is typical. On 21 October he and a friend were in Retief Street when a carload of Inkatha members pulled up in front of them. His friend escaped but Nkomo was forced into the car and taken to Sweetwaters where, after a while, he was stabbed to death. His body was found later, dumped on a hillside.

In the second half of 1988, as the various strongholds became more consolidated and impregnable and the actual business of fighting was confined more and more to skirmishes along the boundaries of different areas, Inkatha and, to a lesser extent, the comrades came to regard Retief Street as a convenient battleground. Warriors would drive into town ready for battle. Their vehicles were packed with weapons and on occasion they brought with them cartons of stones, gathered in the hills, with which they stoned buses going to enemy regions. Groups of Inkatha laid traps for unsuspecting youths and sought out refugees who, by virtue of their flight, were clearly enemies and therefore fair game.

On 26 August, Bongani Mazibuko and Raymond Ngwani were walking in Retief Street when a group of men, shadowy in the dusk, called out *'Heytha!'*, the UDF greeting. They returned the shout, whereupon the men who belonged to Inkatha and were not comrades as they had surmised, fell upon them. Raymond, who was armed, managed to fend off the men, shouting to Bongani to run and save himself. In the event it was Raymond who escaped death while Bongani's body was found some hours later. Other comrades were stabbed or shot in full view of hundreds of people. The attackers took advantage of the crowded and confused conditions to kill and then melt away. Sampala Sokhela, a refugee from Sweetwaters, was cornered at the taxi rank by a group of Inkatha members from Sweetwaters. An informer wearing a balaclava had pointed him out and he had had no time to escape. He was stabbed and left for dead. He was taken to hospital and released after a couple of days and the following week he was back in Retief Street where he was again stabbed by Inkatha members. This time they merely slashed open his back and moved on. Sampala reported neither incident to the police. He was urged to do so but said, 'The police do nothing. That makes it even more frustrating.'

The Retief Street shopkeepers have not appreciated the transformation of their territory from prosperous commercial thoroughfare to dangerous and unstable battlefield. In August a group of people armed with knives and sticks went on the rampage, stabbing and scattering hundreds of commuters who had been queuing for buses. They ran into nearby shops, damaging merchandise in their flight, and some display windows were smashed in the fracas. The shopkeepers were incensed and submitted a petition to the police, calling for a mobile unit to be established near the terminus. After some delay the police acknowledged they had received the petition and said they would consider it. They did; they rejected it. A shopkeeper who spoke to reporters from the *Natal Witness* declared that people were killed near his shop every day. Every Friday he had to summon ambulances. 'People are slaughtered here like cattle,' he said. 'The victims die in the dark as they wait for transport.'

By October matters had deteriorated so much that shopkeepers were forced to close up early in the afternoon on Fridays, forgoing the lucrative evening trade. 'Fridays used to be our big earning day,' they lamented. 'Now we're lucky if we don't make a loss from theft or vandalism.' In December they again appealed to the police for help and described a pitched battle in which, they said, bricks and stones rained down on passersby and destroyed dozens of shop windows. Moreover, the Retief Street violence had badly affected Christmas shopping. Sales were down by 50 per cent on the previous year's figures, despite the fact that in general, the war was far more contained and low key than it had been in December 1987. There were now daily battles. The police stepped up their patrols and made hundreds of arrests, but the killings continued.

Since January 1990 more people have died: refugees, commuters, shoppers. A man has struggled 250 metres along the street, dragging a trail of blood behind him before collapsing for good; another has emerged from a shop to find his car in flames, the old leather upholstery crackling like popcorn. The *tsotsis* prowl around, ripping up goods with their long knives, and smiling contemptuously into the strained faces of their victims; and the fast cars of the vigilantes cruise up and down. There is little prospect of things improving in Retief Street – the pickings are simply too good to pass up.

PART IV
Casualties

16
Case notes

Since October 1987 over two thousand people living in and around Pietermaritzburg have died. Far more have been maimed and injured, and in every township and suburb property and possessions have been wrecked and scattered. The stories of loss, of families decimated, of gratuitous murder and arson are legion. People carry the record of their personal and communal suffering in the grim set of their eyes and in the expressions of their faces in repose. Every week the official unrest report augments the numbers, piling the statistics ever higher and setting the sociologists to work updating and improving their graphs and figures. With the weight of each new week's kill, those who died first, whose stories were once so shocking, are buried deeper and deeper; they become more remote and forgotten. The statistics are disembodied; they tell us nothing about the person to whom they ultimately refer. They tell us nothing about the circumstances of that person's life, nor do they help us build a picture of character or personality.

Sifting through the figures, compiling lists of death per area, per month, per faction, I lost all sense of the people who had died to create these graphs. After a short period of acclimatisation I found it easy to switch off from the real implications of what I was reading. Ideologues from Inkatha and the UDF as well as researchers, journalists and general monitors of the situation refer to the statistics to support political arguments or to derive propaganda value from them. This is legitimate – in this sense the statistics have a morbid utility – but occasionally I would have to remind myself that I was reading about the slash of metal on real flesh, about torches taken to doily-covered furniture, about terrified children shitting their pants, knocked backwards by the blast of a bullet in the legs or guts or head. The cases which follow are presented in an attempt to retrieve a few people from the anonymity of the University of Natal's unrest data base in which I first discovered them. There are almost four thousand incidents listed in these records. I have extracted six, not just because they are so remarkable or unusual but also because they are so representative.

CASE 2

A woman who was married with a family and lived in a house in Edendale arrived home one evening to find she was a widow. Neighbours rallied round. They told her that a white Kombi had come to call that afternoon and that its occupants, well-known vigilantes all of them, had abducted her husband, beating and dragging him from the house into the van. Then both the Kombi and her husband disappeared down the road.

The woman's neighbours poured her cup after cup of sweet tea, transmitted their shock and sympathy through a litany of clicks and head shakes and tried to persuade her that he would return. But she knew with total conviction that the photograph in her wallet was all she would ever see of him again.

In the days which followed, she and her children made enquiries throughout the townships, but drew a blank. She changed to the night-shift at the factory where she worked in order to pursue the search during the day. She took a series of buses to four different hospitals and six police stations and was met with blank indifference and incompetence. She returned again and again to hospital and police mortuaries to examine cadavers. The police mocked and taunted her. 'Leave it, he's left you, Ouma,' they said. 'He's taken up with some fresh little cherrie.' It is impossible to describe the impotent rage she felt throughout this joyless period. She knew well enough, of course, that many policemen in South Africa look through black people and ignore their concerns, but she had not realised that the fight to make them see and hear her would be so painful and humiliating.

Eventually a sympathetic policeman, an exceptional character, became aware of her plight and possibly even of her feelings. He placed before her scores of photographs of all the bodies which had passed through the police mortuary over the last few months and among them she found her husband. The picture was blurred – it was hardly a good likeness – but it was him. The policeman checked the reference number and told her that the deceased had been given a pauper's burial. He did not know whether they had attempted to trace the next of kin. He assumed they had. He shrugged. He was very sorry, but....

CASE 3

Helmina Shange is an old woman whose body is covered with burn scars. At one stage she lived at Mafakatini in Vulindlela. From her bed in the intensive-care unit at Edendale Hospital she related her story to sympath-etic listeners.

'Three hundred men. Yes, the *amaqabane*. I was sitting in my hut with many of my grandchildren when the men arrived. They told the kids to get out, then they came over to where I was sitting, poured petrol over me – my head, clothes, even my feet. They dragged me outside and lit a match, maybe a few matches, I can't remember. They waved a match in front of my face so I could see what they were doing and then they set me alight. I think only God saved me. I was on fire, there were flames on my hands and my face. I fell over onto the soil. I think that's when they must have thought I was dead because they left me and went off to burn the house. I rubbed myself in the soil and put the flames out. I kept rolling until they were all out. Then I crawled through the fence into the field and hid myself. I could not think because the pain was too strong.

'They burnt the house, the car, the TV set. Everything in the house was burnt. Then they left. They were laughing and singing. I sent a message finally to my induna but he never came. He must have been too afraid. Eventually a car came and took me to hospital.'

Helmina Shange was asked whether she planned to seek legal assistance, and whether she would move to a different area when she came out of hospital.

'There's not much point,' was all she said.

CASE 4

Near Thulani's Garage in Edendale there is a general store which opens early and is always full of people. People waiting for buses drop in for food or a newspaper and there is always a group gathered outside to chat or scheme. The composition of the group changes during the day, but the numbers remain constant. Small children kick cans around outside and wait hopefully for largesse from the customers.

At 7.30 on a February morning, Musi Nyide's mother sent him to the store to buy a copy of *Ilanga*, a Zulu-language newspaper with a high circulation, presently owned by Inkatha. He was dressed for school and carried a satchel. In the breast pocket of his shirt he kept a cluster of pens. There was an SAP riot van parked near the store. Preoccupied with the demands of the forthcoming school day, he hardly noticed the vehicle. Musi extracted a pen and began doodling on his hand. The door of the van swung open and a thick-set, square white policeman leapt out clutching a shotgun. He had no neck and the spread of his fingers was wider than the boy's thigh. 'What the fuck you doing with that pen, you kaffir?' he screamed. He grabbed Musi and shook the pen out of his hand. The boy tried to run but the policeman held him firmly and smashed him in the face with a heavy fist. 'I know your shit,' he was still screaming. 'You taking the number of my van to give your friends, you fucking black dog.' He swung the barrel of his gun into his hand and smashed the butt into the boy's face. Musi doubled over and put his arms up around his head to protect himself. The policeman continued to club the rounded curb of his back and neck. Eventually the boy collapsed and fainted. The policeman was red in the face and breathing heavily. He glared round at the people standing silently nearby. 'What you looking at? FUCK OFF!' he yelled. Then he climbed into the van and drove off, revving the engine and spinning the wheels wildly.

Someone picked up Musi and took him to Edendale Hospital. He regained consciousness but his back was on fire and he could not move his neck at all. At the hospital he was told that a bone in his neck had been knocked out of place. He was given six Panado tablets and discharged. Not surprisingly, the pain did not let up. Musi laid a complaint with the police, and said that although he did not know the name of the policeman who had assaulted him, he would be able and was prepared to identify him. He was not called on to do so. The complaint was buried, together with so many other incidents which were 'being investigated'. Musi Nyide now wears a surgical collar and he still cannot twist his neck more than about twenty degrees to the left or right.

CASE 5

One of the most savage and incomprehensible murders occurred early in the course of the war, on 20 October 1987. Unlike incidents both before and afterwards, the nature of this killing caught the conscience of the white population in Pietermaritzburg. Leader articles appeared in the *Natal Witness* and the public wrote letters demanding to know what steps the police were taking to find the murderers.

In the early evening four men arrived at the Shezi house in Esigodeni, Edendale. The Shezis were out, but their two sons were home and hid when they heard the pounding on the door. The men smashed through the flimsy wood and kicked their way into the house. Within minutes they had located the two boys and pulled them out of their makeshift refuges, kicking and biting. One man swung round and hit the 8-year-old Bongani Shezi over the head with a cane-knife. He was knocked flying but recovered sufficiently to twist his way out of their grasp. He reached the door and managed to push his way outside. He fled and hid in the veld. The men turned their attention to his brother Skhumbuzo, who was 4. They took him outside, forcing him along with kicks and blows to his head. Their car was parked nearby; they pushed the child in and drove off.

The following day, in a ditch near the house, the police found his body, decapitated.

The story spread. It was picked up by a number of newspapers and messages of shock and sympathy began to arrive at aid agencies in Pietermaritzburg. The police did not know what to make of the whole affair. They said they thought the murder was a revenge killing aimed at the family as a whole. Possibly the Shezi parents belonged to the wrong group, they surmised. With the decapitation of Skhumbuzo Shezi, people sat up and took notice that there was something bigger and uglier going on around Pietermaritzburg than they had previously imagined. The early warnings of unionists, activists and lawyers now suddenly rang true.

In a report which appeared in the *Natal Witness* on 17 November, the police were quoted as saying that the child's murderer had been killed in Edendale. Two days later, in an editorial, the *Witness* asked, 'In the absence of an inquest hearing or a trial, on what basis was guilt for the crime established? ... Why, in fact does the due process of law appear to have been distorted to the extent that it has?' The police were stung to reply in a letter published in the paper later that week. They said that the file had not been closed and that someone suspected of the killing had been killed in Edendale. The letter writer concluded by saying, 'We do not know who has "distorted the due process of law" but it is certainly not the police. It is clear that the current situation in the Pietermaritzburg area is being somewhat exaggerated by certain media and sensationalised. Some reporters even refer to the "civil war" raging there.'

From Shezi onwards, matters in Pietermaritzburg worsened. The story lost its news value after a while. The killers disappeared – perhaps they had been killed themselves, so many people were dying just then – and the reporters switched their attention to each new week's grim tale.

CASE 6

On the desk in front of me was a pile of fact-sheets and articles all dealing with different aspects of the war. Some were concerned with refugees, others gave statistical breakdowns of the dead and injured over various periods, others looked at the human cost of the war, and yet others were concerned with the way the conflict had effectively brought to a halt the education of thousands of young blacks in the townships. Among the last-mentioned I picked up an article by Mike Hart and John Gultig, both lecturers at UNP, entitled 'The Effects of Violence on Black Schooling in Edendale and Vulindlela'. It was dated October 1988. I opened it and read the frontispiece:

Fifteen-year-old Lucky returns to find a group of people milling around his house. He hears that his younger sister has been stabbed to death at her school and that the 'theleweni' are to 'get' the rest of the family that evening. The attack is unsuccessful, but the next day Lucky's father decides to go into town to see a lawyer about the murder and attempted firing of his home. He turns back when he notices a group of known Inkatha vigilantes at the bus stop. Lucky and a group of friends meanwhile set about defending the home and spend most of Friday manufacturing a crude assortment of petrol bombs as they guard the house. On Saturday the house is raided by the SA Police and Lucky and 15 of his friends are detained. That night the vigilantes attack again and his father is killed and his home burnt to the ground. His distraught mother has to wait for almost three weeks before she is allowed to visit Lucky and tell him the news. She also tells him all but four of the group arrested with him have been released, but that one had already been killed by 'unknown' vigilantes. Three months later Lucky and his three friends appear in court and are convicted of public violence. They receive suspended prison sentences ranging from 3 to 7 years each. Less than a month later, shortly after Christmas, Lucky is redetained and is still being held.

The story rang a bell. I flipped through some of the papers in front of me and found another version, only no name was given in this one, and then another and another. The misnamed Lucky embodied all the ills consequent upon the war – he served as a symbol of all the destructive forces at play. Whenever someone needed an example of human cost they chose Lucky, not because he was unique, but because in his story were combined all the sufferings and misfortunes which sprang up like weeds behind the plough of war.

I mentioned the symbolic nature of Lucky's story to Nhlanhla who had just come in and was standing at the window cracking the knuckles of his long, restless fingers. 'Would you like to meet this Lucky?' he asked. 'I know him well. In fact, I could just take some days to find him and bring him here.'

'I thought he was in detention,' I said.

'He's out now. He's trying to finish his Standard 8.'

'I'd be glad to meet him if it's possible.'

Nhlanhla undertook the task and the following week he introduced me to Lucky in an empty classroom in the Education Building on the New Campus. Lucky stood up to greet me and I noticed that he was dangerously thin. His skin was stretched tightly over his bones and his movements were slow. His handshake was limp and yielding. He sat down and waited. He preferred to speak in Zulu through Nhlanhla although his command of English was good. I was about to ask him the inevitable questions when something about his expression arrested me. He was regarding me with a mixture of watchfulness, boredom and a faint sardonic amusement. I changed my question. 'How often have you been interviewed?' I asked.

Lucky shrugged and smiled for the first time. Nhlanhla interpreted. 'Too many times,' he said, laughing. 'The newspapers, academics, PACSA, lawyers, people like you. And then foreign television people have been here too. He is like an exhibit.' Lucky was laughing too, silently, hardly moving his lips.

I began to question Lucky. He replied in a painfully soft voice, not looking at me but at my notebook. As he spoke – his words almost inaudible, Nhlanhla had to strain to catch them – his eyes swivelled around the room. They were large and sunk deeply in his head. His scalp was shaved and the skin of his face stretched tightly over his cheek-bones accentuating his skeletal appearance. His lips were pulled down, and when he smiled only the corners twitched upwards. A light stubble was visible on his chin. His head and torso were disproportionate to his legs which were short and thin and seemed unsuited to carry the weight of his body. Two silver Parker pens were clipped in his shirt pocket. Occasionally he would extract one of these and look at it carefully as if to reassure himself of its solid, tangible existence.

Lucky murmured something. 'He says he has dedicated his life to revenge,' Nhlanhla reported loudly. I asked where he was living and whether he saw much of his mother. 'He moves all the time in a big circle. A few nights in Nhlazatshe, then on to Howick, a few days with his mother in Sobantu, Ashdown, back to Nhlazatshe. Sometimes he comes in to town to see his mother who works in a store in Retief Street.'

I looked at Lucky. He seemed to be mocking me somehow, challenging me to see something more than just the generic face of suffering sitting opposite me, occupying his skin. I was not sure how to go about this. I was embarrassed by the interview, conscious that I was hacking over the same old ground and poking the same stick interminably in his wounds. I asked him about the course he was taking through SACHED, the South African Committee for Higher Education. He told me that his favourite subject was English. 'Read much?' I asked.

'Not enough,' he said. He spoke in English and his voice picked up in volume. 'Some things are too difficult, some things I understand.' Then, unexpectedly, he asked, 'Have you read *I Am David*?'

'Yes.'

'This book is written by a woman,' he said, 'but it's about a boy. Did she know him, or did she just make up the story?'

'She made up the story, but she probably knew people whose experiences were similar to David's,' I replied. *I Am David* is the story of a boy who escapes from a German concentration camp in Greece during the Second World War and makes his way across Europe to Denmark where he is finally reunited with his mother. David is courageous, generous and, above all, resourceful. He negotiates obstacles and overcomes setbacks and dangers that would weaken and demoralise other people. 'I identify with David,' Lucky said. 'He doesn't see his problems as the end. He keeps struggling, he keeps trying to do things. I would like to be like that.'

At the end of the interview he asked, 'Could you do me a favour now? I need a lift into town.' I drove him in — he was going to meet his mother — and in the car we discussed the independence process in Namibia. I dropped him off in Retief Street and that was the last I saw of him.

Throughout the afternoon I kept returning to Nhlanhla's joke that Lucky was an exhibit. It would be more accurate to say that Lucky's story was the exhibit and that he himself was hidden behind it. And yet he himself gave the lie to this patronising rendition of his circumstances. From what I had seen, Lucky had no intention of becoming anyone's generic victim.

17

Viva Education!

John Aitchison has described the war in the Pietermaritzburg area as one which is 'devouring the youth'. This is accurate as it is the youth, whether comrades, *comtsotsis* or Inkatha Youth Brigade members, who are the primary casualties. They are the ones who kill and are killed, who are turned out of their homes by their enemies and sometimes by their parents, who become homeless refugees, who are forced to steal, who stand in aimless groups waiting for the day to pass. They find themselves debarred from school because they have no money, because the school is full, or because they are of the wrong political camp.

By now it is an axiomatic fact that in South Africa black schools are a site of political conflict and struggle. In Natal it is certainly no different, but the situation is further complicated by the fact that there are two educational departments running schools in the province. The KwaZulu Department of Education and Culture (DEC) administers schools which fall inside the boundaries of KwaZulu, while the Department of Education and Training (DET) of the South African government – the official purveyor of Bantu education – administers schools in black areas not incorporated into KwaZulu. Among the many ironies to be found in Natal is that black pupils actively prefer DET schools and seek a transfer to them wherever possible. According to Mike Hart and John Gultig, educationists at UNP, this preference stems from the fact that DEC schools are over-crowded, understaffed and have poor facilities. Expenditure per student is R198 per annum, as opposed to the DET's R335 (and the R1 710 spent on each white child). Teachers are underqualified and gaps in the teaching staff are filled by Inkatha apparatchiks. Consequently, non-Inkatha students at DEC schools often endure harassment from other pupils and from staff members.

Inkatha keeps a tight hold on education at DEC schools. Ubuntu Botho, a subject devoted to the values and philosophy of the organisation, forms an integral part of the syllabus; and staff members are required to sign pledges of loyalty to the government of KwaZulu. At Sinathing High School in Edendale in April 1986, pupils boycotted the school for a month, but eventually resolved their differences with their teachers. The DEC, however, responded by sending a delegation of MPs from the KwaZulu Legislative Assembly, who arrived one afternoon in the staffroom, armed and angry. They hectored the teachers for allowing the boycott to occur and demanded that each teacher declare his or her political affiliation. When many delcared themselves to be neutral they were told there were no neutral teachers, only those for or against Inkatha, and that the DEC expected every employee to be loyal to Inkatha. This incident effectively split the teaching staff and resulted in the eventual resignation of many of the 'neutral' teachers.

Hart and Gultig conducted an investigation into the state of schooling in the Pietermaritzburg townships and published their findings in the 1988 paper. In the schools in Edendale and Vulindlela, pupils and staff have to make out as best they can under impossible conditions. For example, at the end of 1987, matric pupils at Msimude School in Sweetwaters were attacked while they were writing their final exams. Inkatha vigilantes invaded the school and pupils fled clutching their papers. When the attackers finally left the school, the pupils returned and finished the exam. At another Sweetwaters school, Mpande, pupils arrive late and leave early because they feel it would be too dangerous to travel on the 7.30 a.m. and 2.00 p.m. buses. Hart and Gultig give further examples of education by fear:

Teachers speak of the tension in the schools. They park their cars very near the exit facing outwards and pupils leap to their feet at any noise resembling the chant of a group of raiding vigilantes...

History teachers are not able to express themselves freely because they fear that members of 'certain organisations' will label them as UDF members and they will be in danger. The teachers [are] caught in an untenable position. Their teaching has become increasingly defensive, confined to the syllabus only, with no relationship or communication with pupils outside the classroom. One horrific example of this situation was of a thirteen year old pupil who left the classroom, stabbed a pupil, and returned to carry on with the lesson. The teacher and the school were unable to respond to this incident for fear of reprisal. The teachers felt that they could not disagree with Inkatha and thus felt powerless to protect their pupils or to offer them any sort of assistance in times of crisis.

In this Orwellian scenario, pupils watch teachers who watch pupils, who watch each other, always waiting for a false step, one and all guarded and shuttered. In such a stilted and stifling atmosphere it became impossible to learn and work, so many pupils fled the schools and teachers left their jobs for the reason that it was better to be out on the streets in the open air than in the classrooms.

One school lost senior teachers in English, History, Economics, Accountancy, Business Economics, Mathematics and Biology, all within the space of a few months. Teachers who did not wish to leave the profession, or felt unable to because of the shortage of jobs in other fields, took extended unpaid leave or requested transfers to less dangerous areas.

Pupils who abandoned or were forced out of schools they had always attended tried to enrol at schools in safer areas nearby, but the majority were unable to resume their schooling. They left the country, went to prison or else simply had to make their way as best they could, out of school and unemployed. Hart and Gultig report that 'In the Pietermaritzburg area pupils seeking places in schools in the rural areas were being refused admission because Pietermaritzburg students were seen as troublemakers and students had to give false addresses in order to be enrolled.'

Many pupils fleeing from Inkatha vigilantes in Vulindlela have sought refuge at the Siyahlomula High School in Ashdown. Among comrades the school has a reputation for being non-Inkatha, and the teaching staff is politically non-aligned. The school is administered by the DET and has a capacity of 480 pupils, although many more seek admission each year. Despite the relative political homogeneity of the student body, the school has not been spared disruption and the pupils have not been allowed to pursue their studies in safety: in July 1988 a group of pupils were shot and wounded by *kitskonstabels* stationed on the school premises.

I decided to find out more about this incident so I phoned the headmaster to ask for an appointment. He was extremely hesitant about speaking to me, but said that I could come over the following afternoon, although he could not guarantee he would tell me anything.

I decided to take the chance, and the next day I drove past a couple of lifeless bulldozers, then up a ditch masquerading as a road, and went in through the high gates of the wire stockade surrounding the school. Siyahlomula High School stands right on the Ashdown–Mpumuza border, half-way up the farther, western hillside. On the Ashdown side a buffer of tall grasses and bullrushes separates the school enclosure from the nearest houses, while on the Mpumuza side there is a long stretch of empty hillside before the first of the rural settlements. Looking out to the east from the school carpark there is an excellent view of both areas and of the steep road which serves as a border. The distant, hill-top police mobile unit is just visible, and the damaged border houses cluster in the foreground.

I walked along a brick corridor into the school quadrangle. It was deserted except for a middle-aged white woman clutching a briefcase and pacing about with small steps. She examined my jacket and asked, 'Are you also here for the interview?'

'I'm just a temporary visitor,' I said, and she seemed relieved. She launched into an enthusiastic description of the school and its activities and told me why she was hoping to work there so much. She was practising her lines for the forthcoming interview and I listened briefly before wandering off to look around. At that moment the bell rang for the end of the school day and the pupils came surging out of every classroom. A teacher dispensed soccer balls to a group of older boys. The interviewee and I were standing on the red balcony outside the principal's office, and as they came past on their way to the staffroom, the teachers greeted us with casual politeness. Eventually the headmaster himself appeared. He asked me to wait a few minutes, and ushered the woman into his office. Through the open door I could hear her gabbling rapidly and self-consciously. After about a quarter of an hour she came out again, perspiring, but looking hopeful.

I went into the office and the principal, Mr Nyide, apologised for the delay. I told him that I wanted to talk to him about the *kitskonstabel* incident, and he was silent for a long time, sizing me up. The phone rang. Nyide answered it and went across to the staffroom to summon a young woman. This happened several times in the space of ten minutes, and each time she thanked Nyide with a small curtsey. Returning to my request, he said, 'Look, I'm sorry, but I warned you I might have nothing to say. I'm not authorised to speak about these things to the press.'

'I'm not the press,' I pointed out.

He was dismissive. 'Whatever. You can get a statement from the public relations office at the DET headquarters in Pietermaritzburg if you like.'

The phone rang again, and while he was out of the room I looked about. On the wall above his desk there was a large glossy DET poster entitled 'Education is the Salvation of the Nation'. The poster was divided into eight blocks against a white, orange and blue background. In each block there was a photograph of some educational motif like a laboratory, a soccer match, or a smiling graduate beneath a mortarboard. The words 'Viva Education!' were splashed across the centre of the poster, and at the bottom was written 'Education *is* Liberation'.

On the opposite wall, a second poster proclaimed the teacher's code of dedication, in which were inscribed the values of the DET. The curling edges of a scroll had been drawn around the clauses and there were more photographs of idyllic educational environments on the border of the poster.

Mr Nyide came back in and asked, 'Is there anything else I can do for you?' As I considered my answer I noticed he was fiddling with the empty shell of a shotgun cartridge.

'I think that'll be all, thanks very much,' I said.

Outside, wondering what to do next, I ran into some luck in the shape of a matric pupil called David who wanted a lift into town. I asked him if he had been at the school on the day of the attack by the *kitskonstabels*. 'Sure,' he said. 'Look, let me show you something.' He led me round to the back of the school on the northern side, beyond which lay Mpumuza.

We walked through long, tick-filled grass and my guide pointed out that most of the windows of the classrooms on this side of the school were smashed. 'Vigilantes were coming down and stoning the school all the time, because they know the scholars are comrades, and their kids can't come to school here for the danger. So they had a feeling of jealousy,' he said, 'For some of us it was hardly worth going to school. At night we would be awake for hours, on defence, and then have to be at school by 8 the next morning. Sometimes there were attacks during the school day so we would have to drop our studies and run off to help our comrades and then come back to the books afterwards when we were tired, and maybe some of us might be injured. It was stressful, but in actual fact, it was like a good political education.

'Anyway, the thing is this. Finally the inspector decided the school needs protection so the headmaster asked for a police unit around here to stop the invasions. What happened next was that the *kitskonstabels* came right onto the school grounds but the headmaster asked them to leave because the scholars were finding them to be very threatening, and also because the school did not need people inside, but outside, protecting the border and the fence. So on the first day the police came and took the *kitskonstabels* out of the school but the next day they gathered at the school gates, and then at recess they all came inside.

'Rightfully or wrongfully, the scholars saw this as a provocation against them and there was an exchange of insults. The next thing that happened was that the *kitskonstabels* started chasing children and shooting them. I was coming out of my classroom when I heard the sounds and I started running too. I didn't know where I was going, I just followed whatever direction people were running. The kids who got shot the worst ran to the wrong places near the fence where they were trapped and hit. Many of the students had to be hospitalised.

'Of course the parents heard the shots and they saw their children running around and being assaulted, so they came to the school as soon as they could. Now you must understand this – many of these *kitskonstabels* are from Mpumuza themselves so they have a hatred and a fear of the Ashdown people. So when they saw the parents coming they ran away and vanished. When the SAP came later they couldn't even find their own *kitskonstabels* because they had gone to hide themselves. After that, our mothers went to demand that there should be no more *kitskonstabels* in Ashdown, and in fact they had success because they don't patrol the township like they used to. Also the police put up a unit at the top of the hill there,' he pointed vaguely, 'and the attacks on the school are now much less.'

Just beyond the carpark about a dozen new school buildings were under construction. We walked towards them, and I saw that they were almost in a state of ruin. The metal frames and supports were bent and rusted, and the concrete floors were already split and ragged as tough weeds found their way through the cracks. Brick walls, jagged and incomplete, rose up here and there from a bed of scrub. It was clear all construction had long since been abandoned, and David confirmed this. 'For a long time there was much activity,' he said, 'but then something happened. Maybe the DET lost interest, or they ran out of money, but no one has worked here for six months, maybe more. All of that work has gone to waste. They'll have to start all over again.'

I drove David into town and dropped him off. Later, back at my office, Nhlanhla asked whether I had enjoyed my visit to his old school. In reply I said, 'I've seen a lot of fancy school trophies in my time, carefully displayed and each one with a history and tradition behind it. But in Ashdown the headmaster doesn't keep any silver cups or plates and shields in a glass cabinet. The history of the school is told by the row of empty cartridges lined up on his desk.'

18
Refugees

At the end of the working day, the boys stack the supermarket trolleys in neat rows and throw out any bits of rubbish caught in the wire mesh – crushed lettuce-leaves, broken eggs, plastic bags. Then they pool their tips to buy food and disperse to find a place to sleep for the night. These boys are all refugees, on the run from the fighting in their home townships. Some have friends in Pietermaritzburg itself – they find temporary shelter in domestic servants' quarters in white suburbs – while others root around in the giant skips behind the supermarket and rig up tents out of oil-cloth tarpaulin and discarded cardboard boxes.

Phineas, 16 years old, lanky and with eyes that refused to be still, said through an interpreter, 'I used to live in Sweetwaters and go to school there, but the *theleweni* came and burnt down my house in February. My father and my brother were both killed and my mother fled to Dambuza. I came to the supermarket to make a little money and because I knew I could never stay any longer in Sweetwaters. Right now I'm staying in a room in the suburbs, but I don't know for how long – I can't stay there for ever. I want to go to school, but right now that particular situation for me is hopeless.'

Next to him, drawing deeply on a cigarette, Tom told me his story: 'I lived with my uncle in Mpophomeni, but his house was burnt down and we were both chased out of the township. I've been working here for months now but I have nowhere else to go at night so I sleep out of doors. The problem, for me, with such a life is the cold. Even in summer I feel it deep in my bones.' He clasped his fingers together and sent a rippling crackle through his knuckles. 'You see,' he said, 'you can hear them complain for yourself.'

These boys are better off than many of their peers because they at least manage to earn their subsistence by pushing grocery-laden trolleys from checkout counter to car for white supermarket patrons. When I met them they were not slow to joke about themselves and their lifestyles, and they smoked and kicked a tennis ball around with insouciance. However, such surface indifference to their condition concealed a deeper trauma: these trolley-pushers confine their lives to the narrowest of ambits. They eat, sleep and relax within the space of a few blocks around the suburban supermarket where they work. Some of them go into town occasionally, but most prefer not to venture into what they consider to be dangerous territory. Certainly none of them would dream of returning to the townships, and most are deeply fatalistic about their future prospects.

Since September 1987, tens of thousands of people in the Greater Pietermaritzburg region have been rendered homeless. Some were made to watch helplessly as marauding groups looted and burned their property, others did not wait to see this destructive expropriation, but fled in advance. Jo-Ann Bekker, a reporter on the *Weekly Mail*, met some refugees early in 1988 and described what had happened to them in an article entitled 'A Hill-side Scar Where a House Once Stood':

Themba Ngcobo was about to plaster the brick house he had been building for two years when attackers he claims were Inkatha supporters burnt down the five-bedroomed house....

Ngcobo shows deep scars on his back: 'They stabbed me three times, then they threw stones at my wife.' He says they chopped their hands with a bush knife and he and his wife point to gnarled scars on their fingers....

Ngcobo and his wife, Gertrude, go over an inventory of what was destroyed in the fire and what they left behind: a truckload of sand and 12 bags of cement to plaster the house; furniture, a fridge and a hi-fi; an orchard which produced oranges, naartjies, peaches, pears, loquats, grapes, lemons, apples and sugar cane; and a vegetable patch which yielded mealies, potatoes, sweet potatoes and pumpkins.

Themba Ngcobo remarked that he had been singled out because one of his sons was serving a prison sentence for high treason. 'We have heard that Inkatha says it was good for our house to burn down because it was an ANC house.'

Another refugee, a woman who was living with her children at the back of a house in the white suburbs, told Bekker they had been forced out of their home when her husband was accused of taking part in a fight against Inkatha vigilantes who were stoning buses. She said, 'We had two rondavels and a seven-roomed home made of concrete bricks. It was not yet completed, we were just about to put the roof on. And we had three cows, 28 chickens and three dogs.'

Wendy Leeb, a researcher at the Centre for Adult Education at UNP, has conducted extensive research into the lives of refugees and has documented their conditions in some detail in a number of academic papers. Leeb has described refugees from the war as the 'misplaced, displaced and abandoned', and she maintains that their plight has been worsened by the indifference of white South Africans.

'Part of our problem', she told me, 'is that we can't really comprehend what the life of a refugee is like. We are so easily, but superficially, shocked.

The youth have more fortitude; they are able to bear up and set about dealing with the situation. Most young refugees say that their first priority is to return to school, and this is despite the fact that they have no bedding or clothes or food. Some of them manage to rehabilitate themselves, but most don't.

'Take the case of Lothe Nene. He was 16 years old and came from KwaMgwagwa. He was attacked, stabbed, and forced to flee. He fled from his home fearing that he would bring danger to his family, and became a refugee. When I visited the place he lived in, I found him living in a mud room six metres square with six other young refugees. They had one bed, and one couch with broken springs, one blanket, no food and nothing to cook on, but they were lucky – they had a roof. Ten days later I was invited to his funeral – and I stand in the terrible position of having pictures of him alive and dead. The worst part of it was that all he wanted was to go home and go to school.'

'As a nation,' she continued, 'we purport to care about that great god, the family, but most whites don't seem to give much of a damn about the disruption in family life going on right now in the black townships around Maritzburg. Families who are forced to flee are already in a state of dissolution. Some families may have had as many as three houses destroyed, and some have moved up to five times. Members become disoriented because their roles lose definition, separation occurs and family intimacy is no longer possible. Some family members may have been killed, but the family is prevented from mourning together; and the children drift into isolated and alienated patterns of behaviour.

'Take the example of one family I met. They were forced to flee because a brother had been killed, apparently after having been mistaken for the father. They found temporary shelter in a house together, but the father was very depressed because although he was still the breadwinner, he had lost all he'd worked for for twenty years and he felt that he'd lost his role as head of the family. He became increasingly desperate, largely due to the sufferings of his children, all of whom had to leave school. They were confined, unable to make a noise and very unhappy. They were all depressed and the older ones were becoming difficult. And of course, the worst part is that this is just one anecdote among thousands. For all the people I've met, or cases I've heard about, there must be a hundred unreported.'

According to Leeb, the displacement experienced by refugees is set to have repercussions in the future well beyond the immediate physical difficulties they suffer. She lists three psychological effects of long-term exposure to violence and displacement.

(1)   The trauma becomes long term, and the psychological consequences

become more severe. Anger and grief give way to depression, and the victim becomes unable to act and is paralysed by impotence to change the situation.

(2)   In adults stress levels remain intolerably high, and irritation, alcohol or drug abuse, family violence and social violence become commonplace. In children and youth there is a lack of ability to concentrate, restlessness, feeling of a total lack of self-worth, and resentment against the adults who are seen as letting this happen to them.

(3)   Violence is regarded as the norm, and is seen as a solution. It becomes the one area of life over which the individual has some control and is used for self-assertion.

'Can you imagine the outcry there would have been if thousands of people in the white community had had their property destroyed, seen their families dispersed and been forced to flee their homes?' Leeb asked. 'The response would have been overwhelming: the church, the municipality, the service organisations and youth organisations would have rallied round. But the plight of black refugees has been largely ignored and they have been left to fend for themselves. I don't want to disparage the work done by individuals in any way – hundreds of white employers have sheltered their domestic servants and their families in their servants' quarters for months at a time – but on the whole the official attitude in Pietermaritzburg is to ignore as much as possible, and deny the rest.'

19
The burial of the dead

Just as every week brings its tally of the fresh dead, so every week sees the funerals of the previous week's harvest. The intensity of the war can be gauged from the level of activity at the two major cemeteries which serve the black population of Pietermaritzburg: Sinathingi and Mountain Rise. From December 1987 to February 1988 when the numbers of the dead increased out of all proportion the gravediggers were never idle. They were burying two or three people every day and digging extra cubic slots in the empty cemetery fields, confident that they would be filled immediately. Chris Gutuza, writing for *Die Suid-Afrikaan*, interviewed a gravedigger at Sinathingi who said:

We dig graves every day. Here you see about twenty holes for the day. This afternoon more people will be buried. We bury them every day. I have been here three years. Two more gravediggers are here now. We just dig graves. I never saw anything like the last few months. Sometimes more than ten people are buried a day. Almost all of them die because of the fighting. People of Inkatha and people of the UDF – they all die.

When a comrade is killed in the war, his friends say that he has 'fallen'. By using this word they imbue his death with an heroic quality and drape the mantle of martyrdom over his shoulders. Funerals are invested with a ponderous dignity and they become elongated expressions of tribute and respect. A succession of eulogies and praise poems justifies and affirms both the life and the sacrificial death of the deceased. Ironically, it is at funerals – moments of dissolution – that communal solidarity is most powerfully expressed; they are rallying points for the entire community in whose service the slain activist is said to have died.

Among the residents of non-Inkatha areas, the protocols of burial are inflexible and seldom vary. When someone dies, either an activist or a member of a close-knit community, the local youth or area committee takes it upon itself to facilitate the funeral arrangements. A funeral committee is established and members offer emotional support to the family – they arrive to offer condolences, spread the word and usher others to the home of the bereaved family – as well as physical support. They arrange to identify the body and collect copies of the death certificate. More than that, they set about raising money both to cover the costs of the burial and to see the family through the financial straits of the immediate post-funeral period. After the death of Sipho Maloko, the committee accosted the drivers of all cars coming into Ashdown and offered to wash their cars in return for a contribution. The offer was not negotiable; the cars gleamed and the fund swelled. The name of the donor and the amount of the donation are meticulously entered on the donation list, and all the money is handed over to the family of the deceased.

The funeral arrangements themselves are extremely formal. An expensive coffin is bought – where possible the preference is for a mahogany box with brass handles – but if this is not feasible a simple coffin of polished, varnished pine is acceptable. The lavish coffin and the strict formal dignity of the occasion are all part of the conviction that nothing but the best will suffice in honouring the dead. Where quality of life is lacking – blown away by the insecurities of war, material poverty and political impotence – quality of death is offered in rightful recompense. But a coffin is not all that is needed for the burial of the dead. In addition, a grass sleeping-mat and a blanket, placed under and over the coffin in the grave, are necessary accoutrements. These have to be new, and are donated by close friends.

On the night before the funeral the family hosts a vigil. A core group spend the night in the house while others come and go. Prayers are said, and political songs and eulogies break out spontaneously. The next morning, early, the hearse arrives to transport the family to the church. They squat in the back of the vehicle, around the coffin, which gives off a dull gleam through the curtained windows. Funerals are scheduled to begin early and finish late but this is not always possible either because of police restrictions or because the funeral parlours are overworked and the hearses fall behind schedule as funerals proliferate.

Etiquette requires the family to hire buses that take mourners to the church and then to the cemetery. This is an expensive custom and accounts for a considerable portion of the funeral fund. At the church a mourner steps down the aisle, holding the wooden cross which will mark the grave. Behind him the coffin, draped in the flag of the local youth organisation, is carried in beneath a guard of honour, usually an avenue of comrades standing stiff, fists aloft. The blanket is carried in too, and placed beside the coffin, but the sleeping-mat and the dozens of plastic wreaths sent by friends and neighbours remain in the hearse. The comrades in the guard of honour wear the uniform of their organisation and insist on formal, decorous dress from the mourners. The men wear jacket and tie and the women are required to wear skirts. Older women wrap themselves in black or purple knitted shawls, pulling them about their shoulders and up over their heads. The members of the funeral committee act as marshals:

they wear identification tags, show people to their places, ensure that older men and women are seated, vet clothing and pick up all loose paper left after the memorial service.

And there is a lot of paper to be picked up. Every person is handed a programme that lists the sequence of prayers, hymns, poems, eulogies, general speeches and sermons which take up the entire morning. In addition, the walls are covered with photostatted photographs of the deceased. Other slips of paper contain the words of the hymns, the manifesto of the youth organisation, and sometimes poems which the poet has arranged to have copied in bulk.

Not everyone can fit into the hall, so a crowd congregates outside and people go in or come out in shifts. The mourners put aside the need to eat or drink or go to the toilet, and settle down and concentrate on the programme. The memorial service opens with a prayer followed by a spontaneous hymn. Next, a close relation – father, mother, brother – makes what is part speech and part lament, describing the place occupied by the deceased in the family in emotional as well as practical terms. 'Who will look after me when I am too old to work, who will pay my rent in my old age now that he is gone?' they ask. After this comes a speech by a senior member of the community, followed by speeches by members of all the clubs and organisations with which the dead person has been associated, no matter how tenuous the link. Interspersed with and subsequent to the speeches there are songs, poems and tributes. The committee, or family members, read out the sympathy notices and poems they have received in full, omitting nothing. The names of donors, and of those who have sent wreaths, are read out. Choirs sing hymns of praise and anyone who wishes can add a poem or speech. The programme is a rough guide to the proceedings, not a set order of events.

The service can take anything from two to five hours, concluding with a formal sermon lasting an hour. The sermon is delivered by one of the two or three ministers in attendance, who range in denomination from Zionists to Roman Catholics. At these funerals the religious element plays a leading part, but it is not sectarian. Finally, when the preacher stands down from the pulpit, the congregation gathers to pay its last respects. The two oldest men in the family open the coffin, lifting the lid back to uncover the head and shoulders. The mourners file past. As they leave the church another collection is held, this time for the comfort of the family in the three days of mandatory mourning after the funeral when they will be confined to the house and unable to work.

The memorial service is roughly timed to end at the point at which the hearse again becomes available. These two moments do not always coincide, but once the stretched black car returns, the coffin is shouldered and carried out of the church. The guard of honour runs before it toyi-toying, leading the hearse for the first few paces along the way to the cemetery. Then it is placed in the back, the family climb in, and the mourners cram into buses and Kombis.

Out at Mountain Rise, or Sinathingi, the riot police are already positioned. Their blue denim uniforms, yellow vans and the thin black line of the quirts held lightly in their palms form the backdrop against which the consignment to the earth takes place. At the graveside there are more prayers and reading from the Bible. Under the threatening gaze of the police, youths perform a muted toyi-toyi between the graves of earlier martyrs. The family of the deceased sit on a bench at the head of the grave while mourners gather round, standing on the mounds of the long dead because there is no space between the graves. The sleeping-mat is placed at the bottom of the trench, the coffin is lowered on top of it and then covered with the blanket. Each person, in terms of seniority and closeness to the family, tosses sand down on top of the blanket and no one leaves until the men have completely filled the grave, raised the wooden cross and demarcated the mound with stones and twigs which people have brought in the pockets of their coats. The funeral is over, the riot police give the order to disperse, the next cycle begins.

*   *   *

There is no doubt that funerals make the police nervous. They dislike the occasions, yet they invariably attend them. The spontaneous gatherings, expressions of emotion, affirmation of values and ideals which the police are specifically called in to suppress – all of these factors combine at funerals, leaving the police tense and upset. They do everything they can to limit funerals, short of stopping the killings and bringing down the numbers of the dead. They limit the time allowed for the funeral, the number of mourners, the days of the week on which funerals can be held, but even this is not enough. The police gather outside the churches at which memorial services are held and their vans are parked in row after yellow row at the cemeteries. They break up any group which threatens to become a gathering, and their fingers quiver on the triggers of their teargas launchers.

Khaba Mkhize, the flamboyant chronicler of township life and death, has written about funerals in his *Frontline* article:

Before the violence destabilised Maritzburg there had never been a funeral starting at 8 a.m., undertakers tell me. Now, to allocate policemen to escort the processions, the police commissioner gives the bereaved family a laid-down time for the commencement, usually 8 and 11 in the morning and 2 p.m. The funeral must be concluded in three hours regardless of how long the route takes to the cemetery.

I was at a funeral of an Edendale tycoon whose five and a half grand casket (GST excluded) had to fly into the grave because time was expiring. Family members will never forget the day.

Not everyone regards the actions of the police at funerals with quite so flippant an eye. The UNP data base tells me coldly that at Taylor's Halt cemetery, on 29 December 1987, at the funeral of Thembinkosi Gasa who had been shot by the police, mourners gathered at the graveside were teargassed by a large contingent of riot police. James Lund, Professor of Law at UNP, was present on one occasion when mourners were teargassed on their way to the cemetery.

'From where I was standing I saw the sudden blossom of smoke,' he recalled. 'I heard the pop of the guns and saw the leading group break up. Two of the comrades dropped to the ground, one was hit by a cannister, the other had inhaled a lungful of teargas, and the coffin slipped off their shoulders and fell into the mud. The crowd scattered and the police stopped firing after a short spell. Fortunately it was raining, so the teargas dispersed quickly.

'I went back to my car and drove round behind the police lines. I found the lieutenant in charge of the unit, identified myself, and told him that the action he had taken was totally unnecessary as the ceremony had been entirely peaceful. He responded by saying that the funeral was unlawful in terms of the emergency regulations because it had not complied with the general order restricting all funerals. I asked him to be more specific about exactly which regulations had been contravened but he was unable to do this. He simply said, "Ag, the regulations, man, the emergency regulations." He added that even if he wasn't obliged to disperse the crowd, he was entitled to do so, and had chosen to do so. He said that he did not have to, and was not prepared to give any reasons for taking this action.

'I persisted and then he got really angry. He started shouting – he was very young, you know, he wasn't exactly up to dealing with stressful situations – and demanded to know whether I had permission to be in the township. I said, "Of course not, it's not necessary." He said, "This is an emergency situation. I'm ordering you out, you have three minutes. If you don't get out I'll arrest you." Well, naturally this was ludicrous so I laughed and he became even more angry. He grabbed his walkie-talkie and put a call in to headquarters. He told me to identify myself again, which I did. He relayed the information, listened for a moment, swivelled to look at me and said, "*Ja, hy het a groot snor,*" listened again, put down the radio, shouted an order and drove off without looking at me again.' Lund stroked the thick foliage on his upper lip as he recalled the incident.

The efficient and dignified dispatch of the 'fallen' among the comrades is not only hampered by the police. Inkatha supporters, too, have often attempted to disrupt funerals of comrades and activists, although the methods employed are more brutal and direct.

The most severe attack on a funeral occurred on 30 December 1987 at Sinathingi cemetery. As it turned to enter the cemetery gates, a bus was ambushed by a huge crowd of armed men, and by the time the police arrived there were dozens of injuries to be treated and five fresh corpses to be buried.

A witness who was injured but survived the attack, described the sequence of events. 'Relatives and friends of the family gathered at the house at about 9.30. We were expecting some kind of trouble and the police had given the parents a letter promising to protect the mourners but when we went to the memorial service at the YMCA Hall there were no police. Even after the service, on the way to the graveyard there were no police around. We packed into two buses: the elderly in the first one and about a hundred of youth in the second one. There were also private cars and Kombis.

'In my bus, the second one, we were singing and jumping, chanting slogans. When the convoy reached the graveyard, the hearse, the private cars, the Kombis and the old people's bus went inside, but before our bus could turn in a man ran out and shut the gate. At the same time a whole crowd of men came flooding out of a nearby home. They were armed with guns, stones, pangas and cane-knives; one man had a rifle. They started firing and the people in the bus were screaming and trying to escape. I can say that pandemonium broke out. I ducked and fell to the floor. People were stepping on me and falling; some had smashed the windows and were jumping out, only to be hacked with knives when they landed. I grabbed a knife from one friend and decided to make a break for it. I jumped out, injuring my ankle when I hit the ground, and straightaway three men attacked me with staves and slashed at my head with cane-knives.

'I have been a boxer for years and fortunately I am very fit, although I could not put weight on my leg. I struck back with my own knife, and it and my fighting experience saved the day for me. I was attacked again and again but managed to push through the crowd. I forgot about the pain in my foot and I fled with some others up to the top of a nearby hill. At that point the riot squad arrived with a helicopter which hovered above us and ordered us back to the cemetery. One girl was shot in the buttocks so the police picked her up. I couldn't walk any more and a policeman helped carry me back to the cemetery. We were ordered into a police van and driven to the other end of the graveyard where the bodies were lying on the ground. I saw the body of a young girl lying pitifully across a fence. She had been hacked with bush-knives and her body was covered with blood. Some of it was still oozing out of her wounds. Later I was taken to Edendale Hospital together with three girls who all had knife wounds.'

Other witnesses said that after the initial attacks at least twenty Kombis arrived, bringing reinforcements to the vigilantes, who, they said, had initially been waiting at the home of Jerome Mncwabe, a well-known Inkatha warlord. Moreover, after the attack the police arrived, cleaned up the mess and teargassed a group of comrades who had gathered together to defend themselves against further ambushes.

$\star$ $\star$ $\star$

By contrast with those of UDF supporters, the funerals of Inkatha members provide opportunities for shows of military strength. The mourners arrive decked out in their Inkatha uniforms and armed with sticks and assegais. The speeches are fiery rallying cries, rich with the smell of blood and a taste for revenge. It is precisely after the death and funeral of senior Inkatha personnel that residents of non–Inkatha areas anticipate attacks. Defence committees are placed on full alert and the community digs in and prepares for attack. Under these circumstances, energies are directed towards defence rather than offence: it would be a confident attacking force indeed which dared to disrupt an Inkatha funeral.

$\star$ $\star$ $\star$

I drove out to Mountain Rise cemetery on a March afternoon which was recovering from morning rain. Apartheid is strictly observed among the dead, of course, and although all race groups are accommodated under the broad hillside, it is clear, even without following the signs, which group is buried where. The graves of whites are massy affairs. These enfranchised citizens lie interred beneath thick slabs of marble, surmounted by elegantly engraved headstones. There are wide spaces between the graves and the grassy avenues are neat and well tended. Trees with broad leaves, as well as the inevitable cypresses, provide shade for the fair-skinned faces of visitors. It is a restful place.

The burial ground for Indians sports many ornate monuments, and here too the graves are well spaced, but the dead have been allocated a nether slope of the hill, pushed back from the entrance. I drove along the tarred cemetery drive-way until the road petered out, and bumping over the roots of a clump of pines I found myself at the edge of the section reserved for blacks. The scrub was overgrown and the sun blazed down without interruption. I stepped out into the thick and humid air and made my way over to a cluster of graves which occupied the eastern end of the field. These were the graves of people who had died in the nearby townships since the end of 1987. Over the space of little more than a year, 500 new mounds had sprouted in the coarse grass.

There was only one marble headstone, the rest were all earth mounds marked off by a ring of stones. Each grave had a wooden cross set at the head, two pieces of wood slotted together and nailed into place. The name, age, and dates of the deceased were printed along a strip of plastic Dymotape and stuck down across the join. Occasionally there would be a name picked out on a leather strip, or punched into a thin square of tin, but these were rare. Most of the ages were within the 18–35 range, the generation most affected by the war. It was refreshing, in a morbid way, to come across the resting-ground of anyone over 70, and even this was no indication that the occupant had died of old age.

I wandered among the lots, reading name-tags and trying to keep off the mounds. This was difficult, however, as the graves had been dug right on top of each other, a mere foot-breadth separating one grave from the next. Despite this closeness each grave was carefully demarcated by a border of stones and bricks, and its own garnishing of plastic floral tributes. The original wreaths, encased in Cellophane, Perspex globes or uncovered and half-buried in mud, still lay across the top of most mounds. On some graves mourners had planted daisies, long since dead, and erected shafts of aloe leaves. In this thin soil the only living things were the hardy weeds which somehow found a purchase among the stones.

I found the most recent grave. The funeral had been held a day or two earlier but the wreaths were already spattered with mud. One end of the Dymotape on the cross had begun to curl away from the wood. I pressed it down with my finger but it sprang back up as soon as I released the pressure. Beyond me there were four empty holes, chiselled perfectly out of the ground. I stood on the lip and looked down past the walls with their neat cross-section of soil strata, to the bottom. There was about half a foot of scummy water trapped down there and in each of the others. The wind shifted and I breathed in a lungful of the stench of human decay before I could get my hand over my nose and mouth. There had been so much rain during the summer that the ground was like a sponge. I could picture the water seeping from grave to grave in a vast network until it surfaced at the bottom of the empty slots in front of me.

There was something else that was depressing – the crosses. Neither the wood nor the crude join was designed to withstand the passage of time and season. Along the first row of graves almost all the crosses had either split or collapsed completely. On others, still standing, the strip of tape had peeled off and disappeared, so for at least a third of the graves there was no way of knowing who was buried where.

All those poems of praise, the eulogies and speeches, the fancy coffin, the mantle of martyrdom, the noble death, did not amount to much. Within a pathetically short time the 'fallen' disappeared into anonymity as their crosses fractured and their graves became overgrown. But that, after all, is what this war, like any other, is all about: living people with their histories, thoughts and passions, simply vanishing into the hillside.

PART V
Responses

20

Tea with the Bishop

I found the cathedral easily and promptly got lost. I walked past the windows of a room in which table after table of neatly dressed women were taking tea. They watched me briefly over their cups, indifferent. I went into the new, modern cathedral, built in the round, with interior walls throwing off unexpected planes and angles. I had been warned by people that architecturally the building was a disaster but I thought it was excellent and complete with all the necessary qualities: coolness, calm and space.

None of this was much help to me at that moment. I was getting late and I wandered about some more until I found a man who directed me to the Bishop's office. More than that, he led me there himself, casting glances behind him constantly to check that I was still following. We went up to the third floor of the administrative building, and a receptionist ushered me into a bare room of medium size with a desk cutting slantwise against the far corner. Behind the desk was the Suffragan Bishop of Natal, Alfred Mkhize. He stood up to greet me and then asked the receptionist to bring in some tea for us. I shook hands with the Bishop and took the offered seat, gathering my papers together in a show of efficiency while he watched me impassively.

'And what can I do for you, Mr—?' the Bishop said. I asked him whether the ministry of the church in the war-torn townships had been much affected by the war. He replied, 'Obviously church attendance figures have fallen somewhat, but they are never constant and it is difficult to know exactly what it is that causes them to go up or down at any time. But at all times it is the minister's function to provide for people's spiritual and physical needs and that continues regardless. In our townships there is a tradition of ministers appearing at people's houses without appointment, or other fussy stuff like that. And they rejoice to see us visiting them. These days it is particularly important that we keep up this aspect of our work.'

Then I told the Bishop that I was interested in his views on the war, at which he smiled mirthlessly. 'I'm afraid I can give you no views on that,' he said, and sat back to wait for my next question.

'Why is that?' I asked. 'I'd have thought you'd be a man with strong opinions on this matter.'

'Oh, views! I have views,' he replied. 'Personal opinions, but nothing I can share. As Bishop Suffragan I am part of the reconciliation process, you must understand. I am involved in trying to bring the groups together.'

'And can you tell me how you're doing this?' I asked, but without much hope.

He shook his head and smiled again. 'I'm afraid I can't tell you that either,' he said. 'The matter is very delicate, very, very delicate indeed, and for me to comment would be to inhibit the process.' I noticed that the Bishop's mouth moved slowly when he spoke and that he had a lazy right eye, whereas his left eye regarded me keenly.

Just then the tea arrived. The receptionist brought in a tray with two cups, a silver sugar bowl, a jug of milk and an enormous teapot, the size of which made me wonder whether some tea party was about to take place in the Bishop's room. The Bishop said, 'Ah, the tea. Please help yourself to tea. I know some people prefer coffee, but I always take tea.' When he had refreshed himself, he continued. 'I know my response might be a little disappointing to a researcher such as yourself, so I might expand just a little. When dealing with this violence – or any other problem for that matter – is it helpful to destroy the symptom without destroying the causes?' He paused and poured himself another cup, gesturing with the pot for me to do the same. I shook my head. 'Exactly,' he said. 'We in the church often find it useful to speak metaphorically, in conjured pictures, so I might say to you if you want to cut the tree down, don't worry about the branches. Cut the stem and the branches will fall. Isn't that so?'

I agreed with him; he drank his cup and poured another. 'Are you sure you won't have any more?' he asked. 'I find in this hot weather— What I'm saying is that we're just playing marbles if we don't address the state's policies in this regard. If we don't, we may deal with these symptoms – just these, mind you – but the cause will be there to reproduce another kind of problem. It is like the treatment of tuberculosis – TB – destroy the *germs* rather than worrying about the sores on the lungs.

'In South Africa the system of apartheid is so pervasive that it takes up every aspect of our lives and dictates our actions and responses, often in negative and destructive ways. In America they have a machine for corn-beef which wastes no part of the cow. The animal goes in one end and out of the other comes corn-beef, steaks, leather and suede for clothes and shoes, glue, offal, pet food, fertiliser. In South Africa apartheid is like that machine. It takes in people and fragments them, dividing them and setting them against each other. We've reached the point where the machine stands, but we destroy ourselves. It is no use trying to bring about concord unless we see the machine for what it is. If we can transcend that, then the symptoms I was talking about will take care of themselves.

'Do you see now how difficult it is to live in South Africa? When I talk like this, people say to me, "All right! All right! Now hang on, just a minute. You don't have to be a politician in Bishop's robes." But this is not politics, it's life, and the church's first concern is with life and the way it is lived.'

Bishop Mkhize emptied the pot into his cup and we chatted about his tough travelling schedule: as Bishop Suffragan he has to travel huge distances every week to preach at different parishes throughout the province. Eventually he said, 'Well, Mr—, er? If there are no further questions—' I took my cue, gathered my notes together and thanked him for his time. The Bishop walked me to the front office where the receptionist handed me the *Bishop's Newsletter* for March, a pamphlet which described itself as 'a monthly newspaper for the Diocese of Natal'. I put it into my pocket and opened the door. As I stepped out I saw the Bishop cross my name off the list in his diary and ask the receptionist for another pot of tea.

I went back to my office and thought about the church. I pulled the crumpled newsletter out of my pocket and skimmed through it. Michael Nuttall, the Bishop of Natal, had devoted his message to the subject of the war. He said:

My dear people,

Make no mistake, conflict, violence and death continue unabated in various parts of our Diocese. There are those who like to claim or pretend that this is not so....
    At the request of the Diocesan Council I have been in correspondence with the State President·about the matter during the past twelve months. It has been a sobering correspondence which has just now come to an end. My chief purpose was to get him to appoint a judicial commission of enquiry into the unrest, so as to get to the root causes of the conflict and violence. He refused, claiming that senior police officers had carried out extensive investigations and that 'there are now clear signs that calm has returned to the area'. How wrong this analysis was....
    'This speaks to us of a problem of major proportions which continues to deserve serious and impartial investigation,' I pleaded in a further letter to the State President. I also said that the root cause of the conflict was, in my opinion, the dislocation and resentment caused by forty years of apartheid, and that real healing could only come with the courageous and rapid dismantling of this policy. He replied, 'How you succeed to reason logically in this regard is beyond my comprehension.' Again I wrote, trying I hope, to reason logically so that he could understand how many people are feeling. In his final letter he said: 'I do not intend corresponding with you in perpetuation of your wrong perceptions of South African history.' I am afraid we were now a far cry from my original request for a judicial commission of enquiry.

Given the Bishop's attribution of the conflict to apartheid, the State President's response was disappointing, but hardly surprising.

In October 1987, just as the pace of the conflict began to accelerate dramatically, a meeting was held in Johannesburg at which it was decided that various church leaders would hold an ecumenical service in Pietermaritzburg to call for an end to the violence. Dr Lizo Jafta of the Pietermaritzburg Council of Churches called on people of all political persuasions to attend. Velaphi Ndlovu, KwaZulu MP for Imbali, responded by saying that Inkatha would not attend because they had not received a formal invitation. 'We must talk first and pray about it later,' he added.

The meeting was held in Edendale on 1 November, and speakers made it clear that both parties faced a common enemy, namely apartheid, and should not be fighting each other. After the ecumenical service there was a smaller meeting between church leaders and some community leaders which Inkatha again did not attend.

However, in Durban on 6 November, Chief Buthelezi met various church leaders including Desmond Tutu, Archbishop of Cape Town, and Denis Hurley, Archbishop of Durban. At the meeting Chief Buthelezi presented a long memorandum in which he questioned whether those present were committed to peace or not. He said, 'I did not ask for this meeting. It is your meeting. I have always said that I will speak to the devil himself if it is for the good of South Africa.' Chief Buthelezi ended by calling for a joint initiative for peace and declared that those present at the meeting should stand together on a platform at the biggest rally for peace the region had ever seen. Archbishop Tutu did not take up the suggestion, a lapse which Chief Buthelezi attributed to his reluctance to be seen sharing a platform with Inkatha. 'I have always been shunned as some kind of South African pariah by the UDF both in this country and abroad. The truth of the matter is that the UDF's leadership dare not share a platform with me because they would be shown up politically,' he commented later.

In January 1988 church leaders reported a 'dramatic breakthrough' in the form of a joint UDF–Inkatha statement calling for an end to the violence. After the statement had been issued, the Catholic churches in Pietermaritzburg held a twelve-hour vigil. Unfortunately, the statement turned out to be neither 'dramatic' nor a 'breakthrough', and in February, Dr Khoza Mgojo, president of the Natal West District of the Methodist Church of Southern Africa, was commissioned by the South African Council of Churches to convene a peace meeting at Botha's Hill on 23 February. Chief Buthelezi sent a long letter in reply, setting out his reasons for declining to take part in the meeting. Among other things, he said:

As you are no doubt aware, the hierarchy of the SACC has, for a considerable time, shown precious little Christian charity towards myself, Inkatha and Kwa-Zulu. Its support for the UDF, COSATU *et al.* is undisputed. This is something which has hurt me deeply as it is ordinary men, women and children who have had to suffer the consequences of the opposition to my leadership and the support Inkatha receives from the people....

It is because I am so deeply concerned about restoring peace to the Pietermaritzburg scene that I have reservations about attending the proposed meeting. We just dare not put our hand to that which will fail in the terrible circumstances which confront people in the Greater Pietermaritzburg Area....

My advice to churchmen who earnestly seek peace for the Greater Pietermaritzburg Area is for them to do a lot of homework and a lot of behind-the-scenes lobbying and at all costs to avoid high profile attempts to make the futile look feasible.

Without the participation of Inkatha this round of peace talks would have had little chance of taking place, but in the event no meeting was held because on 10 February the police detained a number of key UDF activists which set the schedule back, and on 24 February the state passed restrictions prohibiting the UDF and COSATU from participating in any political activity whatsoever.

*   *   *

For much of 1988 and part of 1989, the church appeared to be paralysed and unable to intervene effectively to stop the violence. However, in May 1989, a team of Anglican churchmen was instrumental in setting up five-a-side peace talks between Inkatha and the UDF–COSATU. Although that initiative foundered, the Natal Church Leaders Group – comprising representatives from the major churches in Natal – has continued to work towards a settlement of the conflict.

In January 1990 the Group met the Minister of Law and Order to lobby for a commission of inquiry into the violence. The police were naturally reluctant to accede to such a request, knowing that any formal inquiry would be bound to reveal police improprieties. Nevertheless, the delegation insisted that an inquiry would be an indispensable step towards achieving peace. The churchmen pointed out that a commission of inquiry would be seen as a signal from the government, a genuine commitment to peace on the part of the authorities. The psychological impact of such a move would be extremely positive and would help restore the faith of war-abused people in the process of justice.

Eventually, the Minister agreed to consider the request. If one bears in mind that he has rejected all previous requests out of hand, even this small concession represents a victory for the persistence of the Church Leaders Group.

*   *   *

The exigencies of peace aside, the war presents the church with other problems. Churchmen in the townships have to preserve their ministry in the face of declining numbers of congregants and have to persevere in a situation in which spiritual well-being is at a low ebb and prospects for its revitalisation are bleak. The ministers must decide what stance they choose to adopt. They may opt for neutrality, or throw themselves behind the cause of one or other party. In some places – unstable areas where the balance of power is not set – there is little choice; you are either neutral or you leave. As a result, sermons tend to be bland, calling for peace, togetherness, brotherhood, fraternal love, harmony and good neighbour-liness, but beyond that making no specific reference to the war. Ministers who remain neutral out of choice or through force of circumstances are able to preach to a wide constituency, but are limited in what they can say to general comments and allegory.

On the other hand, those who do take a side can only preach to their own political congregation – ministers who preside at the funerals of comrades do not preach at the funerals of Inkatha members, and vice versa – but they can say more. They are not shackled by metaphor, allusion and oblique reference. They can speak directly to condemn, expose and advise. They brand themselves as partisan and have to take the consequences. In this way they come to identify not only spiritually but also physically with the sufferings and hardships endured by their war-stricken parishioners.

I was still caught up with matters of the church and the war when Exodus dropped in to see me one day and asked me to stand him a beer. At the bar counter, he said, 'I'm taking something of a risk, you under-stand. As a restricted person it is not necessarily possible for me to be here, but I suddenly thought I would like to see how you were coming along.'

I told him that I was glad to see him and hoped that there would be no unpleasant consequences following his impulsive gesture. Then I asked him whether he was a regular churchgoer and, if so, whether he had found the practice of religion impaired in any way by the war.

He said, 'To you I would call myself a devout Christian, but lately I find I have been unable to attend my church. You see, as a restricted person I have to attend only the church near my home, that is the Methodist Church in Imbali. But the Inkatha warlords of Imbali go to that place, which of course makes me feel uncomfortable. But the reason I really cannot sit in that place of worship is that Constable – no, I don't want you to write his name down – goes there to pray. He's a security guard who assaulted me in detention and I can never forget about that.

'I don't feel the atmosphere is good for me to pray in that church. With him in there I still feel spat on: it makes a mockery of my prayers.'

21
The data base

In April 1988 the Centre for Adult Education at the University of Natal, Pietermaritzburg, hosted a seminar on violence in the Pietermaritzburg area. The seminar was attended by academics, diplomats, businessmen, churchmen, welfare workers and a number of security policemen in light blue suits carrying concealed tape-recorders. Initially, Brigadier Büchner, the head of the security police in the region, asked for an invitation and was given one, but he was subsequently disinvited after pressure was applied by groups who refused to come if the police were present.

Papers were presented by academics, who were mostly on the left of the political spectrum, and each examined a specific aspect of the war, ranging from vigilantism to the plight of refugees to the limitations of the law and the role of the press. Most of the analyses put forward found Inkatha primarily responsible for the war and for its worst excesses, and attributed a secondary and cynical role to the police who were accused of collusion with Inkatha vigilantes. Given the extent to which police actions and motives were discussed, it was unfortunate in retrospect that Brigadier Büchner was not there. In the event he found himself in the enviable position of hearing, through the tape-recordings of his undercover plain-clothes men, the comments of his detractors without having to respond to them publicly.

John Aitchison, head of the Centre for Adult Education at UNP, and a convener of the seminar, told me that its object was to expose prominent outsiders to what was going on around Pietermaritzburg. The seminar was aimed at diplomats and businessmen, city councillors and members of parliament – people with a voice and the ability to exert some pressure on the police or the government. 'The UDF wasn't able to put forward its own case because of the February restrictions on its activities, so we decided not to invite any of the key parties, but to keep the seminar strictly academic. Aside from the practicalities involved we thought people were more likely to be influenced by the conclusions of dispassionate observers. It was our intention to present the facts as baldly as possible, on the basis that the facts more than any polemic would show people that Inkatha was less than righteous.

'I think the day was a success: more than two hundred people came and afterwards I got a lot of informal, positive feedback. We succeeded in our primary intention which was to publicise as widely as possible the iniquitous situation in the townships. We wanted businessmen and politicians to understand that the situation was not merely bad, but that it was more complex and political than they imagined. We also wanted them to understand that positive intervention on their part meant taking on Inkatha, that it was not enough just to talk to them. We wanted local business to put pressure on the police to investigate alleged atrocities by Inkatha warlords with the same fervour with which they follow up complaints against the UDF.' Aitchison paused. 'In that regard I can't say we were particularly successful,' he conceded.

The CAE was a natural choice to host the seminar as it has been the academic institution most involved in monitoring the course of the war in the Pietermaritzburg townships. To the chaos of conflict, staff members at the Centre have brought the academic's urge to contain and enclose on paper the complex forces at work. They have shifted the war zone from the dirt tracks and overgrown hills of Edendale and Vulindlela and brought it into the neat and tidy realm of university lecture theatres, conference halls and computer centres.

The University could not be more different from the townships. In place of dirt tracks there are straight paths of brick or concrete flagstones; and the lush foliage is manicured. From my own office window I could see broad green lawns sloping up to a wide road. Further along, a traffic warden ushered white children across the road to their school. Wherever I looked I saw students in brightly coloured clothing wandering about unhurriedly. The sounds that reached me were soft and restful. In the canteens people sat in the dim light reading newspapers and sipping cups of coffee; the architecture of the campus is interesting and welcoming, inviting people to linger in the concourses of buildings, or to sit on benches and steps.

I thought that those activists who come to the campus, taking the bus in from Edendale and avoiding the second round of dangers at Retief Street, must find it a strangely muted environment, almost ridiculously safe. When I asked Nhlanhla about this, for once he was not very articulate about his feelings but said eventually that he did find the place fairly relaxing. 'Peaceful,' he said.

This paradox – coming to a place of peace to talk about war – was not confined to the experiences of fieldworkers. The very practice of academic research and analysis to some extent necessarily involves a manipulation and sterilisation of the phenomenon studied. Academic papers dealing with Pietermaritzburg can tell you quite a lot, but they never manage to evoke the stink of the war, or the cryptic flash that memory sometimes causes to appear in the otherwise bland expression of a survivor. These papers took the flexible and amorphous state of conflict and rendered it into stiff language. The stuff of war becomes the stuff of articles and special conferences.

In this war the academics at the Centre for Adult Education are well placed to play the role of general commentators. They are close to the cusp of battle, familiar with the terrain, with the protagonists and the political history of the area, and yet at the same time, they have the advantage of distance. They are allowed the luxury of perspective denied to those actually caught up in the fighting. For the latter, their view of the whole, by contrast, is distorted by the closeness of their personal experiences, which are so vivid that they illuminate one small patch and obscure everything round about.

I cornered John Aitchison at tea-time one day and asked him why it was that the Centre for Adult Education at UNP had become the chief recorder of the progress of this war. 'Why you and not some other department, or some other agency?' I asked.

He told me that the Centre had been drawn into the conflict right from the start. In mid-1987, organisations affiliated to the UDF approached staff members with the request that it run a course on organisational skills for comrades and activists. The Centre agreed and set up a programme to teach accountancy, typing, computer literacy, and to improve media production, communication skills and committee work. Aitchison described the process further: 'We started the course and immediately encountered a series of crises. One morning, a woman on the course arrived in tears because an Inkatha warlord, Sichizo Zuma, had threatened to kill her. Then shortly after that, another of our students reported that someone had tried to kill him in the night by firing shots into his bedroom. The following night his house was attacked with petrol bombs and his mother and brother were killed.

'We knew by then that the violence was on the increase, although we had no idea it would escalate into a full-scale war, and after these incidents we felt that we had a personal stake in the matter. At that stage PACSA was monitoring the incidents, but in quite a time-consuming way, so we got together to pool our resources. At the CAE we had the necessary infrastructure: computers and the know-how to set up a systematic data base, and between us we had links with people in the community.'

The next morning I went into Aitchison's office and greeted the research assistant hard at work updating the data base. The weekend just past had been violent, and the warring parties had issued a fresh set of declarations calling for peace and deploring the attitude and actions of their opponents. Consequently, Monday morning found the assistant seated at the computer console surrounded by dozens of newspaper clippings, police unrest reports and glossy Sunday magazines folded back to the relevant article. Where clippings simply repeated each other he noted the duplication and copied out whichever was the more detailed. It was midday, and he was sweating as he worked with painstaking concentration from one source to the next.

I took care not to disturb him and walked through into the next room, in which the latest printout of the data base was kept. It was stacked two feet high and sat squat and heavy on the floor of the office – a tremendous fat thing. And yet, in another way, it was pitifully small and thin. Reduced to black dot-matrix typeface on white, standard-sized computer paper was the whole course and progress of the war. Countless deaths, incidents of violence and destruction, comments, appeals – sanctimonious or sincere – were registered within this paper tower. I walked round it in a circle, uncertain as to how I should proceed. I tapped it; it gave off a muted rustling sound.

I lifted the top page and pulled up after it a long streamer of paper which I then allowed to subside back on top of the base. I knelt and began to flip through the entries. Some were only a few lines long – nothing was known but the barest of details, neither the names of the perpetrators nor the victims or their political affiliations – while others went on for pages, crammed with press reports and eyewitness accounts and weighty pro-nouncements by professional commentators. The information contained in the data base was so densely packed that reading it was a process of learning and forgetting simultaneously. Each incident superimposed itself on the one before, saturating the memory and numbing the senses.

I squatted down on the floor besides this monstrous chronology and wondered how to tackle the mass of information. I was still sitting blankly when Nhlanhla dropped in. He read a few pages and looked at me sceptically. 'Do you have to read all this?' he asked.

I hesitated.

'I'd rather take my chances on the streets than go through that lot,' he said.

22

The last outpost

There are some whites in Pietermaritzburg – journalists, politicians, academics, clergy, people who have sheltered refugees and provided material assistance where possible – whose lives have been profoundly affected by the war. They have recognised the problem as their own and responded as best they could. The Pietermaritzburg branch of the Democratic Party, for one, despite suffering setbacks in its previous incarnation as the PFP in the 1987 general elections, has been active in monitoring and exposing the situation in the townships. Senior party officials have toured the troublespots and local MPs have ensured that the war has remained prominently on the parliamentary agenda. The Minister of Police has been regularly challenged on the police record in the townships, although to little effect: to each allegation the Minister replied courteously, responding with a brief denial. Nonetheless, the DP has maintained its involvement, and, general policies aside, is highly regarded by the black population of the city.

The Pietermaritzburg Chamber of Commerce, for another, in the first few months at least, devoted energy and goodwill to brokering peace between the warring parties. These efforts eventually came to nothing thanks to the combined efforts of certain parties who quickly found reasons for obstructing and delaying what had been an encouraging process.

However, this conceded, it is fair to say that whites in Pietermaritzburg have had an easy war. So easy, in fact, that many of them have no idea that anything unusual is going on at all. Many white-owned cars in Pietermaritzburg display a bumper sticker which reads 'Natal: The Last Outpost' against a background of the Union Jack. For these people, the anachronistic symbols of the British Empire are closer to home than events in Pietermaritzburg's black townships. In general, they endorse the comfortable line which says that it is wrong to describe the 'black-on-black violence' as occurring in their patch. According to this view, the strife takes place outside the boundaries of the City of Pietermaritzburg and is therefore foreign.

For example, the kidnapping, assault and murder of children in the townships caused a ripple of concern at first, but soon lost its news value.

The abduction of a single white child in Pietermaritzburg in January 1989 remained front-page news for a month, and a fund of more than R20 000 was established to help secure her recovery.

Business, usually sensitive to political upheavals in black areas, has suffered no ill effects. In Pietermaritzburg, the Chamber of Industries, when asked to intervene by COSATU, declared itself neutral and apolitical. When workers were forced to absent themselves from work in order to ssafeguard their houses from attack, or arrived late, and even when workers were killed in the fighting, the PCI still chose to ignore the war. Members of the Chamber did not investigate the appalling home situation of their workers, they did not donate money to refugee relief. In short they absolved themselves of any reponsibility for the welfare of their employees outside the workplace.

The mayor of Pietermaritzburg, Mark Cornell, at first leapt into the fray, but then rapidly retreated. In October 1987, shortly after the devastating Natal floods of September, he said of Inkatha's campaign of forced recruitment: 'If Inkatha had wanted to make friends they should have gone and helped people instead of going and saying to them at three o'clock in the morning – sign this card or I'll kill you if you don't.'

For these strong, accusatory words, Cornell was soundly castigated by Chief Buthelezi. Cornell said later: 'We, that is some members of the City Council and myself, went on a courtesy visit to Ulundi and we were given hell in the council chambers. He's a sensitive man.'

In January 1988, Cornell complained that the press as well as the police in their unrest reports were tarnishing the image of the city. 'Several of the townships are far away from the city itself, but the impression is given that the whole place, including Pietermaritzburg, is burning. This can't be good for our image.' This remark provoked a strong and jeering response from the UDF, COSATU and their sympathisers who pointed out that those living in these 'far-off' townships still work, and spend their wages, in Pietermaritzburg. Cornell's attempt to distance himself and the city from the fighting was dismissed as a feeble exercise in wishful-thinking.

In February, Cornell again trod on some important corns, this time those of the Minister of Law and Order, Adriaan Vlok. Cornell called for the South African Defence Force to deploy a larger task force in the townships because the police were unable to control the situation, and because the population had more faith in the army than the police. Vlok rounded on him and said that the police were entirely up to the job – in fact had the situation under control – and rejected the idea of a greater army presence. 'I spoke to Vlok, Roelf Meyer, his deputy, and Stoffel Botha. We were treated like very small little boys, I can tell you,' Cornell remarked after his meeting with the Ministers.

After six months of these unfortunate interventions, Cornell shifted his attention and concentration to the big event oof 1988: Pietermaritzburg's 150th anniversary. In celebration, millions of rands were spent redesigning the city centre into a complex and confusing system of pedestrian malls and one-way streets. The white inhabitants of Pietermaritzburg favoured this development because it took their minds off unpleasant realities.

The police also participated in this sustained exercise of pretending nothing was wrong In February 1988, days after the banning of the UDF and COSATU, and as the war in the townships proceeded in all its squalor and confusion, the station commander of Town Hill police station in Pietermaritzburg was awarded the trophy for the neatest police station in the country, by the Minister of Law and Order, Adriaan Vlok, specially present for the ceremony.

Also in honour of the city's auspicious anniversary, the business magazine *Financial Mail* brought out a special supplementary survey on Pietermaritzburg. The cover showed a cartoon of Queen Victoria, sceptre in hand, holding the Union Jack aloft over the city. Not surprisingly, among the articles on the economic resources at the disposal of the PCI, the flavour of Britain still permeating the capital, the agricultural show and the city's famous sporting events, there was no mention at all of the war in the local townships. As the mayor said, 'In a supplement aimed at attracting investment, it's hardly sensible to advertise the problems.'

23
Mr Average Journalist

I noticed early on in my researches that a good many people had no idea anything untoward was taking place in Pietermaritzburg, and those who had an inkling that all was not well had no idea of the scale of the trauma. I also observed that people tended to excuse their ignorance on the grounds that the newspapers had not provided sufficient coverage of the war. This failure they ascribed to a variety of reasons, ranging from cowardice in the face of the authorities – or, more likely, Chief Buthelezi's writ-issuing attorneys – to a simple lack of interest in the whole affair. In short, the press was receiving a bad press itself and taking a lot of flak from people who like to think of themselves as well informed about South African current affairs.

Since a substantial component of my research involved reading and collating thousands of articles on the war published in a variety of newspapers over the previous two or so years, I thought this attitude uncharitable. The problem lay not in any lack of reporting, but in the fact that people were not reading the articles which did appear. Moreover, although some newspapers unashamedly avoided the issue altogether, other newspapers went to considerable trouble to seek out and, what is more important, to disseminate the news.

In his article, 'Reporting the Violence', presented at the CAE's seminar on violence, David Robbins, a deputy editor on the *Natal Witness*, set out some of the problems facing a reporter in the South Africa of the late 1980s:

A reporter's task is to present the facts as accurately and even-handedly as possible. The facts are normally gathered by answering the following questions: What happened? Where? When? How? Why?…

In short, the rules that govern reporters' activities under normal conditions are simple. They are:
— get there if possible;
— double check the facts;
— quote the opinions of the relevant parties.

However, the rules under which newspapers are obliged to operate when it comes to reporting on so-called 'unrest' are, thanks to the emergency regulations, another matter altogether. They are:

— under no circumstances get there, and if by chance you happen to be there anyway, leave immediately;

— try to check facts afterwards, but don't expect verification from the authorities, especially the police, of facts they don't want published;

— quote the opinions of people involved, but not if their opinions contravene the emergency regulations, and especially not if they are restricted from expressing opinions;

— under no circumstances describe security force action.

This refreshingly ironic code of practice impelled me to go over to the offices of the *Natal Witness* in Longmarket Street to talk to the press.

I hurried up to the receptionist on the mezzanine level and waited as she paged David Robbins. Robbins arrived, white-haired and affable in glasses, and ushered me into a small boardroom. I asked, 'Would I be right in inferring from your article that the police don't care what they do or who knows it, as long as it can't be reported or proved?'

'That's about it,' Robbins replied. 'They're a cynical bunch. They don't give a stuff that you know they're lying. Once they're armed with the emergency regulations, they rule, and there's an end of it. In the same way, the state makes a lot of noise about being neutral in this conflict when they manifestly aren't. There's a lot of evidence of police assisting Inkatha, but we can't report it. I mean, it gets ridiculous: last year the mayor went to see Vlok and said, "Look, can't you stop this?" and Vlok says to him, "You mean to tell me you don't want Inkatha to win?"'

'Mainly, though, if you want to see which side the police are on, you can see it in their attitude to the warlords. Those guys are supremely arrogant, completely cock-sure of themselves, because they know they can get away with it. I once saw Sichizo Zuma in a blind rage because someone had accused him of killing twenty people. He was yelling, right there in the foyer of the Supreme Court, that that was libel because he'd only killed eighteen. I mean, look at it this way: if Alec Erwin or any of the other COSATU or UDF guys were running with guns, they'd shoot him, gun him down. The warlords break the emergency regulations every day, but none of them have been arrested.'

I decided to steer the interview back to the issues raised in his paper. 'In some ways it must feel like a self-defeating exercise, running a newspaper under these conditions,' I hazarded.

'It is bloody hard, yes,' he agreed partially. 'We have to deal with the regulations and a system of verification which is either pure Orwell or pure Laurel and Hardy, I can't decide which. In the past, and even now with regard to normal crime, we confirm incidents with the local police. With unrest incidents it's a different matter, because only Pretoria can confirm unrest incidents. So we phone or fax through a request for confirmation to Pretoria, who contact the local police to find out what's going on. The local police then submit a report to Pretoria who then get back to us, but this can take forever, so the news gets buried.

'Those are problems of getting the news out, but before we get that far we have all the problems of finding the news in the first place. We've had times when our reporters have been harassed by *kitskonstabels* – the usual bully-boy tactics: people ripped out of their cars, cameras smashed on the ground, that sort of thing. Or they may try more subtle forms of intimid-ation, like investigating us for infringements under the emergency regu-lations to scare us off going into troublespots. They've even been on to us for publishing pictures of damaged buildings. As far as they're concerned, the matter is simple: we're not allowed to have been there; we're not allowed to have seen anything.

'What's worse is that we can't afford to take these threats lightly. We can't survive being shut down for three months, the way a paper like the *Weekly Mail*, say, survives. They're a desktop operation, they can go in with stuff we wouldn't dare publish. The *Witness* is a huge established business with a thousand employees.... But you should speak to Richard Steyn if you want to know more on that score.

'Anyway, what was I saying? Oh, yes, the problem is reaching the news in the first place. Well, there's the terrain – I expect you've been out there yourself – very hard to get to stories out in the rural area, or to hear about them in the first place. People don't have telephones, or useful contacts, not to mention a basic reluctance to talk to the press for fear of reprisals. But I don't want to sound over-pessimistic – we have got a lot of stories out; our reporters have sent stories to papers all over the country and overseas – we're still doing our damnedest to perform our function.'

'As a journalist on a paper catering for a largely white readership, are you aware of any alteration in local white attitudes towards Inkatha?' I asked.

'Damn right,' he answered frankly. 'If there was doubt about the acceptability of the Indaba ★ before the violence, now there's masses of doubt. This whole business has been the worst possible advert for Buthele-zi. Look, in the past Buthelezi has been able to maintain his image as the

---

★ The Indaba is a political alliance between white Natal business interests and Inkatha, the KwaZulu government. At a conference held in 1986, proposals for an intergrated, federal Natal–KwaZulu provincial government were endorsed by participants. However, the proposals were rejected by the South African govern-ment and the scheme fell into abeyance. The future of the Indaba remains unclear. On the one hand, the new political environment in South Africa appears to have superseded the Indaba, rendering it an outmoded political experiment. On the other hand, the government appears to be moving towards some sort of federal constitutional dispensation, in which case the Indaba may enjoy a revived vogue.

archetypal moderate black leader, which won him a lot of support from faded NRP types ** who reckoned they'd seen the light. At one time everyone was saying, "Buthelezi is the way to go," but you don't hear much of that any more. I'm not talking about a swing against him to the left, but a conservative reaction. They look at the warlords, the vigilantes, the retribution against anyone challenging the Inkatha line and they say, "They're violent buggers, just as bad as the radicals." No, Buthelezi is looking shaky in the PRO department at the moment, which is tough for someone as dependent on public image as he is.'

Robbins left shortly for his next appointment and I went down the corridor to meet Richard Steyn, the editor of the *Natal Witness* and a newspaperman of the highest repute, who consistently infuriates both the left and the right by his doggedly liberal editorial policy.

I found Steyn extremely cordial. After exchanging several polite comments, he came to the heart of the matter: 'How much bad news do you give your readers?' he asked rhetorically. 'If you give them too much, keep pumping in the horror and bleakness all the time, they switch off. But of course those aren't decisions unique to our circumstances, every editor faces the same problem. Here in Maritzburg we do our best to perform our function despite the restrictions. We have to inform people of what's going on even if it's not always 110 per cent accurate or timeous. But we can't be accused of being unaware, at least.' He tapped his desk with a warning forefinger.

'In the last three months,' he continued, 'we've been investigated fourteen times by the security police who warn that charges are being prepared. Of those fourteen, six have been withdrawn, leaving eight we have to deal with, six under the emergency regulations and two under the Police Act. The police move pretty quickly, I'll say that for them. They have a sophisticated monitoring system and anything suspect goes up to Pretoria. If they don't like it, we hear from them next morning.

'Mostly, I'd say, they don't prosecute, it's more of a softening-up process. Wasting our time writing statements, finding potential witnesses, trying to force us to self-censor ourselves out of existence really.' He shrugged, but smiled. I had the impression that he was a man who did not find his job too much for him.

On 2 February 1990, a year later, the State President, Mr F W de Klerk, lifted certain emergency regulations restricting the press. This bodes well for future reporting but cannot redress the fact that for more than two

---

** The now defunct New Republic Party (NRP) was a white political party whose constituency consisted of conservative, English-speaking Natalians caught indecisively between the PFP and the NP. Many old NRP supporters are now in the NP.

years coverage of the war was suppressed and reporters and editors severely hindered in carrying out their proper functions. Writing in the *Natal Witness* in March 1990, Richard Steyn praised a recent report on the Natal war zone in the SABC news programme *Network*, but added, 'One wonders whether similar coverage a few years ago might not have jolted the authorities into making more serious attempts to curb the hostilities before they got out of hand. Well do I remember the complacent judgement of a local MP that the violence was only a form of faction-fighting – traditional with these people, you know.'

★   ★   ★

Though it was lunch-time I did not feel like joining the hordes of office-workers outside in the heat, eating pavement hotdogs, so after leaving Richard Steyn I went along the passage to the *Echo* newsroom to find Khaba Mkhize, editor of the *Echo*, and Lakela Kaunda, his chief reporter. As black supplements to white daily newspapers go, the *Echo* is particularly successful, reaching a huge readership in the black townships, and boasting a circulation far higher than that of the *Witness* itself.

In the newsroom a lone reporter was typing at the far end of the room. He told me that Mkhize and Kaunda would be back shortly, so I sat down in front of Khaba's desk to wait for them. The room smelled faintly of print and stale smoke. Khaba's desk looked like the archetypal newsman's desk, spilling papers from every corner. The confusion was so complete it seemed almost studied.

Behind his chair, on the far wall, there was a square pinboard covered in postcards and large-size glossy news photographs, many of them depicting Jesse Jackson on the 1988 campaign trail. There was also a picture taken at the Gorbachev–Reagan summit in Reykjavík and, next to it, a group photograph of singing toddlers at an Edendale crèche. Further along, an ancient poster peeled slowly away from the wall, announcing some innocuous event, while a *Natal Witness* calendar as well as a few religious pictures took up the rest of the wall-space.

I had read a fair amount of Khaba Mkhize's writing on the war in Pietermaritzburg. Like his journalistic role model, Casey 'Kid' Motsisi, Khaba favoured an idiosyncratic writing style which had the advantage of ensuring that his work could never be described as dull or staid. It might be confusing, fantastical or plain ridiculous, but it was never boring. He, Khaba, tended to feature centrally in everything he wrote, referred to either in the first person as the lower-case 'i', or in the third person as 'voteless', a reference to Motsisi's collective term for South African blacks: 'non-voters'.

Soon after the outbreak of hostilities, Khaba devised a set of generic characters through whom he charted the effect of the war on the population of the Pietermaritzburg townships. There was the 'Average Smoker', forbidden to smoke on buses or taxis by puritanical comrades; the 'Average Soccer Fan' no longer able to watch his favourite team because the stadium was situated in enemy territory; the 'Average Chatterer' who had to be careful of the political connotations attached to his blithe words; the 'Average Nurse' who faced attack because the Edendale Hospital was associated with Inkatha control; and the 'Average Shopowner', taking flak from all sides because he sells to all sides.

However, Khaba had reserved his most comprehensive character examination for 'Mr Average Journalist', a vital figure in the life of the township, one who takes himself and his job extremely seriously and is not given over to self-irony in any measure.

Mr Average Journalist must satisfy each camp that he is not a propagandist for the other. He may also collapse from the strain of meeting the spate of demands. People do not understand the stress and the tightrope. He loses friends. His wife is angry that he no longer eats the supper she has prepared – every day he is taken to the glamorous restaurants for hefty free luscious lunches by guys from all over the world on fact-finding visits.

Later in his paper to the CAE's seminar on violence entitled, 'Reporting the Violence – An Insider's Problems', Khaba set out in more detail the peculiar travails of Mr Average Journalist:

The Average Journalist has lost valuable friends and made new valuable friends while the violence was at its peak. Some old friends could not understand the pressure of working under trying and taxing conditions and felt they were being ignored. They also interpreted the many appointments one had in the diary of important overseas and local people as a snobbish reason to 'mix' with important strangers.

One Johannesburg journalist remarked angrily in his newsroom after leaving this area that 'those folks at the *Witness* office think the world revolves around them'.

We were busy helping the foreign press with information. Reporting the violence as an insider you have to accept the fact that everybody pages through you as if you were an encyclopaedia on violence.

On the other hand – after giving assistance to the very many people – one gained an ocean of quite useful friends. i made my count as to the number of people i had given interviews to and found that the more than a million words i have spoken on just one topic – VIOLENCE – proved useful to more than 60 representatives from abroad and locally.

Mr Average Journalist had to put on a face of boldness, yet deep down inside his human mechanism lay a fear…. One had to live the life of a Scarlet Pimpernel. i had to change 14 cars – through an arrangement with a friendly connection in the motoring world – to avoid being spotted easily. Mr Average Journalist had to devise a set of disguises. About a dozen different baseball caps and other shapes, as well as different hats, in order to survive the harsh violent season.

Reading this sensational account I was not sure whether Khaba was merely being self-effacing in describing these circumstances as the lot of the average journalist, or whether he was saying that the war effected so great an upheaval in the life of the average journalist as to catapult him from days of monotony and trivia into the harsh spotlight of international media attention. Some of it might even be made up, I reflected. When I read the cool orthodox journalism of Lakela Kaunda, Khaba's right hand and foil, I thought this not only possible, but probable.

I was thinking along these lines when Khaba and Lakela returned clutching chicken-mayonnaise sandwiches which sat precariously on tiny polystyrene plates. We had all met before so we settled into a relaxed discussion right away. 'There's something I've been meaning to ask you, Khaba,' I said, taking some papers out of my briefcase. 'In your *Frontline* article you begin by saying this: "What is actually happening to the lives of the ordinary people of Maritzburg? That is the question the editor of *Frontline* asked me to answer. My first thought was: To live in this place is to endure the torture of having to dutifully answer such questions as yours, while all around is pain." Don't you think it's a bit strong to describe answering that kind of question as "torture"?'

'Look,' he said with his mouth full, 'for me the telephone is already a cliché. It rings and I know in advance what the question will be. Even my dreams will be formulated in the same way, the same question follows me around even in my sleep. If I sleep sober I wake tired because my sleep has been an extension of the day's work and questions. I must go to sleep with drink. Then there's the perpetual anger. If I sleep sober, then at 2.00 a.m. when a car passes, or a dog kicks the rubbish bin, I won't regain sleep. And during the day I'm up and down all day with meetings and appointments, always trying to make sense of the chaos. I can't even keep my desk clear. My wife complains, she says, "You don't even care about family matters." All this because I am relentlessly pursued by that one question.'

'Your tea's getting cold, Khaba,' Lakela put in pragmatically when he paused to swallow.

'Strain,' he continued, 'that's the long and the short of it. I don't just report, willy-nilly I have to educate too. I meet comrades in the street who ask me why I've published a pro-Inkatha letter, or I run into the top brass vigilantes, armed to the teeth, who want to know why I've run a COSATU ad. They say to me, "Khaba, why do you help the *amaqabane*? Why do you give space to those dogs?" Then very patiently I have to explain to them that it is "you who created the UDF in this area because you are the ones who labelled everyone UDF who didn't join Inkatha." They look at me open-mouthed, gaping, "Is this true? Is this true?"

'I say, "Before all of this, I knew about five UDF here. UDF was non-existent, now they bask in the glory of having blocked Buthelezi."

'Then I have to teach both sides about newspaper objectivity, and I have to do it very, very carefully. It's one of the hazards if you're someone whom everyone comes to for advice and information, you have to watch out if they don't like what you have to say. One of my jobs is to teach both sides how the state of emergency works, but that's a cover for me. It covers up the way I water down my own position for both sides because I can never give my true opinion. I manipulate the emergency for my own protection.'

'Or the emergency manipulates you, Khaba,' Lakela said, laughing.

Khaba picked at his teeth with a match and spat thin splinters into the ashtray. 'I'm so used to death threats,' he said, 'when I don't hear one for a while, I say, "Hey, what's going on, why so quiet?" If you're a journalist you have to take the rough with the smooth, you can't run away from difficult things. I hold to the view that you should take risks for what you believe to be the truth.'

'I thought you said that you could never allow your true opinion to be known, Khaba,' I interrupted.

He ignored me. 'As far as I am concerned, one should not worry if your shadow is crooked so long as you are standing upright – because at the end of the day, when the sun has set, your real image will remain.'

I was still digesting this opaque truth when Lakela said, 'Last year when the hit squad was out to get you, you hopped off pretty quickly.'

Khaba nodded. 'I thought it was time to take a well-deserved rest and the opportunity came. I told the Canadians, "You have to get me out of here by Wednesday." Thursday I was already at my first speaking appointment in Toronto.

'Anyway, I was three months away, and now I'm back in harness, still around. Christmas has been and gone and I'm still around,' he concluded with immense satisfaction.

We chatted on for a while, but Lakela's and Khaba's lunch-break could not be prolonged indefinitely, so I got up to leave. Khaba said, 'Just wait a second, I want to give you some things.' He began to poke around the paper middens on his desk and eventually came up with a bundle so crumpled it looked like rice-paper. 'These are a few of the poems we've published in the *Echo* Poet's Corner over the last year,' he said. 'People use it to open out, air their grievances. They can be anonymous if they like, or give their names – it's up to them. It's a specific service to let them release some of the pent-up emotions that build up when you live in a war zone.'

I thanked him and took the poems back to my office where I read through them. Khaba was not exaggerating when he said the poems came from the heart. They exuded the quality of needing-to-be-said.

Two poems particularly attracted me. The first, 'It's a Weekend Again' by Afropoet from Imbali, because of the strength right at the end, with which the poet both invoked and railed at the monstrous, arrogant appetite of the two insatiable cemeteries, Sinathingi and Mountain Rise. The second poem, 'Blessed are the Dead' by B M Tenza, also of Imbali, for its simple but savagely fatalistic logic: 'Blessed are the dead/ For they will/ Never be transformed into firewood/ Never be killed'.

It's a Weekend Again

It's a weekend again
Execution time
Daggers ready to obey orders
Our townships like a hive
Ever swelling with anger
Death staring at us like a hungry wolf
Women wail through the night
African women.
Bullets fly in the air
Unleashing death
Children lying in tatters

Blood flowing profusely
Fresh yet new blood
Wolves parading our streets
Their teeth dripping with blood
It's yet another procession
Sinathinge!
You have seen nothing
The worst is yet to come.
Mountain Rise!
You rose and the mountains echoed
Haughtily you swallowed them.
It's you and I
Locked up there
Peeping through the key holes
Watching revolution live.
Is this freedom?

Blessed are the Dead

Blessed are the dead
For they will:
Never be suspected,
Never be chased,
never be unmanageable,
Never be transformed into firewood

Never be killed
For they are now:
Protected from adversaries
Saved from opponents
Secured from the persecution of this world
Blessed are those who are dead
For they have the benediction
Of living eternal and everlasting life

24
Before the courts

Towards the end of September 1987, COSATU commissioned a legal team to go to down to Pietermaritzburg to investigate allegations that Inkatha was committing acts of violence against the people in the local community and, in particular, against members of unions affiliated to COSATU. The legal team soon concluded that these acts of violence were part of a concerted effort on the part of Inkatha to win the political allegiance of the people in the area, and that the violence, moreover, was self-perpetuating as rival political forces organised themselves to resist and retaliate. More than this, two other early features of the war became apparent: first, the Inkatha attacks were orchestrated by a number of key actors, dubbed 'warlords'; and second, the police were not merely unco-operative about investigating allegations of attacks and harassment by Inkatha warlords, but appeared to be positively obstructive.

Consequently it fell to the legal team to do the job of the police, namely interviewing and taking statements from victims and witnesses of attacks, corroborating accounts, documenting the evidence, and making cases against the main perpetrators of the violence. In the first phases of the investigation, almost a hundred statements were taken from people, detailing dozens of incidents in which Inkatha warlords had assaulted, attacked and generally intimidated residents of the township perceived to be anti-Inkatha. The lawyers gathered relevant medical records, and in some cases undertook on-site inspections. They photographed material evidence of attacks such as damaged property, bullet holes and cartridges, bullet wounds and the physical scars of beatings. The lawyers also estab-lished that charges had originally been laid with the police and were able to see that the police had taken no steps whatsoever to investigate any of these complaints.

As the scale of the problem became clearer, the lawyers realised that a concerted legal strategy comprising interdict applications would be needed to counter the depredations of the warlords. In his paper, 'The Law and Its Limitations', Professor James Lund sets out the conditions under which an interdict may be granted, and the extent of its restrictive power on the parties involved.

The [interdict] order is often sought as a matter of urgency. It will be granted only if the applicant has (i) a *prima facie* right, (ii) a reasonable apprehension of irreparable harm if the relief is not granted and (iii) no alternative remedy. The court will also weigh the interests of the applicant against those of the respondent in deciding whether to grant the interdict. The granting of an interim interdict does not mean that the applicant has established that his version is the correct one. An interdict may be made final when the applicant proves his clear right, but that may take some time.

In Johannesburg I went to see Halton Cheadle, senior partner at Cheadle Thompson and Haysom, the legal firm acting on behalf of COSATU, and the man centrally involved in devising the interdict strategy in the first place. Cheadle sat squarely across the desk from me. He looked like a boxer who unexpectedly finds himself in a suit. Nevertheless, he was friendly and said, 'We set out to pinpoint the warlords by bringing interdicts against them. These guys were completely lawless because they knew there would be no come-back to their actions, but once the Supreme Court spotlight was on them they'd be curbed. Taking this thinking further, we reckoned that if we brougght many applications, the effect would be overwhelming. We knew that bringing interdicts against Inkatha warlords would not bring about the immediate arrival of the new dawn, it wasn't a panacea. But what the interdicts could achieve, or rather what we hoped they would achieve, would be to force the top Inkatha leadership either to take responsibility for its members, and in particular for those warlords who held leadership positions in Inkatha, or to distance themselves completely from their actions.

'If you look at the first wave of interdicts you see that we never cited Inkatha itself, in order to give the organisation the leeway to distance itself from the thugs, but far from doing that, Inkatha defended them all the way. So we ended up citing Inkatha as a respondent in one of our applications in order to say, 'Right, you've had your chance, but now we're holding you responsible for these acts of violence.' There's no doubt that Inkatha suffered propaganda setbacks here and overseas because of the interdicts, but then what did they expect? You can't play in the dirt and come out looking clean. Local opinion, I think, began to shift away from Inkatha. People started to ask questions about Inkatha's role in the violence. Their image as this non-violent, moderate organisation started to look a bit worn. And overseas as well, people were suddenly having second thoughts about just what kind of an organisation Inkatha really was.

'Another part of our approach', he said, 'was not to cite the police directly, but still present horrendous allegations against them in the papers. We wanted to make it very clear that the reason we had to bring the interdicts was because the applicants could get no relief from the police in the first place. All in all, COSATU filed eleven court applications in the

Maritzburg Supreme Court for restraining interdicts on various Inkatha members. But if you want more detailed information you should speak to Matthew Dontzin. He did a hell of a lot of the leg-work down there.'

More than a dozen phone-calls later I managed to locate Dontzin and arranged to meet him one morning, in my office. Dontzin proved to be a loud and frenetic American. As he spoke he seemed to cover great distances, although in reality he did not move much from his chair. He did accompany his words with wild hand gestures, however, and this contributed to the illusion. In general he liked to sit back with his legs up and crossed on the edge of my desk, but he would drop them emphatically when he wished to make a particular point.

'You know, bringing one interdict even, forget eleven, is a fuckload of work, and for a while we were working twenty-hour days, day after day, to get the applications prepared. OK, hang on, let's take it step by step. We had all these statements, right, but you can't just bring hundreds of affidavits to court and hope they all hang together. You have to be selective. So from the evidence we'd gathered we pinpointed a number of specific incidents and focused on them. We basically set up a centre of operations to bring together all the resources we'd need to build the strongest possible cases.

'We took at first a few rooms, and then a whole floor at the Capital Towers Hotel, brought down articled clerks, secretaries, typists from Johannesburg, and gathered together a team of fieldworkers to go into the townships and find the witnesses. There were activists from COSATU and the UDF involved, always on the move, bringing in new people to make statements, taking others back to the townships, organising food. We had marshals patrolling the hotel floor, checking for Inkatha spies. Then there was the whole business of switching cars, working out ways of protecting the witnesses, finding places for them to stay — a lot of these guys were refugees already — you see what I'm saying, it was just fucken madness the whole time, like a fucken nightmare.'

In fact, I could visualise the scene even without Dontzin's description, as I had been to the headquarters of the legal campaign at the Capital Towers on a visit to Pietermaritzburg in late October 1987. There had been nothing particularly unusual about the hotel corridor, but as soon as I started opening doors it was as though I had inadvertently wandered onto the set of a surrealistic film. In each room there were crowds of people sitting patiently and silently waiting to be called to dictate their statement. Some had been there for hours on end, and as I opened the door all heads turned immediately in the hope that I had come to summon them. Further along, typists were furiously transcribing affidavits, and in some rooms attorneys were grilling witnesses, probing each statement and making sure that they were absolutely certain of their facts. So great was the urgency of the exercise that shifts of attorneys, clerks, interpreters, drivers, and typists were working round the clock to prepare the documentation for the applications, the first of which had been set down for the first week of November.

On that occasion I had met Dontzin too, fleetingly. He had been racing around coordinating everything, collapsing, swearing, eating and taking a shower before rushing off again.

In my office, eighteen months later, I reminded Dontzin of this brief meeting and he said, 'Right, so you know that shit. But you have no idea of the time it all took. We had to see that people got to the offices of the local Maritzburg attorneys who were working with us; and we needed lawyers to accompany our witnesses who went to make statements with the police. The main point, though, is that we didn't just take the statements we were getting at face value. We examined our witnesses more thoroughly than they would ever be cross-examined in court. We went over and over each claim looking for inconsistencies, weak points.'

Dontzin paced about, raised and dropped his hands. 'Eventually we got it together and brought the applications,' he beat his hand into his fist, 'we were pumping them out, every ten days, wave after wave of interdicts, keeping the heat on....' He looked at his watch and exclaimed, 'Hell, man, I'm history! Catch you tomorrow same time if you like,' and was gone.

The various applications brought by COSATU called on the court to interdict particular Inkatha members from killing, assaulting, threatening or attempting to kill, intimidating or attempting to intimidate by word or conduct any of the applicants on whose behalf the applications were brought, and from instructing or inciting others to commit any of these acts. In all but one of the applications, temporary interdicts were granted on the basis of the affidavits submitted by both sides. In each case the respondents contested the claims of the applicants, pleading innocence of all the allegations against them. Consequently the cases were referred for oral evidence to be heard, at which point the judge would decide whether the interdicts should be made permanent or not.

Towards the end of 1987, interdicts were secured against a number of Inkatha leaders in the following applications:

— *Sililo* v *Mncwabe*, alleging murder by Inkatha leader and Imbali town councillor, Jerome Mncwabe;
— *Hadebe* v *Shiyabani Zuma*, alleging assault, kidnapping, theft and intimidation against Slangspruit Inkatha leader, Shiyabani Zuma;
— *Mkhize* v *Zuma*, alleging murder, attempted murder, assault, arson, kidnapping and intimidation against the chairman of the Harewood branch of the Inkatha Youth Brigade, Sichizo Zuma;
— *Mkhize* v *Zuma*, alleging contempt of court by Sichizo Zuma;
— *Zulu* v *Zondi*, alleging assault and abduction by Inkatha members and

accessory against Inkatha leader, Abdul Awetha;

— *Mkhize & Others* v *Ntombela & Others*, alleging murder against the chairman of the KwaMncane branch of Inkatha, David Ntombela.

In the early months of 1988, COSATU brought yet more applications to the Supreme Court for interdicts against Inkatha warlords, many of them already restricted by earlier interdict orders. Among the second wave of interdicts were the cases of:

— *Zondo, COSATU & Others* v *Inkatha, Ntombela & Others*. This application arose from the events surrounding the Inkatha meeting held at KwaMkhulu on 31 January 1988, Inkatha's so-called Operation Doom. The applications brought allegations of murder, assault and damage to property against Inkatha members, and incitement to murder and assault against David Ntombela;

— *Mthembu* v *Mncwabe & Others*, alleging intimidation by Inkatha leader and Imbali town councillor, Jerome Mncwabe; Inkatha member and KwaZulu policeman, Thulani Ngcobo; and the chairman of the Harewood branch of the Inkatha Youth Brigade, Sichizo Zuma;

— *Mthembu* v *Zuma*, alleging murder and contempt of court against Sichizo Zuma;

— *Zondi* v *Zondi*, alleging intimidation and assault against Inkatha patron, Shayabantu Zondi.

Despite these successful applications and the adverse publicity which consequently attached itself to Inkatha, the Inkatha leadership took no action on its own either to investigate the charges against the warlords, or to discipline them for any infringements. Instead, Chief Buthelezi attacked COSATU for making use of the courts maliciously for the purpose of waging a propaganda war against Inkatha. In the case of *Zondo, COSATU & Others* v *Inkatha, Ntombela & Others*, Inkatha the organisation had been joined with individual respondents on the basis that the alleged crimes had been perpetrated by Inkatha members during and following a meeting organised by and under the auspices of Inkatha. Chief Buthelezi submitted a long answering affidavit on behalf of Inkatha, the first respondent, in which he said:

Since the beginning of November 1987, numerous applications have been brought by members of the UDF and COSATU for interdicts against members of Inkatha. The relief inevitably is an order seeking to restrain the members of Inkatha cited in those applications from murdering the members of the UDF or COSATU. As such illegal acts may carry capital punishment, no meaningful advantage can be obtained through a court order in civil proceedings with its sanction of committal for contempt. Accordingly, such applications I submit have been brought as political strategy.

When the initial cases were brought before court certain leaders of the UDF and COSATU became deponents including Jay Naidoo, the leader of COSATU.

Immediately after interim interdicts were obtained, a 'Press Conference' was held by COSATU and UDF leaders to ensure that their organisations obtained maximum publicity from such facts.

In subsequent speeches throughout the country, officials of the UDF and COSATU have been using the fact of the court orders as propaganda and proof of the fact (as they allege) that the court has found Inkatha responsible for all the violence in the townships surrounding Pietermaritzburg and the UDF and COSATU supporters are portrayed as the innocent victims.

The next day when Matthew Dontzin burst into my office as arranged, I showed him Chief Buthelezi's comment, but he brushed it aside and began speaking very fast. 'No thanks, buddy, I've seen that many times,' he began, 'but I think we'd better get some things clear. First of all, the interdict campaign was not some kind of elaborate game which COSATU was playing for its own purposes. The stakes were incredibly high; we were dealing with people who had been attacked, had all their possessions destroyed, seen members of their families murdered, been threatened, and when they'd gone to the police to complain they'd been ignored, insulted and ridiculed. And their attackers and tormentors continued to walk around freely and commit crimes with total impunity. All the applicants came to us as a last resort when the normal channels – I mean investigation by the police resulting in prosecution of criminals – had proved useless. And don't think it ended there either. By submitting affidavits and agreeing to testify against warlords in open court, our applicants and witnesses were opening themselves up for new and greater dangers.

'Look at what happened in the *Mthembu* case. On the day before the application was due to be heard in court, one of the applicants was shot by Sichizo Zuma, one of the respondents, and injured so badly he subsequently died. And then there's the case of Johannes Nkomo, one of the applicants in *Zondo* v *Inkatha*. He was murdered by Inkatha members days before the application came to court. And what about what happened later? When the *Zondo* case came up in court, David Ntombela threatened to shoot one of our witnesses if he testified against him.

'Then in July, as we were getting ourselves ready for the first of our interdict applications to come up for oral evidence – the *Mthembu* case – our key witness, Ernest Mthembu, was shot outside his house. Officially he was killed by unknown attackers, but who the hell else could it have been other than Inkatha members? As it is, Sichizo Zuma, one of the respondents, had killed Ernest's brother Simon in January, just before the first round of the application was heard.

'Look, you have to understand that was a hell of a blow to us, and I don't mean just in terms of losing our key witness, but we had to start asking whether it was worth pursuing the strategy, thereby further endangering the applicants and witnesses, or whether we'd got as much as we could out of the whole exercise. Well, you know what happened next; at the beginning of September 1988 COSATU reached a settlement with Inkatha – the COSATU–Inkatha Accord – and dropped all but one of the applications. We had to let *Mthembu* v *Mncwabe* carry on because it was already part heard. But it's very important you understand exactly why we stopped when we did.

'First of all, what had we achieved? We had temporary interdicts restraining warlords from attacking specific applicants or operating in certain areas, but this wouldn't stop these guys from going into other areas and attacking other people. So obviously we needed proper criminal prosecutions of these people. But despite the pressure on the Attorney-General to get on with it, there were very few prosecutions, and those that were heard were handled so incompetently, in my opinion, it would be laughable if it wasn't so pathetic. Warlords guilty of serious crimes like murder and kidnapping would be acquitted because the prosecution was so ham-fisted, which only reinforced their opinions of themselves as being above the law and invulnerable.

'Second, there was the fact that applicants and witnesses had been attacked and killed after bringing actions against warlords. We found that people who had been willing to testify when the interdicts were first brought were increasingly reluctant to come to court eight months later to give oral evidence, because they'd been threatened, or they'd seen what happened to other witnesses.

'Then there was the fact that the cost in terms of money and time of bringing ten cases wwas prohibitive. I don't know – maybe if all the other factors were working with us we'd have found the time and the money, but as it was....' Dontzin shrugged.

'Then there's the attitude of the courts,' he continued. 'At the beginning there were some judges who were concerned about what was going on, who shat on the Attorney-General for not investigating and prosecuting, but these were exceptions, man. For the most part the judges who were assigned weren't the senior judges who really command respect, but acting judges. Then we found that they were antagonistic to us using the civil courts to hear criminal matters. But, hey, that's not our problem, that just says something about the criminal courts. And then you get the judges who reckon the interdicts are just a waste of time. In one of the early applications, a Justice of the Supreme Court, no less, said, "Why bring all of these applications? The Zulus have been fighting for a hundred years."

'The real problem was that the courts simply didn't take the matter seriously enough. We had to wait eight months for oral evidence to be heard in just *one* of the applications, and then what happened was this: the trial was heard for two weeks, adjourned for two months and then heard for another two weeks, adjourned for four months and heard for three days, adjourned for another month, and so on. As far as I could see, the counsel for Inkatha was dragging it out as long as possible, filibustering, spending days on cross-examination he could have completed in a couple of hours.

*   *   *

When Dontzin left I reread James Lund's paper 'The Law and Its Limitations', which he had presented at the seminar on violence organised by the CAE. Lund had written:

Over the past six months the Supreme Court has issued a number of interim interdicts in terms of which named individuals are prohibited from e.g. killing, assaulting or threatening or attempting to kill or assault other named persons or attacking or destroying their property. Is such conduct not in any event prohibited by the ordinary law of the land?

Lund concludes with the obvious, pessimistic answer to his own question:

The need for the victims of violence in the Pietermaritzburg area to resort to the dangers and expenses associated with the interdict applications in order to claim the fundamental human rights and protection that should be theirs in any sane society, shows that the courts and the legal process have become a mockery. The judges, still fiercely proud of their independence, have been turned into impotent second-rate – may I say independent – press agents. And while this might be a sad spectacle for many, a sadder feature is that the disillusionment created can only serve to promote further violence and disrespect for law on all sides.

I phoned Lund and asked, 'What did you mean by calling the judges "impotent second-rate press agents"?'

He answered, 'In my paper I said that one of the reasons the interdicts were necessary was because the normal channels of information had been closed off in South Africa. First you have laws like the Group Areas Act which effectively separate the races and keep whites from knowing what is going on in black areas; then you have the whole battery of emergency regulations which completely emasculate the press and screen the police or, here, the warlords from any independent scrutiny. The only way victims could get their stories heard was through the courts, even though the material improvements in their situation remained limited. In this sense, then, the judges were not so much providing relief for the applicants, as acting as press agents, facilitating the dissemination of information.'

'So do you think the interdict strategy was a failure?' I asked.

'Well, that remains to be seen,' Lund said. 'The warlord question had to be raised, and the interdicts were as good a strategy as any. It's only when peace has been achieved and maintained that we'll be able to look back and see which forces were vital.' He sighed. 'But the long term will bring its own problems. The police, the prosecutors, the judges totally out of touch with the gravity of the situation, none of them realise the repercussions of their actions. In the long run we'll find that the real casualty in the conflict is the rule of law. The people in the townships experience law as a negative, predatory force, not as a protector or enabler.'

25
Peace-broking

There has been more than one attempt to bring the warring parties in Pietermaritzburg together to talk about peace. Right from the start, from September 1987, each side has consistently presented itself as the party of peace and taken steps with greater or lesser enthusiasm to bring about a ceasefire.

Peace negotiations are delicate, touchy affairs. The negotiators on both sides manouevre slowly and with extreme care, constantly trying to second-guess their opponents and desperately anxious not to relinquish any advantage through some unguarded compromise or admission. If there is enough common ground between them for a joint statement to be issued, this is hailed as a 'major breakthrough', but when deadlock is reached, as is more often the case, each side then accuses the other of bad faith and of betraying the cause of peace.

I went in search of some of the people who had sat around the table trying to find the magic formula that would bring an end to the killing. First I spoke to Paul van Uytrecht, managing director of the Pietermaritzburg Chamber of Commerce until March 1988. Van Uytrecht chaired two sessions of peace negotiations between Inkatha and the UDF in November and December 1987, and over a plate of chicken biriani and a few beers he told me how the local palace of commerce had become (briefly) the place of peace.

Van Uytrecht sat uncomfortably in the low armchair in the bar, his knees practically up to his shoulders. I put him somewhere in the late thirties, and waited while he ordered a refill. 'We were first approached by Inkatha in about September 1987. Vitus Mvelase, the KwaZulu Urban Representative in Pietermaritzburg, is a member of the Manpower Commission – it's now called the Industrial Relations Commission – so he's had a lot of contact with the Chamber for a long time. He told us that he was worried by the escalation of violence and wondered whether there was anything the Chamber could do.

'Shortly after this, a matter of days, no more, we were approached by COSATU to discuss the matter, so we met a COSATU delegation, and after that, some people from Inkatha. Defining the Chamber's role was not that easy as both parties were looking for partisanship, which was ridiculous as the Chamber had no power to make or enforce any unilateral decisions about the fighting. I mean, Inkatha would say, "You're an employer organisation, you've got clout with the unions, so get them to stop the violence," and COSATU would say, "Look, you capitalists understand Inkatha, use your influence with them to get them to stop." In effect what COSATU was saying to us was "Do something about it or we'll call a strike in Pietermaritzburg."

'In the end the Chamber took the role of honest broker, but it's very hard to be a completely impartial mediator between two warring parties. One can't help being critical of the way one or each goes about seeking peace. And that's forgetting as well the flak we took from our own members in the business community, many of whom said things like, "This is politics, you shouldn't get involved," or they said, "You're wasting your time refereeing squabbles between savages; it's in black nature to be violent." Still, I think a large majority of the members of the Chamber were in favour of our actions.

'Our task was made that much harder in November when the police detained the secretaries of the UDF in the Maritzburg region, Martin Wittenberg and Skhumbuzo Ngwenya, but we kicked up a hell of a fuss and a whole lot of embassies which had been watching the progress of the peace negotiations put pressure on the police as well. For once that kind of thing worked and those guys were released, although with restrictions. They could participate in peace talks, but that was all.'

The first meeting was held on 24 November at the Imperial Hotel and seemed to go well. 'I organised coffee, but no alcohol,' said Van Uytrecht. 'Only afterwards, when we'd drawn up a joint statement, I ordered in some drinks and people seemed pretty happy and relaxed. I mean, there were UDF guys and Inkatha guys swapping stories, laughing; there was banter between guys who'd never met before.'

Amongst other things, the joint statement said the following:

The parties to this joint meeting i.e. Inkatha–UWUSA, UDF–COSATU, and the Chamber of Commerce have reached agreement on the following points:

1. We publicly condemn and dissociate ourselves from the current violence.
2. The police and security forces must allow meetings of the different organisations which are part of the peace process.
3. All parties who are part of the peace process must publicly endorse and accept the principles of freedom of expression and association and publicly condemn such actions as forced recruitment and will take immediate disciplinary action against those individuals who violate these principles.
4. There are certain points related to the details of the perpetrators of the violence where agreement could not be reached and the parties have agreed to reflect on those points and to raise them again at a future meeting.

After the meeting COSATU and the UDF issued a call for an end to the violence in which they repeated a number of the points made in the joint declaration, but also added a few specific appeals of their own. In their broadsheet they wrote:

We wish to make the following calls on the community:
— Ordinary members of Inkatha should dissociate themselves from the warlords;
— Our activists must not treat warlords and ordinary Inkatha members in the same way. Let us isolate the warlords and assure ordinary Inkatha members that they have nothing to fear from COSATU and UDF;
— The policies of COSATU and UDF have been deliberately distorted. Our policies must be carefully explained to Inkatha members so that they can decide for themselves;
— The leaders of COSATU and UDF must ensure that we act with discipline and restraint. Our task is to unite and lead people to a democratic South Africa. We will not be able to do this if we are provoked into using the undisciplined and violent methods of the warlords.

This appeal by COSATU and the UDF made it clear that they saw the existence of Inkatha warlords as the major obstacle to the return of peace to the area. Indeed, by the time the first meeting was held, a number of Inkatha warlords had been issued with interim interdicts preventing them from assaulting or otherwise harassing members of the community. Inkatha had at all times denied that warlords were operating in the area and had strongly opposed the interdict applications. Consequently they were not prepared to accept the UDF–COSATU demand that the warlords be restrained and their vigilante armies disbanded.

The existence and role of the warlords remained a major point of contention as the two parties went into the second round of peace talks on 9 December. However, whereas the first meeting had been smooth and amicable – too easy, some people thought – the second degenerated into one bitter dispute after another and then fell apart completely. Paul van Uytrecht, chairman of the meeting, tried to explain the causes of breakdown. 'Well, first of all there was no agreement about the warlords, but the second meeting also introduced a contentious theme which has remained an issue ever since, and that's the question of who exactly should be doing the talking. As far as I was concerned, the people present at the first meeting were representative of the parties concerned.

'Suddenly, though, we learned that Inkatha was not happy about the composition of the two teams of negotiators. They wanted higher-ranking people in the organisations to be doing the talking: the secretary general of COSATU, the president of the UDF, the president of Inkatha. I think Inkatha wanted to make Pietermaritzburg a national or at least a regional issue, rather than have it seen as just a local conflict, and they wanted the negotiations to reflect that by involving the national leaders of the various organisations, rather than the local office-bearers.'

As it happened, the second meeting broke up for a different reason. The Inkatha delegation brought with them an article that had appeared in the October edition of the journal *Inqaba yabasebenzi*, which is produced by a tiny extremist group called the Marxist Workers' Tendency of the ANC. The gist of the article was simple: the UDF and COSATU were called upon to take all possible steps to expose Chief Buthelezi as a puppet of the government, and to destroy Inkatha in any way possible. The Inkatha delegation insisted, as a prologue to the meeting, that the UDF–COSATU delegation repudiate this article in order to re-establish their good faith at the peace table. The UDF and COSATU people said that they had nothing to do with the document and that it was irrelevant to the matter at hand, but Inkatha insisted.

Van Uytrecht continued: 'The UDF–COSATU delegation assured the Inkatha people that they dissociated themselves from the content of the article, but that wasn't sufficient. Inkatha demanded that they make a public repudiation of the article, so the UDF people said they would make an announcement to the effect at the press conference after the meeting. But that was not enough either; Inkatha said that people in the townships wouldn't see the advertisement. The UDF and COSATU people eventually agreed to place a prominent advertisement in the *Witness* repudiating the article, but again Inkatha wasn't satisfied and demanded that the UDF convene a rally in the townships to declare their repudiation. The UDF–COSATU delegation balked at this. They said that the issue of the article was a red herring, raised by Inkatha merely to delay the peace process, and that they weren't prepared to organise a rally for the sole purpose of repudiating a banned article which no one was likely to see or care about. And at that point the talks deadlocked and there were no further meetings convened by the Chamber, even though the UDF and COSATU did stand by their agreement to place a full-page ad in the paper.

'But speak to people from Inkatha – I'm sure they've got a different line on the matter.'

When I met Vitus Mvelase and Velaphi Ndlovu of Inkatha in the lounge of the Imperial Hotel in Pietermaritzburg, they were quick to dismiss the UDF–COSATU repudiation of the article as mere lip-service, devoid of any sincerity. I suggested it was unusual that the second round of talks had been so unsuccessful given the positive outcome of the first round. 'Positive in what sense?' Velaphi Ndlovu demanded. 'That is the introductory talks, there can never be the obstacle. Negotiation is only the second or third round.'

'On the question of the *Inqaba* article …,' I began.

'Yes, now that is the negotiation,' Ndlovu agreed. 'After the introduction. That was the article denigrating Inkatha. In this meeting—'

'—they refused to dissociate themseves—' Mvelase suggested.

'—we laid down the rules as to how they should repudiate this thing.'

'I thought that they had repudiated the article,' I said.

'No, no, no, no, no,' Ndlovu corrected me indulgently, wagging a forefinger. 'They haven't. They've advertised in a paper the way they think it's right. We wanted a letter direct to ANC, and we wanted them to call the mass meeting for their members to say to them, "See here, we're repudiating this pamphlet now." '

'And did their members even know about this pamphlet?' I asked.

'Of course, yes,' said Ndlovu.

'Even though it was banned?'

'You call it was banned,' Ndlovu said, 'but other people have it.'

Mvelase added, 'There are so many pamphlets which are banned and which are distributed. It was our agreement, and they don't want to do it because they want their boss, which is ANC, to see they are doing their work.'

'Well, it's history now, I guess,' I said, 'but you know there are a lot of people out there who think Inkatha raised this issue just to sabotage the talks.'

'We haven't done that. We could never do that. How could we do that?' Ndlovu asked comfortably, still smiling, and turned to other topics.

After the abortive second meeting, in December and January, Paul van Uytrecht gave a number of interviews to journalists from local and foreign papers in which, unwisely, he commented on Inkatha's behaviour at the negotiating table.

'I was quoted – or misquoted, I should say,' said Van Uytrecht, 'criticising Inkatha in an article in the *New York Times*, and immediately Chief Buthelezi announced that he would have no further dealings with the Chamber unless it repudiated me and my comments. But if you really want to know about this business you must read Buthelezi's speech on the matter. It's part of his opening speech to the KwaZulu Legislative Assembly, March '88. He goes on about it for about twenty pages, I think.'

I sat in my office that afternoon and sweated my way through Chief Buthelezi's account. His policy speech, with which he had opened the sixth session of the fourth KwaZulu Legislative Assembly, ran for 217 pages, of which he had devoted 20 to the Van Uytrecht affair. He felt bound to place all the facts before the Honourable Members of the Assembly. Apart from his own views, he also read into the record all the correspondence that had passed between him and various officials of the Pietermaritzburg Chamber of Commerce (PCC) and of the Associated Chambers of Commerce of South Africa (ASSOCOM).

Mr Speaker, I would like to share with the House exchanges that have taken place between myself and the Pietermaritzburg Chamber of Commerce. The Chamber mounted a peace initiative in which it presented itself as an honest broker between the UDF and COSATU on the one hand, and Inkatha on the other hand....

We soon came to realise, however, that the Chamber had tackled something which it was ill equipped to handle. Preliminary meetings served only to define the intractable nature of the problem the Chamber was facing. It was being used by the UDF–COSATU alliance to cast aspersions on Inkatha's sincerity in seeking peace.

Then to compound the Chamber's problems, John F Burns in an article in the *New York Times* publicised the attitudes of the Manager, Mr Paul van Uytrecht, of the Pietermaritzburg Chamber of Commerce....

Here we had the Manager of the Chamber itself taking sides in a situation in which the Chamber was purporting to be neutral. I therefore wrote to Mr Stewart Smith, the President of the Pietermaritzburg Chamber of Commerce.

Chief Buthelezi's letter began by setting out for Mr Smith the aims and achievements of Inkatha over the years. Once his credentials had been suitably established, Chief Buthelezi turned to the substance of his dissatisfaction with the PCC.

When John F Burns publishes an article in one of the world's largest mass circulation newspapers, the *New York Times*, in which he reports that Paul van Uytrecht, the PCC's Manager, says 'Inkatha warlords had tried to enforce loyalty to the Zulu group at schools, hospitals and work places, even insisting that disaster relief after floods in October be channelled exclusively through its hands', I am appalled at the kind of organisation which the Pietermaritzburg Chamber of Commerce must be. Mr Van Uytrecht is reported to have said: 'Over a period of time communities that were not politicised have begun turning over spontaneously against Inkatha. Now things have swung in a way that is very unsatisfactory to Inkatha, and they may in fact be left with very little.'...

A great many around me are shocked by Mr Van Uytrecht's reported statements. It is being repeatedly said to me, and I convey the idiom of what is being said, that the Pietermaritzburg Chamber of Commerce is covering its arse because it is shit-scared of the UDF and possible commercial action that the UDF so desires to specialise in. Is the PCC simply the tool of small-minded businessmen who think they can make a few extra bucks by appeasing revolutionary forces?

Stewart Smith wasted no time in replying to Chief Buthelezi's letter, dissociating himself from the report.

Later in February, Chief Buthelezi sent a letter to Mr Alec Rogoff, the president of ASSOCOM, complaining of a further impropriety on the part of Van Uytrecht.

Last night I received a copy of another article by the same Mr John Burns written for the *New York Times* in which amongst other things, Mr Paul van Uytrecht is quoted as saying: 'The Indaba is dead.' This statement is put in an article the gist of which is that Pietermaritzburg has shown that my political base is in jeopardy and that the Indaba has no future because the gap between moderate whites and major black groups has not been bridged.

The Pietermaritzburg Chamber of Commerce now really does need to declare publicly where it stands. Does it hold a brief for the UDF and COSATU? Does Mr Van Uytrecht reflect the Chamber's views about the Pietermaritzburg violence and about the Indaba?

Mr Rogoff replied as soon as he could, and faxed his letter down to Ulundi. He said: 'ASSOCOM recognises the vital role you are playing in upholding the free enterprise system and in seeking a solution to South Africa's problem through peaceful negotiation and dialogue and has a positive attitude towards the KwaZulu–Natal Indaba.' At this point the correspondence appears to have ended – at any rate, there were no further letters deemed by Chief Buthelezi sufficiently important to be read into the Assembly record.

Naturally I immediately confronted Paul van Uytrecht with this lengthy and damning indictment of his actions. I found him, a year on, only moderately contrite about the incident. 'I realise now that a mediator shouldn't give any interviews because remarks can be taken out of context – as in this case – and the repercussions are tremendous. All I had said is that these were allegations against Inkatha warlords, and allegations made by neutral people such as the mayor, moreover; I wasn't giving an opinion, although my own feelings may have been apparent.'

'What about your comments on the Indaba?' I asked.

Van Uytrecht shrugged. 'Well, for one thing,' he said, 'I didn't say that the Indaba was dead, but I did say that it wasn't looking as healthy as it had a year earlier. In saying that, I was reflecting views I'd picked up here and there from people who had formerly been staunch supporters of the Indaba. People were saying things likke, "Well, if this is what Inkatha does when it's in dispute with black groups, what'll it do to whites if there's dissension in the Indaba?" Suddenly whites were saying that there hadn't been enough attention paid to safeguards for white interests – stuff like that. I wasn't endorsing, or agreeing with these views, I was merely commenting that there had been some change of attitude.

'Look,' Van Uytrecht gently spun the glass in his hand, 'it's also not as if I didn't pay a price. Buthelezi, as you know, threw all his toys out of the cot; the Chamber acceded to his demand that I take no further part in the peace negotiations, and basically the general atmosphere at my work became so hostile and tense that I left in March.'

Whatever the merits of Paul van Uytrecht's explanation of the motives and consequences of his actions, the attitude of Chief Buthelezi was itself questionable. The Chief Minister accused the PCC of betraying its role as honest broker in the dispute, and yet on the strength of his statements, one could argue that he was seeking from the Chamber not so much neutrality as an endorsement of and alignment with the policies of Inkatha.

In his letter to Alec Rogoff of ASSOCOM, Chief Buthelezi declares that the PCC needs to declare publicly where it stands. In reply, Rogoff says that ASSOCOM – and by extension the PCC, since it is a member of ASSOCOM – 'recognises the vital role that you are playing in upholding the free enterprise system and in seeking a solution to South Africa's problems through peaceful negotiation and dialogue and has a positive attitude towards the KwaZulu–Natal Indaba'. Every one of these sentiments is contentious and contrary to the views of COSATU and the UDF, and for Rogoff to express them implies a partisanship towards Inkatha which far exceeds any real or imputed bias on the part of Van Uytrecht towards the UDF and COSATU. However, Chief Buthelezi either failed to see this contradiction, or else he recognised it but chose in this instance to hold his own counsel.

Notwithstanding the extent of the Chief Minister's bluster and indignation, the episode proved itself to be no more than the proverbial storm in a teacup. The February meeting did not take place but this was not simply because the question of Van Uytrecht's participation remained unresolved. Instead, the state stepped in and closed off the option of further talks by banning the UDF and COSATU from taking part in any political activity.

At this point the PCC's peace initiative foundered completely and there were no further attempts at a rapprochement between the two sides for six months.

★   ★   ★

In August 1988, oral evidence was heard in the *Mthembu* case, the first of eleven interdicts brought by COSATU against various Inkatha warlords. However, before long the COSATU representatives were of the opinion that through a mixture of court adjournments and filibustering on the part of the Inkatha legal team, the process could well go on into the indefinite future and would cost an enormous amount of money. Consequently, when the possibility of settlement between the two parties was mooted, COSATU, instead of rejecting the suggestion, entered into discussions with Inkatha. The result was the declaration of an Accord between Inkatha and COSATU and the establishment of the Complaints Adjudication Board (CAB).

The CAB was mandated to hear and adjudicate disputes arising from violence in the townships. It was convened like a court: the sessions were chaired by two retired judges of the Supreme Court who sat with two assessors, one each appointed by COSATU and Inkatha. The real advantages of the Board lay in the fact that the probity and competence of the joint chairmen was beyond dispute, which meant that the Board could be relied on to make just findings, and to do so quickly and at a fraction of the cost of litigation in the courts.

The chief problem with the CAB, however, was its relative inability to compel either of the parties to abide by its findings. The first case brought before the Board was a complaint against the Inkatha leader of the Inadi region, Shayabantu Zondi, and his induna Lawrence Zuma, who were alleged to have prohibited non-Inkatha meetings in their area, in contravention of the principle of freedom of association espoused by both Inkatha and the UDF–COSATU. In addition, the men were alleged to have harassed non-Inkatha supporters with threats of violence and forced removal if they refused to join the organisation.

The Inkatha leaders named as the respondents refused to attend the hearings on the grounds that they might prejudice criminal investigations currently being carried out by the police arising from the same incidents.

The hearing went ahead in the absence of the respondents. The Board found that a *prima facie* case had been established against the two respondents, and recommended that Inkatha take disciplinary action against them. However, towards the end of February 1989, Inkatha informed the applicants that it would take no action against the respondents so as not to prejudice any criminal prosecutions that might follow at some stage.

The ease with which Inkatha was able to disregard its recommendations illustrated the Board's limitations as an adjudicatory body. There was nothing in its articles to induce either party to abide by its findings except good faith, a rare and unreliable commodity in times of war.

Apart from the fact that its findings could be followed or ignored as a matter of convenience, the CAB was also incapable of dealing with all the complaints that might have come before it. At best, its interventions could have pinpointed and neutralised a few of the main perpetrators of violence, but the impact of such actions was necessarily limited. In April 1989, a witness who had given evidence before the CAB was murdered by unknown assailants, after which the Board ceased to operate.

*   *   *

In the same month, however, there was a new movement towards peace. A much publicised letter from Nelson Mandela to Chief Buthelezi expressed hopes for more cordial relations between Inkatha and the ANC, and said:

Far more information than I possess at the moment is required before I can blame any of the parties involved in the deplorable conflicts now taking place in Natal. All the same, I consider it a serious indictment against all of us that we are still unable to combine forces to stop the slaughter of so many innocent lives....

In my entire political career, few things have distressed me as much as to see our people killing one another as is now happening. As you know, the entire fabric of community life in some of the affected areas has been seriously disrupted, leaving behind a legacy of hatred and bitterness which may haunt us for years to come.

It is a matter which requires the urgent attention of all people in this country. Nothing will please me more than to know that my concern and appeal have not fallen on deaf ears.

Shortly after Buthelezi had released the text of this letter to the press, the local papers announced that a new peace initiative had been set in train by Chief Mhlabunzima Maphumulo of Maqongqo, near Table Mountain in Natal. Chief Maphumulo was already well known as a maverick chief who had gained considerable notoriety for himself by consistently refusing to toe the Inkatha line. Towards the end of 1988, he was summoned by Chief Buthelezi to appear before him for the purpose of an inquiry into the administration of his area.

Chief Maphumulo refused to comply on the grounds that the summons was vaguely worded and imprecise, and he warned that any action taken against him would be challenged in the Supreme Court. The matter was left to rest, but many political commentators believe that Maphumulo was being called to account for his avowed policy of neutrality in the conflict. In his area of control, hundreds of refugees from the Pietermaritzburg townships have sought and found safety.

In Maqongqo, UDF and Inkatha supporters live together without tension or acrimony, and it is reported that this liberal policy, together with the chief's current ban on political recruitment in his area by either party, has incensed military elements within the Inkatha hierarchy who do not like chiefs who break ranks. Chief Maphumulo appears to be unmoved by the umbrage he provokes in Inkatha circles. He declared, 'Anyone who wants to stay among my people must accept the condition of peace. Unlike other chiefs I refuse to get involved in the violence. I have chosen to be neutral. That is the only way to peace for my people.'

In early April, Chief Maphumulo drew up a petition calling on the then State President, P W Botha, to recognise that there was a breakdown in law and order in the Pietermaritzburg region, and to appoint a commission of inquiry into the causes of the violence. He flew to Cape Town to deliver the petition in person to the State President, and it was not long before he began taking flak from both the state and Inkatha. Chief Buthelezi came out strongly against the idea of a commission of inquiry, saying that he hoped Mr Botha would not allow Chief Maphumulo to muddy the political waters when the country's people were trying to find one another politically.

Chief Buthelezi need not have worried. The Minister of Law and Order dismissed out of hand any possibility of establishing a commission of inquiry as he had done on all previous occasions when petitioned to do so. From his statements it seemed as if the Minister was thoroughly satisfied in his mind that to find the causes of violence he need look no further than certain 'radical elements' associated with COSATU and the UDF, and therefore to set up a commission to discover what he already knew would be a redundant exercise. Vlok described the UDF and COSATU as a 'revolutionary alliance' and said that activists in these organisations were taking instruction from the ANC. He also scoffed at the efforts of clergymen involved in peace initiatives, and said they had been 'inspanned by the ANC–SACP to do their devilish work'.

Vlok also made it clear that he was preparing to crack down further on UDF and COSATU activists and announced that yet more personnel and equipment would be deployed in Natal. He mentioned that he had discussed the matter with Chief Buthelezi during a recent visit to Ulundi, an announcement which alarmed many people and led them to surmise that between them Vlok and Buthelezi had jointly devised an 'iron fist' strategy to deal with progressive organisations in Natal.

Despite these ominous harbingers of things to come, by the end of April 1989 there were fresh moves to convene peace talks between Inkatha and the UDF–COSATU. Chief Buthelezi publicised a peace plan which called for an enormous public relations operation in the townships to be subsidised by large-scale national and international funding. In a letter to Archbishop Hurley, Chief Buthelezi wrote:

The people on the ground must be bombarded with educational material and messages of a committed leadership acting in concert with other committed leaders. We must be in a position to buy radio and television broadcasting time, to buy large-scale newspaper advertising space, to do air drops of hundreds of thousands of peace pamphlets, to use loud-hailers and pre-recorded messages which can be taken to the people on the back of trucks.

At the same time COSATU and the UDF released a peace plan of their own, which was considerably less ambitious. The two organisations called for a conference to be convened by a number of church and community leaders. In addition they declared, 'We share with Inkatha a common view and commitment to a mass movement for peace. Whilst COSATU and the UDF largely share a common political position which differs from that of Inkatha, all three organisations share an abhorrence of apartheid and are committed to achieving peace in Natal.'

Despite the conciliatory nature of this pronouncement, Inkatha's initial response was not particularly encouraging. Chief Buthelezi called for a 'moratorium on mudslinging', saying, 'We are maligned by the very parties who now want us to join in peace initiatives with them.' However, at a meeting of the Inkatha Central Committee (ICC) during which both peace plans were discussed, it became clear that what Chief Buthelezi had in mind was a selective moratorium on invective: he could employ political polemic but his opponents could not. During the debate on the COSATU–UDF plan, several wits among the KwaZulu MPs observed that some priests were behaving as if 'drunk on communion wine'.

Chief Buthelezi also referred to a memorandum passed between lawyers acting for COSATU and for Inkatha as being full of 'ugly lies and insinuations', and said too, 'I do not want to stoop now to pick up the filth you are flinging around.'

At the end of their meeting, the Inkatha Central Committee issued a resolution writing off the COSATU–UDF proposal as 'undemocratically conceived' while wholeheartedly endorsing Chief Buthelezi's plan. Nonetheless, there was sufficient common ground between the two proposals for the new peace initiative to continue. The ANC also agreed to play whatever role was requested of them by the other parties in the peace process, and by the middle of May, Chief Buthelezi had written to COSATU and the UDF suggesting a meeting at Ulundi on 20 May. COSATU and the UDF replied, saying that they found the date acceptable, but would prefer to meet at a neutral venue, such as Durban.

Chief Buthelezi, who maintained that it was 'vitally important for the sake of peace' that the meeting be held at Ulundi, wrote back stating, 'I have no intention of going to Durban or anywhere else in order to fulfil your wish to meet me.' This categorical statement sat uneasily with an undertaking he had made in an earlier letter to Denis Hurley, Catholic Archbishop of Durban, to 'go to the ends of the earth if need be' to bring about peace.

As the peace process lapsed into stalemate over the question of a venue for the first round of talks, the Minister of Law and Order, Adriaan Vlok, again disrupted matters by placing national leaders of the UDF under virtual house arrest, thereby restricting their possible participation in peace negotiations. Archie Gumede, joint president of the UDF and a key figure in the talks, was prohibited from leaving his house between 8 p.m. and 5 a.m., with the result that he could attend no night-time meeting, and no meeting outside Durban, without breaking his curfew.

The Minister was accused by churchmen, leaders of the extra-parliamentary organisations, and MPs of once more trying to sabotage the peace process, but as usual he disregarded these voices. The official police public relations officer, Brigadier Leon Mellet, said that Vlok's only concern was to bring peace to the region.

Fortunately, despite the Minister's best efforts to bring peace to the region, 'five-a-side' peace talks did commence in Durban in mid-July. Chief Buthelezi did not attend, but sent a memorandum which was read out at the meeting by the Inkatha secretary general, Oscar Dhlomo.

Although as usual the Chief Minister's remarks were far from conciliatory, a second meeting was held four days after the first. Delegates who attended the talks were reticent about their content, but it seems clear that this first round of talks was designed to lay the groundwork for a joint peace initiative involving Inkatha, COSATU, the UDF and the ANC.

In the meantime, the peace roadshow got under way in the townships. Inkatha members were reported to be going door to door in UDF areas like travelling salesmen for peace, trying to persuade their erstwhile foes to lay down their arms and to be reconciled with Inkatha. In addition, both Inkatha and the UDF–COSATU held several peace rallies in townships around Durban and Pietermaritzburg.

In a report in the 21 July edition of the *Weekly Mail*, Thandeka Gqubule described an Inkatha peace rally in Imbali. She claimed that the peace initiative had as much to do with promoting the stature of Chief Buthelezi as it did with ending the violence in the region. She said:

In contrast with UDF and COSATU rallies, where no single leader stands out, the Inkatha rallies are marked by a 'personality cult'....

This week an Inkatha peace rally in Imbali … was characterised by frenzied praise and showers of gifts for the man who is at once Inkatha president, KwaZulu's chief minister and minister of police, and chancellor of the University of Zululand....

Buthelezi's elevation above the political organisation of which he is president was evident, as the legislative assembly of KwaZulu and members of the cabinet sat forgotten in the grandstand, while Buthelezi basked alone in the limelight.

Gqubule went on to describe the gifts received by Buthelezi and the various songs and speeches in his praise which preceded Buthelezi's speech. In his speech the Chief Minister alternately attacked the Mass Democratic Movement and demanded the incorporation of Inkatha into its ranks. He demanded too the release of all political prisoners and the unbanning of the ANC and then went on to claim that he had been vilified at a recent UDF–COSATU rally in Pietermaritzburg. Gqubule concludes: 'Drowned out by the applause were Buthelezi's references to the cycle of violence and revenge in Natal, and the need for peace in the region. Such concerns were lost in the spectacular gimmickry of the rally.'

Chief Buthelezi was predictably incensed by the report and wrote a strong letter, which appeared in a necessarily abridged version in the next edition of the *Weekly Mail*:

The whole article is a vicious attack on the best I am doing to bring about peace in strife-torn areas of KwaZulu and Natal. For the *Weekly Mail* to present my personal commitment to peace as developing a 'Buthelezi cult' is vicious political propaganda of the kind which actually produces the killing....

In this whole article there is not one word of praise, not one word of recognition that I and Inkatha are actually working for peace. There is only denigration and ridicule. Not only is the article a shame to black South Africa and indicates that Miss Gqubule is totally unfeeling about her fellow blacks, but the article also represents an attitude of the *Weekly Mail.*

There is no doubt that in the present context of moves towards peace, Gqubule's article falls into that well-known sphere of political operations known as 'shit-stirring', but in the same way, the Chief Minister's response falls into an equally well-known political category, namely 'self-righteous indignation and outraged innocence'. In fact, the Chief Minister should consider himself fair game for some sniping criticism of his role in the history of peace attempts in the Pietermaritzburg war. At times his preoccupation with trivia has been so disproportionate to the main concerns that it has seemed almost as though he and Inkatha were intent on side-tracking the process down the culs-de-sac of irrelevant issues.

Gqubule's article notwithstanding, by the beginning of August hopes were riding high. Monitors at the CAE at the University of Natal reported that by the end of July 1989 the death toll had dropped significantly over the previous three months. They said that while this might reflect no more than a cyclical slowdown in the rate of killing – a break for exhausted fighters before the start of the next round of hostilities – it was probably largely attributable to the peace drive.

The 'five-a-side' negotiators came up with an agenda for a meeting of the presidents of Inkatha, the UDF, COSATU and the ANC to be held at an unspecified overseas venue. However, at this point, when it seemed that Chief Buthelezi's most fervent wishes were coming true, a new set of factors impinged and the peace process once again broke down. Chief Buthelezi and the ANC traded accusations of stalling; and the UDF and COSATU devoted all their energies over the next two months to a national defiance campaign in protest against apartheid laws and the whites-only general election.

Then, just as negotiations were set to resume, Chief Buthelezi discovered two pamphlets allegedly issued by local comrades and by the exiled South African Congress of Trade Unions (SACTU) which called on comrades in Pietermaritzburg to exploit the peace negotiations in order to gain an advantage over Inkatha. The message was simple: lull them into a false sense of security and then hit them hard.

The UDF and COSATU delegations immediately repudiated the pamphlets as did a spokesperson for SACTU. According to the UDF the pamphlets were sophisticated forgeries introduced by some malicious third party to sabotage the peace process. They pointed out that no copies other than those in the possession of Inkatha had been found anywhere. However, Chief Buthelezi was not prepared to accept their repudiation and placed a moratorium on all further rounds of talks.

Recent events have considerably changed the terrain on which peace talks were formerly conducted. The Church Leaders Group has managed to wring from the Minister of Law and Order a promise to consider (albeit grudgingly) the establishment of a commission of inquiry; a group of Hammarsdale industrialists had temporary success in concluding a peace treaty between Inkatha and the UDF–COSATU in Mpumalanga; and the whole fabric of the political order in South Africa has changed since 2 February 1990.

Indeed, the most hopeful development in recent times has been the release of the imprisoned ANC leaders including Nelson Mandela, opening the way for peace talks at the very highest level between Inkatha and the ANC. Both Chief Buthelezi and Nelson Mandela are charismatic and influential leaders, and to the extent that their words hold force among their supporters, a joint call for peace would have more effect than any previous one.

However, that said, it is also true that March 1990 saw the worst upsurge of violence in the Pietermaritzburg area since the outbreak of hostilities, and this in the wake of peace calls by both leaders.

Past experience has shown that the process of translating the decisions of top-ranking leaders into action at the grassroots level is fraught with difficulties. The fact that this is an unofficial war means that such conventions associated with peace as surrender, armistice, and demobilisation, do not apply. There is no organised and mobilised army, and no military structure to be dismantled. Instead the fighters are individuals, or disparate groups who may choose to heed the calls to end the fighting, or they may choose to ignore them because they find the claims of vengeance or of power more attractive and compelling.

One clear implication is that a diplomatically negotiated peace is at best only a first step. The establishment of disciplined and responsible political structures – on both sides of the conflict – to implement this peace is of far greater urgency. Moreover, although the root cause of the war may have been of a fundamentally political nature, the solution must include and transcend political considerations. Without a development plan to reincorporate displaced and disaffected people into the economy of the region, and more important, to repair fractured physical communities, there is no prospect of a lasting peace.

At this stage, in advance of a long-term strategy to heal and revive the region, perhaps the best that can be hoped for is that the appeals by high-ranking political actors in COSATU, the UDF and Inkatha will have some influence on their local membership in the Pietermaritzburg region, and that these will coincide with and reinforce a natural reduction in the level of conflict caused by war-weariness and a desire for rest.

PART VI

Inkatha and the police

26
The brass people of Inkatha

I put a phone call through to the offices of Vitus Mvelase, the KwaZulu Urban Representative for Pietermaritzburg, and the chief spokesman for Inkatha on local matters. I introduced myself to Mvelase and asked whether it would be possible for me to interview him. There was a long pause while he considered my request. At the other end of the line I could hear papers rustling and a confused background murmur of voices. Eventually Mvelase said, 'I can give you Thursday three weeks.'

'Nothing earlier?' I asked.

'I'm a busy man,' he replied, 'many responsibilities and calls on my time. Shall we say 8 o'clock at the Imperial Hotel? I will ask my colleague, Mr Velaphi Ndlovu, the KwaZulu MP for Imbali, to join us.'

On the appointed day I parked in the lot next door to the headquarters of the security police. It was 8.01 a.m. as I crossed the road to the Imperial Hotel. Outside a sign said 'Welcome to the Biggest Little Hotel in Pietermaritzburg!' I went inside and found that I was late. Vitus Mvelase and Velaphi Ndlovu were already seated in the entrance lounge waiting for me. They were accompanied by a Mr Ngcobo, a local businessman and Inkatha member who had come along as well.

Mvelase brushed aside my apologies and led us into the main lounge where we arranged ourselves in a square around a coffee table. As we settled into the low velvet plush of armchairs and settees, I appraised the Inkatha delegation. The three men were immaculately dressed in well-cut suits and sober ties. They chose to wear their trousers a little short, exposing the tops of their raised leather shoes. The fold of white sock over the top of his wide black shoe made it seem as if Ngcobo was wearing spats. Both he and Mvelase were stout men. They sat well back in their chairs, with their jackets unbuttoned, the wings pulled aside over their paunches, on which they rested their clasped hands comfortably.

Velaphi Ndlovu, by contrast, was a thin, wiry, active man with a sharp beard and bright eyes. He smoked Dunhill cigarettes incessantly, stubbing them out one by one in an ashtray at his feet. Ndlovu sat on the edge of his seat and spoke with flamboyant hand gestures. He tended to dominate the conversation, his voice at all times cajoling and persuasive, striving to convince the listener of the logical inevitability of his position. He and, to a lesser extent, Vitus Mvelase dealt with all the points raised, while Mr Ngcobo was content to listen in, only occasionally intervening to make a point, or correct a minor error of fact.

Thus it was, when after prolonged formal introductions the interview began, that Ndlovu answered my request for an Inkatha analysis of the causes of the war.

'General views, Mike,' he said, 'is that unemployment is high and schools limited. You find drop-outs from schools who can't find jobs because of these sanctions affecting most blacks, as well as that force done by the radicals to overpower the innocents. If I can just elaborate, most of the peoples they don't want to fight, don't want to kill, but because of the other bunch of people who want to really force people, they must defend themselves.'

'What "other people" are you talking about here?' I asked.

Ndlovu said, 'If we talk about other people we talk about organisations. You will recall, Mike, there was a pamphlet issued by ANC that they are controlling COSATU and UDF, and all instructions they apply is taken direct from ANC.'

'The ANC claimed this in a pamphlet?' I asked, astonished.

'This is what ANC says, not claims,' he corrected me sternly. 'There is in fact a direct link between these organisations. This is the reality, the practical things observed.'

Vitus Mvelase cut in at this point to confirm his colleague's statement. 'Jay Naidoo, the COSATU secretary—'

'—secretary general—' said Mr Ngcobo.

'—travels every two months reporting back to Lusaka, and then he reports to his membership. This proves any move of COSATU is the instruction of the ANC. But, if I can just say this, as my colleague Mr Ndlovu said, unemployment is the main cause of violence because people are unemployed and frustrated. The UDF and COSATU capitalised here because they know people are stranded. One member of Inkatha who has crossed the floor told us, when we said, "Why, why are you joining UDF?", he said, "The UDF is paying us money to buy cigarettes, but Inkatha only wants to take money from us for subscriptions."'

Velaphi Ndlovu leaned forward and spoke solemnly: 'In this violence, the most people that are being used are the youth. It's easy to buy a child—' he paused for effect and then repeated deliberately, 'It's easy to buy a child, to manipulate him.'

'If the reason for the violence is unemployment, which is a problem across the country, why has Pietermaritzburg, in particular, been such a flashpoint?' I asked.

Mvelase said, 'The rate of unemployment here is very high.'

'I know, but it's high elsewhere too,' I replied. 'Why is Pietermaritzburg singled out?'

'The agitators who foment violence can hide in Pietermaritzburg,' Mvelase suggested. 'We have flushed them out of other areas, the agitators. They are the ones who initiate fighting. They organise the youth and then they are pinpointing weak points of the recognised authority body. After that they start fomenting grievances. We are not stooges,' Mvelase concluded, 'but our fear is violence.'

Here Velaphi Ndlovu smiled like a cat, hitched up his trousers exposing cream socks, crossed his legs and began to explain. 'You see, Mike—' he began.

Across the table, Ngcobo murmured a deprecating correction: '—Martin—'

'—violence is in three categories,' Ndlovu continued. 'There is the physical violence, when the majority defend themselves. The second is the mental violence, where they phone you up with the death threats – such things like, "We will come at night and kill you, Mvelase."'

I turned to Mvelase, 'Is that just an example, or did that happen?'

Vitus Mvelase, leaning back, gently stroked the bulge of his stomach. 'Oh, yes,' he said complacently. 'A group of sixteen people came, but fortunately I was away at the time. They told the security guard that they were looking for me. Another time the guard went to the shop and he heard youngsters talking about my name. They were saying there was a sum of R15 000 for any person who might kill me.'

'That's a very large sum.' I said. 'Do you have any idea who might have staked it?'

Mvelase shrugged. 'This I cannot say. I really have no idea. I presume some member of the UDF.'

'Couldn't the police take some sort of action here?' I asked.

Ndlovu picked up the thread again. 'We are dealing with the professionals here. You can't arrest on basis of rumour. Now the third violence, that is the propaganda war, when you are writing to the press and saying, "Mr Ndlovu has done this and Mr Mvelase has done that and that and that." These are the lies to denigrate our organisation and ourselves as human beings.'

'But what motive is there for this kind of campaign of denigration?'

'It is for trying to pull out Inkatha from the stance of peace to the struggle of fighting,' Ndlovu replied. 'There are two ways – a peace one and fight one. And there are two ways of trying to pull fight to peace or peace to fight. The ANC discovered that the mass of people are followers of Inkatha so they are losing their stand. They have to use another alternative ways, so now the feeling of ANC and UDF is that Inkatha is delaying freedom because of using non-violent methods. They say the Inkatha leadership must be eliminated. They want to get rid of Inkosi Buthelezi, president of Inkatha, and the other top leaders. The UDF failed to succeed their ambitions. Now they are calling us collaborators, stooges, sell-outs—'

'—puppets and so forth—' Mvelase added.

'—but no matter,' Ndlovu continued. 'We are fighting for liberation as they are. That is the practical situation, not the theory; the practical situation as it applies to our organisation. The Honourable Chief Minister, the president of Inkatha, Dr Mangosuthu Buthelezi, must be hit on the head because he is a snake, and a snake must be hit on the head, that is what they are saying. You see, they mean not just Inkosi Buthelezi, but all the brass people of Inkatha and the brass people of the leaders. This is because you can't succeed to hit the person until you have got down to the toe of the person, and the toe of the person is us, the officials.'

'The practical reality of the situation is this,' Mvelase remarked; 'you can't fight the whites by weapons. It was proved in Soweto in 1976 when they killed children – armless children – so it would be foolishness for us to try and fight them with weapons. But if we bring them to the table, there they can't fight, because they have no facts.'

'You will recall, Mike,' said Ndlovu, 'if you are doing the history, we did fight whites in many wars by the Zulus to prove their innocence of the oppressions. We can't go by the same path that doesn't prove anything.'

'I'd like to ask you a question more specifically about the war in Pietermaritzburg,' I ventured. 'Inkatha has been accused of fielding an army of vigilantes led by warlords who conduct terror campaigns against any person who refuses to join Inkatha. I'd like to hear your response to such allegations.'

Mvelase replied, '"Warlord" is simply the insult used against any strong member of Inkatha fighting against violence in his area. It is a term only, a term from Jay Naidoo [COSATU general secretary]. I ask you, what about their so-called defence committees? Those are warlords, not Inkatha.'

'We don't want to talk about the word "warlord" because it is not a term which applies in our constitution,' Ndlovu added. 'No one has it on his ID. We don't want to talk about it because that is the insult. Remember, Mike—'

'—Mark—' Ngcobo murmured gently.

'—they have been calling us so many names, but we have never ever called anybody in a bad name.'

'Their aim is just to provoke,' Mvelase added. 'To provoke so you'll fight. Once when I was playing soccer, another chap when he realised his opponent was too strong, he used to swear him. Then the other chap would hit and the ref would stop the game and send him off so it would be easier for him to score goals. That's what these chaps are trying to do.'

'Nonetheless a lot of evidence has been gathered against these warlords – or whatever term you prefer. For example, the interdicts brought by COSATU against Inkatha set out the details of a number of incidents involving intimidation, harassment and criminal behaviour on the part of senior Inkatha members.'

Ndlovu shook his head slowly and said, as though speaking to a child, 'Interdicts, Mike, are the propaganda thing. They are the propaganda of the ANC. I can interdict anyone anytime. It is up to that person to prove his innocence in a court of law. Therefore, in one sentence, interdicts are the propaganda to denigrate the organisation and the person involved. There is no proof in all this.'

'And then after failing in proof they came to us and asked if they could sort things out, out of the court because it was too expensive. But that was not true. It was because they knew they would fail, because they knew everything laid down in these so-called interdicts—'

'—the affidavits—' said Ndlovu.

'—were all lies because the intention was simply to publicise themselves in the world, that's why.'

'I'm told that the COSATU legal team had hundreds of affidavits of people who claimed to be victims. Are you suggesting they were all fabricated?' I asked.

'Yes,' said Mvelase.

Ndlovu explained: 'You know, as I said, the propaganda system. You see, if you are issuing interdicts you need a lawyer, you need the advocate – someone who is very high – to make it. And tell me this: where do they get the money?'

'Are you saying then that COSATU has a propaganda wing which devises, creates and pays for a strategy like this?'

'Yes, because they had the money,' said Ndlovu.

'But who would be employed in such a unit?' I asked.

'Lawyers, Mike,' Ndlovu said slowly, 'can be posted from anywhere. They are using every lawyer they can put their hands on.'

'And do you think these lawyers actually spoke to the witnesses and victims, or do you think they just made everything up?'

'No, it was on the instruction of COSATU. In the court the witness tells our advocate that the legal advisor of COSATU will pay all the costs.'

'I remember that at one point Inkatha was thinking of bringing its own interdicts,' I said. 'What became of that idea?'

'Yes, we thought of it,' replied Ndlovu, 'but we didn't because there was too much at stake involved. You must bear in mind that our organi- sation is based on membership. Money collected from us is used to pay for the administration of the leadership, to administer the administration of the leadership. You cannot put aside R100 000 to pay for an interdict, the way COSATU can. You see, they have the money for this propaganda.'

'But the attorneys representing COSATU belong to a reputable law firm, they're not part of some kind of advertising agency spewing out propaganda for the sake of it,' I pointed out.

Ndlovu said, 'It is part of the ANC strategy. They bring these things because of the leadership of Chief Buthelezi, because it is too prominent, because it is too high, because—'

'—they are jealous!' Ngcobo called out.

Ndlovu ignored the intervention: '—it overwhelms their ambitions, it overrides their authority, it overrides their techniques. Therefore they cannot succeed if Chief Buthelezi is going up and up and up and is recognised by the whole nation. And he has succeeded. He has succeeded in resisting the independence for KwaZulu. And he has done that. He has done a lot of good for the people. He has been involved in peace negotiations with COSATU – he was personally involved because he sent Musa Zondi, the national chairman of the Inkatha Youth Brigade, with all his wishes to be involved, because he and Dr Dhlomo who are the brass level of Inkatha have agreed to do that and the masses have asked us to go to the table.'

Mvelase added, 'Yes, and during those days we are the ones who made their leaders to be released. Martin—'

'Witterberg,' said Ndlovu.

'—and Skhumbuzo Ngwenya, who were detained, so they could come to the negotiating table. We – myself and Mr Ndlovu – our team, you know, requested the what-d'you-call-it? – the Security Branch: "We can't go on if these people are inside. They must be released straightaway." Then they agreed.'

Ndlovu said, 'At their meeting at Wadley stadium Mr Ngwenya told his followers we are negotiating, but if the *theleweni* attack you must still defend yourselves.'

'Yes, and on the same day our people were killed at Dindi,' noted Mvelase.

'How do you like that?' Ndlovu asked. 'I mean, are we really negotiating or are we just playing games?'

I put in: 'I'm afraid I don't see the connection. Surely Ngwenya telling his people to defend themselves is the same as you in Inkatha telling your people to defend themselves?'

Ndlovu made an impatient gesture. 'How can they do that?' he asked irritably. 'How can they be the defenders when they are the attackers?'

'Well, no doubt Ngwenya wouldn't see it that way,' I said. 'For him Inkatha would be the attacker.'

'How can that be when he is the initiator?' Ndlovu persisted.

'It seems to me that in a conflict like this it is impossible for one side always to be defending and the other always to be initiating,' I commented. 'There has to be a certain amount of give and take on both sides. I'd think....'

'No, you are wrong,' said Ndlovu firmly. 'You're totally wrong, Mike, because if you see the basic of this violence you will see that the other side is attacking. You have never ever in the court of law found a member of Inkatha in charge of going and killing another person in that person's house. Ever! Ever! Never ever in Pietermaritzburg has there been found a member of Inkatha in somebody's house killing that somebody. Never ever. Therefore you cannot say that it is two ways. Inkatha people have never been the ones of attack. They are the people of defend, always.'

As he said this, there was a painful screeching sound behind us. A waiter was struggling to open the sliding glass door out onto the patio. Ndlovu swivelled in his armchair and admonished him roundly. 'Hey, there, we are having an important conversation here,' he called out. 'This noise is bad for the tape-recorder.' The waiter abandoned his efforts and quickly left the room.

'Well, let me try a different argument,' I suggested. 'It's common cause that in this war there are displaced persons on both sides. People who have had to leave areas under both UDF and Inkatha control. You would agree with that?'

'Yes,' they agreed.

'Right, then,' I followed up, 'why would refugees have fled Inkatha areas if not because they have been attacked by Inkatha?'

Again Ndlovu adopted a tone of infinite patience. 'You see, Mike,' he said, 'in the first place when the war was started, Inkatha people didn't want to kill the people, they didn't want to defend themselves because they didn't know what is going on. A chap, he doesn't know the people are coming to kill him, he knows them as neighbours and he sits down with them at his house only to find that he is being killed. When we told our membership that they should defend themselves, when we told them that life comes just once – just once – that's how the ball has tended to the other side. If they're in our premises we chase them out, they come to the road, and nobody stays on the road.'

'Why don't they simply return home? We're talking about people who have left their own houses in Inkatha areas.'

Ndlovu replied, 'If I defend myself in my premises, that guy who fights me, because he doesn't know anything, and maybe he's drugged or something, he will go back. Maybe he gets disciplined by his father or his mother because of what he is doing, and burn his own house, because he is afraid to face the parents because of what he did to me. The unplaced people are running away from their parents.'

'I see,' I said. 'It may look as though they're running away from Inkatha but in fact they're running away from their own parents.'

'Yes, that's right,' Ndlovu confirmed.

At this point I suggested sending out for some tea but the idea was quickly scotched by the others. 'If we have finished with the questions, I have to get back to the office. I am a very busy man,' Ndlovu informed me. 'I am a very *busy* man.'

'Actually, I still have some questions,' I ventured.

'Then we must finish the conversation,' Mvelase said briskly. 'You can have coffee or the tea-bag later.'

I asked, 'When members defend themselves, do they adopt any military tactic or formation? For example, do they organise themselves into impis?'

Ndlovu said: 'What they do is simply the neighbours' watch, you call it that way. You whites call it neighbourhood watch. If you are my neighbour and someone comes to attack me, my neighbour should help me.'

'There is no such thing as the Zulu impi any more,' Mvelase remarked.

'What about armed marches of Inkatha members at rallies and functions?' I asked.

'That is the necessary cultural thing,' Ndlovu replied. 'That is our culture. We don't like to be called impi, let's make that quite clear. There is no impi.'

'You know,' Mvelase said, 'there are these photos taken at tribal celebrations—'

'—the cultural thing—' Ndlovu repeated.

'—when we are dressed in traditional attire. They take those photographs and use them, you know, for propaganda. They say, "Here are the impi killing people in Pietermaritzburg."'

'We haven't got time to march in impi,' Ndlovu interjected.

Mvelase continued, 'You only hear about these things in the press which is biased. Like biased newspapers, like the *Natal Witness*.'

'Would you call the *Witness* biased?' I asked in some surprise.

Ngcobo, who had been silent for some time, cut in here. 'Yes, a biased newspaper. It belongs to so-called liberals. They think they can think for us and do things on our behalf.'

Ndlovu agreed, saying, 'Yes, and they can say words that we haven't uttered.'

Mvelase continued: 'In fact there is a campaign even now that this matter should be taken to parliament for this and that, and because they say some things are not being done properly. The PFP – or what are they now—?'

'—Democrats—' Ngcobo supplied.

'—they are behind the whole thing because they have lost the election and now they just want to gain.'

'I thought there was a good relationship between the PFP and Inkatha,' I interposed.

'Yes, there *were*,' Ndlovu said, emphasising the tenses, 'but now there *is* not.'

'Everyone who wants popularity in South Africa is attacking the Kwa-Zulu government,' Mvelase complained.

Ngcobo leaned over and said, 'Perhaps you don't know that there are five other self-governing territories, but you'll never hear a word against their governments.'

They shook their heads and a small silence ensued. I was coming to the end of my questions and my stamina, so I asked drearily, 'Tell me, gentlemen, do you think the police have done a good job in Pietermaritz-burg over the last two years or so?'

Ndlovu, also beginning to look a little weary, responded: 'The police, you see, can sort out the physical violence, but they can do nothing with mental violence and propaganda.'

'In those townships which have been handed over to the KwaZulu Police, the ZP, there is still maybe a little bit of violence,' said Mvelase, 'but mainly you find order there because the ZP are so strict. They want to see everyone, treat everyone alike. They don't want to see anybody running about killing people. But the SAP, you see, some come from outside and they are scared because they know the Zulu people are the very brave people. They use vehicles because they are scared to patrol on foot.'

'Why do you think this war has gone on as long as it has, and do you see prospects of it ending in the near future?' I asked.

Ndlovu replied: 'The chain of communication from the president of Inkatha, Dr Mangosuthu Buthelezi, to the membership is very good, it is well organised – on our side. There is no such a chain of communication to the other side, therefore there is a lack of communication, therefore the membership do what they feels is right – on their side.'

The three men stood up to leave on this note. As he shook my hand, Ndlovu said, beseechingly, 'You see, Mike, by way of conclusion, you cannot compare the UDF guy with the Inkatha guy. You cannot compare the radical with our guy, who is a peaceful, and stays at home doing what the police tells. Because there is nobody who is over the law. Remember, there is nobody who is over the law.'

27
Warlords

Velaphi Ndlovu had dismissed the term warlord as an insult. I sought out John Aitchison at the Centre for Adult Education and asked him whether he thought the word was accurate or merely abusive.

'It's up to you whether you want to enclose "warlord" in inverted commas or not,' Aitchison said. 'Of course Ndlovu is right: the word "warlord" is pejorative – after all, the word is archaic and its modern sense is generally derogatory – but in my opinion it is still sufficiently accurate to justify its use as a description of the local Inkatha leaders and their *modus operandi*. Oh, and I'll tell you another thing, whatever the official Inkatha position on the matter may be, the warlords themselves seem to take a certain pride in the label; derogatory or not, it is still an acknowledgement of their power and importance.'

'But why use "warlord"?' I persisted. 'Couldn't you call them gang or vigilante leaders?'

'That's all right as far as it goes,' Aitchison said, 'but it doesn't go far enough. Warlords are powerful local leaders who rely on the force of arms to maintain their power. They tend to gather a group of professional strong-arm men around them and they pay for their services by screwing the local populace. Now to that extent, you could say that they are no more and no less than gang leaders, but the key difference is that they are not motivated *exclusively* by the acquisition of personal wealth and power, but in addition they owe allegiance to a central power, namely Inkatha. You could say the difference lies in the form of extortion: gang leaders fight for money and territory, whereas warlords are also crusaders for a political cause. There's one other reason for calling these people warlords, and that's the hype that surrounds them, and I don't just mean in the media, I mean among their own communities. Their exploits become the stuff of modern-day legend, like fairy-tale villains, attributed with special powers, personal invulnerability. I don't want to press this point too far, because I don't know how important it is, but certainly the fact that they are larger-than-life figures contributes to their larger-than-life title.

'I know I've said that it is their ideological position which differentiates them from ordinary gang leaders, and certainly it's true that these guys are

Inkatha warlords, but that doesn't mean they're a completely unified bunch. There are plenty of reports of groups of vigilantes fighting each other, of jealousies and rivalries between warlords. Here in Maritzburg they've managed to maintain quite a cohesive front in the face of a common enemy, the comrades, but in Durban where they face less political opposition, they tend to turn on each other.'

In the past the word 'warlord' referred to a feudal relationship between leader and followers, the latter providing their manpower in return for protection and other services. Something of that feudal relationship is still implied when we describe certain Inkatha leaders as warlords. Inkatha leaders in the Durban area were the first to be called warlords and the label spread. In Durban the struggle for land is more pronounced than in Pietermaritzburg, and the warlords earned their reputations from the ruthless way they manipulated the land under their control, offering or withholding it according to circumstance, and using it to establish a complex system of patronage.

One example is the case of Thomas Shabalala, warlord – or perhaps shacklord would be more accurate – of the squatter camp of Lindelani near Durban. According to his tenants, Shabalala runs the settlement as his personal fiefdom; nothing happens without his say-so. He allocates land, evicts people, squeezes them for protection money, insists that they join Inkatha, and runs a private army.

Shabalala's methods were exposed to me when I read the affidavits of Belinda and Simon Mfeka, two Lindelani residents who had brought an interdict application against Shabalala in 1986. They claimed that Shabalala had threatened them with death and banished them from the area for failing to join Inkatha. In total he demanded the following annual subscription from them: R5 Inkatha membership fee; R1,50 membership fee for the Inkatha Women's Brigade; R3 membership fee for UWUSA; R2 Inkatha building fund; and R3 subscription towards Shabalala's bodyguard fund – all this despite the fact that they were not supporters of either Inkatha or UWUSA.

The Mfekas were ordered to present themselves at Shabalala's house to account for themselves. Shabalala's stronghold resembled nothing so much as a military compound, swarming with armed men, many of them in uniform, some wearing Inkatha and UWUSA insignia on their clothing. They were verbally abused by Shabalala who told them he did not tolerate people who were not Inkatha supporters in Lindelani.

On 26 May 1986, the Mfekas were granted a court order restraining Shabalala from attacking or harassing them; yet within hours of the application the Mfekas' house was wrecked by a group of about a hundred people who used axes and iron bars to tear the house and vegetable garden to pieces.

Shabalala was not prosecuted for breaching his restriction order: on the contrary, he was appointed shortly afterwards to the Inkatha Central Committee, the highest policy body in the organisation. However, in 1988, even Inkatha could no longer ignore the universal disapprobation attached to Shabalala, and he was called before a disciplinary committee and expelled from the Central Committee.

In Pietermaritzburg, by contrast, many of the warlords do not control any land and have to base their power either on brute force or on access to other resources.

The warlords can be divided into three groups. The first is simply the bully-boys, tough fighters, mobile with impressive fire-power and enough backstop to frighten off most challenges. They are the closest to being ordinary gang leaders – they make their money through evictions, looting, conventional protection rackets, and they also maintain the trappings of gang bosses with smart clothes, cars, drink and women. In this category one finds someone like Sichizo Zuma, the former chairman of the Harewood branch of the Inkatha Youth Brigade.

The second category consists of the urban warlords: Jerome Mncwabe, Abdul Awetha and Patrick Pakkies, who are all Inkatha town councillors in Imbali and consequently have a degree of political clout in the township. They control the allocation of housing and services and the granting of trade licences.

The last category is that of rural warlords, the true Pietermaritzburg equivalents of Thomas Shabalala. These rural power-brokers tend to be chiefs and their indunas who have extensive control over the allocation of land in their areas. Originally indunas were traditional officials in the tribal system, but under the present Bantu Chiefs and Headmen Act they are salaried officers whose stipend is so meagre that it is accepted practice for them to augment their salaries by dispensing patronage. The tribal authorities already have a feudal aspect to them which for the most part is accepted begrudgingly by the inhabitants of the various Zulu chieftaincies. They are prepared to pay for services, but not unreasonably they become unhappy when faced with extortion for its own sake. For example, if the induna comes round demanding an Inkatha subscription fee, it is simple coercion, there is nothing offered in return.

Once the induna adopts a more aggressive political profile, gathers an army behind him and begins to rule by force, he becomes a warlord. He may no longer restrict himself only to his own territory, but might offer his services to other areas in need of some military power: he and his men become a roving band of trouble-shooters for Inkatha.

One description of the mode of operation of David Ntombela, a rural warlord who was Inkatha branch chairman of KwaMncane out in the Elandskop region of Vulindlela, and who has recently been appointed the

KwaZulu MP for Vulindlela, can be found in the affidavits in the *Mkhize* interdict application.

In his affidavit, Mandla Mkhize says:

The first respondent's [Ntombela's] association with Inkatha goes back some years and during his period as chairman of the Maswazini Inkatha region he has introduced a number of new 'customs' into our community. An illustration of this is a 'custom' that he introduced that if any member of the community who is not a member of Inkatha, wants to slaughter a cow, then he or she has to pay a R5,00 Inkatha membership fee to him as the Inkatha chairman. If anybody should refuse to pay that fee then he or she is taken by Ntombela or his supporters to the Chief of the larger area and then fined R150,00. If, on the other hand, a member of Inkatha wishes to slaughter a cow, then the only requirement is that he or she has to report the slaughter to Ntombela. Another 'custom' that Ntombela has introduced is that if a member of Inkatha has a wedding it is obligatory that the wedding be reported to him, who then allocates an Inkatha observer or guard to the wedding at a fee. If, on the other hand, anybody who is not an Inkatha member has a wedding, then the wedding proceedings and festivities are frequently disrupted by persons who are known to support Ntombela's administration.

There are many warlords operating in the Pietermaritzburg region, some more feared than others. I collected a bundle of reports and affidavits on the two most notorious, Sichizo Zuma and David Ntombela, and began to sift through the allegations against them.

*   *   *

I started with Sichizo Zuma, in 1989 still only 26 years old. From a recent photograph I noted his fresh-faced and youthful looks, and an expression almost gentle in repose. His reputation, however, belies his appearance: Zuma is considered to be one of the most fearsome of the warlords operating in the townships around Pietermaritzburg. Until the beginning of 1989 he was chairman of the Inkatha Youth Brigade branch in Harewood, Edendale, but was later voted out of his official position and relegated to the ranks. Zuma was named as respondent in four court applications. In the first of these, *Mkhize & Others v Zuma*, the applicants set out in their affidavits a long list of crimes allegedly committed by Zuma and his accomplices. Zuma was alleged to have committed murder, attempted murder and arson, kidnapping and assault. Moreover, he was alleged to have carried out his actions with impunity and without fear of arrest or prosecution.

The abduction of Jaminah Mthiyane, a resident of Harewood, is a case in point. It was rumoured in the townships that Sichizo Zuma had threatened to 'fix her up' several times because she was a UDF supporter and because she had resisted his seduction attempts. Jaminah Mthiyane fled the township in July 1987 and in August even went so far as to join Inkatha. All this to no avail, however, as she heard that Zuma was still intent on harming her in some way, so she moved on again. On 9 October, at a bus stop in Macibisa, she was abducted by a carload of Zuma's supporters, who took her to his house. There she was held prisoner and interrogated about the whereabouts and activities of local UDF activists. She was doused with paraffin and threatened with rape and immolation if she refused to cooperate. Fortunately, the abduction was witnessed by several people who alerted her family, who in turn reported the matter to the police. The police arrived at the Zuma residence and freed Mthiyane but did not arrest or even question Zuma.

To compound her injuries, the following week she was taken from her house to the Plessislaer police station by two officers of the SAP accompanied by Sichizo Zuma himself. At Plessislaer, the officer who had taken her statement after the abduction now asked her a range of questions concerning a UDF activist. When she proved unable to provide the requisite answers, the police threatened to leave her alone with Zuma, but they eventually allowed her to return home unharmed.

Jaminah Mthiyane was 15 years old at the time.

Zuma was also named as the second respondent in the case of *Mthembu & Others* v *Mncwabe & Others*. This application for a restraining interdict was brought by Johannes Mthembu and his four sons, Elphas, Smalridge, Simon and Ernest Mthembu. The affidavit of Johannes Mthembu set out a history of conflict between Inkatha members in Imbali and his family. Mthembu described an attack on his family by Inkatha members, particularly those linked to Inkatha town councillor Abdul Awetha in August 1987. The Mthembus defended themselves, and in the ensuing fracas, some Inkatha members were injured, including Awetha's son Dumisani. After the fight, Johannes Mthembu made a statement to a plainclothes policeman in which he stated that he was the victim of an unprovoked attack by Inkatha members.

In his affidavit to the Supreme Court, Mthembu set out the treatment subsequently meted out to his family by the police and prominent members of Inkatha in Imbali. In November he and his sons were arrested at a memorial service for his four dead daughters. They were severely assaulted by the police and told they were under arrest for assaulting Dumisani Awetha in August. They were driven to Plessislaer police station and held overnight. On the way they passed the house of Abdul Awetha, who stepped outside and waved at the policemen as they drove past.

In January, however, matters reached a head when Elphas Mthembu was shot by Thulani Ngcobo. Johannes Mthembu subsequently made the following statement:

On Saturday, January 16, during the early evening I was visiting relatives near my home in Imbali. I received an anonymous phone call to the effect that Second and Third Applicant [Elphas and Smalridge Mthembu] had been shot near the Roman Catholic Church by Third Respondent [Thulani Ngcobo, an Inkatha member and KwaZulu policeman].

I rushed home. As I reached my yard, I saw a blueish station-wagon, driven by Third Respondent, draw up outside. Fourth Applicant [Simon Mthembu] was with me. The light was sufficiently good for me to identify First and Second Respondents [Jerome Mncwabe, Inkatha town councillor in Imbali, and Sichizo Zuma, chairman of the Harewood branch of the Inkatha Youth Brigade] who were with Third Respondent in his car. Third Respondent emerged from his car and pointed a gun at me across its roof. First Respondent pointed a gun at us out of the car window. Third Respondent called that they would kill everyone in the house. I and Fourth Applicant fled inside, whereafter Respondents left.

Mthembu went on to recount how a short while later, Ngcobo, Mncwabe and Sichizo Zuma returned and threatened him again, and that shortly afterwards his sons Elphas and Smalridge Mthembu had returned, Elphas with a bullet wound in his foot. In his affidavit, Elphas Mthembu said that he and a group of friends had been accosted and chased by Thulani Ngcobo for no reason whatsoever. Ngcobo had fired a number of shots, one of which hit him in the foot. However, he managed to get home and found that the bullet had passed through his foot and been caught in his sock.

Johannes Mthembu then phoned the police, who took Elphas to Plessislaer where he made a statement before being taken to Edendale Hospital. While at Plessislaer, he observed Ngcobo chatting and joking casually with the police.

On the basis of these attacks, the Mthembu family decided to bring an application for an interdict restraining Jerome Mncwabe, Sichizo Zuma and Thulani Ngcobo from attacking or threatening them in any way. The matter was set down to be heard on Monday, 25 January 1988. Zuma himself was known to be in possession of the court papers apprising him of the application on Saturday, 23 January. However, on Sunday, he went to the Mthembu house, together with some associates, apparently in a rage at having been cited as a respondent. He shouted from his car that he had been wrongfully cited and then drew his gun and shot Smalridge Mthembu, who was on his way home, through the shoulder. Zuma then drove off, pursued by Simon Mthembu who was wielding a knife. As Simon drew level with the car, Zuma shot him. Simon Mthembu fell to the ground bleeding heavily. Zuma stopped the car, got out, took aim carefully, and shot Simon again where he lay. At this point, Johannes Mthembu and his sons Elphas and Ernest ran up. Zuma had run out of bullets so he and his associates fled. In his rage, Ernest Mthembu smashed the back window of Zuma's car with an axehead. •

Both Simon and Smalridge were taken to Edendale Hospital. Smalridge was treated for a bullet wound in the shoulder, but Simon was immediately admitted to the intensive-care unit. However, the COSATU legal team, representing the Mthembus, received information that Zuma and his men had been seen at Edendale Hospital shortly after Simon and Smalridge were admitted. Late at night, and under cover, the two were secretly moved to Northdale Hospital in Pietermaritzburg, a hospital which normally refuses to admit black patients.

Smalridge was subsequently discharged, but Simon died a month after the shooting, without ever fully regaining consciousness.

The follow-up to the shooting was drearily familiar to the Mthembus. The SAP again neither arrested nor charged Zuma, despite a statement made by an off-duty policeman who had witnessed the event. In fact, the only police response was to arrest Ernest Mthembu, who was charged with public violence for smashing Zuma's car. The charges were later dropped without explanation.

The Mthembus therefore joined their application for an interdict against Mncwabe, Zuma and Ngcobo with a further application against Zuma alone, restraining him from murdering or attacking them in any way, and calling on him to give reasons to the court why he should not be held in contempt of court for acting in defiance of the court papers served on him the day before the shooting.

The judge granted the order, although he indicated that he did not want to impose unduly onerous terms on Zuma. Moreover, despite the gravity and urgency of the case, the first available date that could be found for the hearing of oral evidence was in August, eight months away.

In July, a couple of weeks before the hearing, the Mthembu house was again attacked. Ernest Mthembu, the fifth applicant and a key witness, went outside to investigate. As he stepped through the front door he was hit by a salvo of shotgun fire and died shortly afterwards. Before he died, he identified his killer as Thulani Ngcobo, the third respondent in the first application. Thus in the space of a year, all four of Johannes Mthembu's sons had been shot, two fatally.

Although it may appear from events like the *Mthembu* case that Sichizo Zuma is exempt from various fundamental laws which prohibit people from committing murder, assault or other forms of social violence, he has in fact been prosecuted in the past. In 1987 he was charged with attempted murder, but was acquitted after the state failed to muster together the most basic elements of a prosecution. For example, in the months between the incident in question and the criminal trial, the prosecutor did not interview any of the seven eyewitnesses who had come forward; Zuma's alibi was not tested; no forensic evidence had been gathered; and the key witness was not interviewed before the trial date.

Then in September 1988, Zuma was convicted of illegal possession of a firearm and ammunition. Despite the fact that he was still facing charges of murder and contempt of court, he was given a minimal fine and a suspended sentence.

★   ★   ★

I met Nhlanhla one afternoon punting a soccer ball against a University wall and I asked him whether he had ever had dealings with Zuma. 'I know that boy,' he said. 'He used to be a taxi-driver with the ITA – the Imbali Taxi Association – which was UDF in the old days. The Inkatha drivers went to see Abdul Awetha to complain that the ITA was UDF – there was violence between the drivers. I know Awetha laid a charge against Zuma and some of the others. They were charged with public violence. Next thing, Awetha approaches Zuma, very quiet quiet and recruits him into Inkatha. Zuma agrees to work with Awetha and by magic his charges are dropped.' Nhlanhla gathered in the soccer ball and spat.

'First thing he shot Gibson Msomi, the PRO of the ITA, next thing he was elected chairman of the Harewood Inkatha Youth. He tried to force the youth in Edendale and Sweetwaters to join Inkatha but people resisted. He realised he could be in jeopardy so he changed his tactic to attack specific people who are anti-Inkatha. And the other warlords use him too. I could say they don't like him – between him and Shayabantu Zondi, the warlord of Sweetwaters, they say one day one will die – but they use him because he is a fighter. Also the people, the community, believe he is protected because he escapes all the death attempts on him.'

The more I heard about Sichizo Zuma, the keener I was to meet this legendary figure, but I had no idea how to contact him. I was pondering about this when he again made headline news. Radley Keys, of the Pietermaritzburg Democratic Party, issued a statement to the press, claiming that an Inkatha warlord was responsible for up to 25 murders, none of which had been investigated by the police. His statement caused a tremendous commotion. Questions were asked in parliament; the police issued shrill denials of the allegations; and Inkatha representatives in Pietermaritzburg were livid with indignation. Although Keys had not named the warlord in question, it was common knowledge that he was referring to Zuma, who had not, as yet, made any personal comment on the matter.

A week later, however, a full-page interview with Zuma by Lakela Kaunda appeared in the *Echo*.

Sichizo Christopher Zuma is the most talked about young man in Pietermaritzburg, the various embassies of countries with an interest in South Africa and in newsrooms around the world as well as in legal circles....

Sichizo looks much younger than 26, looking at least 18 and is extremely talkative. He has seven children, and all live with their mothers. The eldest is eight years old and the youngest two.

Near hysterical, he said the DP statement had renewed violence: 'The DP statement was distasteful, defamatory and extremely embarrassing. At first they mentioned no name, and talked about a certain mass killer. The next thing I saw my name. I was shocked.'

I phoned Lakela to get some background information on the story. 'Well, I don't know how shocked he could have been,' she said. 'After all he hasn't sued either the PFP or us for defamation. But I'll tell you this much – his image is very important to that boy. He wears a big hat, a zoot suit, wide-banded ties. All of this, together with his aquiline features, makes him look like those sentimental gangsters of the '40s and '50s – you know, Lucky Luciano, Baby Face Nelson, that sort of thing.

'Anyway, he just walked in, blazing mad about that DP statement. But here's another thing about him, he's a polite boy. He was very respectful, very courteous, only sat down when we offered him a chair. You find the comrades tend to overlook the titles of respect but he's his own PRO. Of course, he doesn't answer questions, he just goes on his own rave, and checks to see that you're taking it down. I must say, he was immensely irritated and agitated, it was hard to keep him focused on anything.'

I put down the phone and reread the article. With a certain disbelief I learned that Zuma sees himself as something of a peacemaker:

He was disturbed that he was not invited to take part in the peace talks held last year because he believes he has some solutions to ending the violence

Encouraging sports, especially soccer, would gradually end the local violence, he asserts.

*　　*　　*

For all his close ties with the police and his bullying tactics, Zuma is not ranked as a warlord in the same class as David Ntombela, the induna of Maswazini in Vulindlela and the KwaMncane Inkatha branch chairman. Where Zuma is representative of a youthful, transient warlordism, Ntombela has the benefits of age and status on his side. He is considered to be perhaps the most powerful of the warlords operating in Pietermaritzburg, relying not merely on personal fire-power and fighting prowess to see him through, but on a political power base which he has built up in his area over a long time. His near-legendary reputation is founded on years of laying down the law, of issuing ultimatums and following up any infringements.

Ntombela was not slow to become involved in the current war. He threw himself into the recruitment drive with enthusiasm, and set about winning souls for Inkatha.

On 9 October 1987, in Maswazini, he and his brother, a local store-keeper, together with seven other men, are said to have killed Angelica Mkhize and her 11-year-old daughter Petronella in an act of cold-blooded murder. Angelica's sons, Mntu and Mangethe, were members of a local youth group affiliated to the UDF, and on the night of the murders, Ntombela and his men had come to the Mkhize homestead to seek them out. It was well known to residents of this area that Ntombela tolerated no UDF activity in his fiefdom and that he was committed to flushing out and cleansing his area of UDF support wherever it emerged.

Angelica Mkhize and other members of her household were asleep when the vigilantes arrived. They pounded on the door demanding entry and called out that they were looking for the *maqabane*. They searched the main hut and the outer huts and satisfied themselves that Mntu and Mangethe were not at home. As they left, Angelica Mkhize followed them out into the yard to relieve herself. As she stepped outside, Ntombela and his men stopped short and turned to face her. Anatoria Ngcobo, who was living with the Mkhize family at the time, describes what happened next:

I remained in the kitchen. I saw Mrs Mkhize enter her hut and then come out again. She was surrounded by Ntombela and his men. I stood next to the window in the kitchen which, although it is boarded up, has a hole on the one side of it. I then saw David Ntombela shoot her as she stood next to the door. He did so with a small handgun.

I am not sure if she was shot more than once as I immediately turned and tried to escape from the kitchen. I ran straight into the man whom I know as the shopkeeper [Ntombela's brother]. We met in the doorway and he shoved me back into the hut with the butt of his gun. It was extremely painful. I told him to be careful as I was pregnant.

After shooting Mrs Mkhize, the men returned to the outer huts and went into the kitchen hut where Kathula Mkhize and his sister Petronella were sleeping. According to the affidavit of Kathula Mkhize, the men then killed Petronella before leaving:

After they shot my mother I heard someone tell her to get up and open the door. I did not hear her answer as I hid under my bed.

A short while later some of the men entered the room. I saw Sibongi Zondi aim his gun at my sister, Petronella, and fire one shot. She fell to the floor and I heard more shots. I remember her crying out, 'Awu weMa'.

She lay bleeding on the floor. She was moaning. I closed my eyes and after a short while the men went outside and I heard David Ntombela say that they should burn the house. One of the men argued against this, saying that they already had two of us.

A few minutes later my sister Patricia came into the room. We fled from the hut and ran into the bush far from the house where we spent the night. It was cold and as we were only wearing very light clothes we piled dry grass on top of us and hugged each other to keep warm.

When we awoke early in the morning we made our way to the house of my uncle, Stofile Mkhize, who also lives in Maswazini. We told him what had happened and then returned to our kraal.

On the way to the house we saw a number of policemen around a corpse and my uncle told me that it was Sithembiso Khumalo, a good friend of our family.

According to the testimony of his girlfriend, Patricia Franz, Sithembiso Khumalo had been abducted and killed by Ntombela and his men some time after the Mkhize killings, apparently in a case of mistaken identity for his brother. Sithembiso was only in the area for a brief holiday to visit his family, on leave from his job in Johannesburg.

The police took statements from the various witnesses and arrested Ntombela and his eight accomplices. All were immediately released on bail of R100,00 each, at which point the investigation foundered. After a month in which the police took no further action against the alleged killers, the family approached the COSATU lawyers in Pietermaritzburg with their complaint and the incident became the substance of the first interdict application, *Mkhize & Others* v *Ntombela & Others*, brought by COSATU against the Inkatha wwarlords.

On 2 November 1987, Judge Thirion of the Natal Provincial Division of the Supreme Court of South Africa granted the restraining order against Ntombela and the eight other respondents in the action. Almost eighteen months later, in March 1989, the magistrate presiding over the inquest into the Mkhize murders found that Ntombela and several others were responsible for the deaths. He referred the matter to the attention of the Attorney-General. Despite the inquest findings, Ntombela has still been neither prosecuted nor even indicted.

At the end of January 1988 David Ntombela was one of the speakers at an Inkatha rally at KwaMkhulu in Mpumuza. At the rally, Ntombela allegedly declared that anyone who refused to join Inkatha should be killed. He asked the conveners of the meeting to stop the rally so he could lead out the assembled people to drive the UDF and COSATU from the area. He was later seen directing a group of vigilantes who were pursuing and assaulting Ashdown residents with vigour.

On 12 February 1988, the events of January 31 were brought before the Natal Supreme Court in the interdict application, *Zondo, COSATU & Others* v *Inkatha, Ntombela & Others*. At the hearing, several witnesses heard David Ntombela, the fifth respondent, threaten to shoot a man who had assisted the COSATU legal team in serving papers on him.

Ten days later, on 22 February, the inquest into the deaths of three COSATU supporters in Mpophomeni township in December 1986, began in the magistrate's court in Howick. The three were allegedly murdered by Inkatha supporters attending a rally in Mpophomeni, an allegation upheld by the presiding magistrate.

On the first day of the hearing, counsel for the families of the deceased stopped the proceedings and informed the magistrate that David Ntombela, seated near the witness box, was carrying a gun on his person. Ntombela was taken outside and disarmed. Following instructions from the magistrate, every person seated in the public gallery was searched and four other guns belonging to Inkatha members were confiscated.

In February 1988, Ntombela was a respondent in two interdict applications, and in addition, was out on bail for the murders of Angelica and Petronella Mkhize, as well as that of Sithembiso Khumalo. Needless to say, no action was taken against him for either courtroom incident, nor was his bail revoked.

*   *   *

Ntombela's star continued to shine: in February 1989 he was elected unopposed to the KwaZulu Legislative Assembly as MP for Vulindlela and the translation of his exploits into the stuff of local myth proceeded apace. I arranged to meet David Ntombela at the Inkatha headquarters in Edendale, located on the ground floor of Marawa House, a modest block of flats next door to the Edendale Hospital.

The Inkatha offices bear a discreet, almost self-effacing sign on the door. I was met by Vitus Mvelase who led me into a small office, where David Ntombela was seated on a plastic chair near the window and two women were sitting at the desk. One perched on the corner, her arms braced behind her, and swung her legs idly in the air; the other sat behind an old typewriter, laboriously picking her way along the keyboard. She stopped when I entered and looked up. Mvelase waved vaguely at the women and said, 'My associates, you understand. You don't mind if they sit in.' I realised that this was not a question, and shook my head.

Mvelase then introduced me to David Ntombela, who stood up and shook my hand with a limp grip. He was wearing a wide smock with black embroidered edging, which effectively concealed his girth and exposed his powerful arms. I could see at first glance that he was a man who expected others to take him very seriously. In fact, throughout the interview he was clearly ill at ease in the cramped office, far too small to accommodate so large a personality.

I switched on the tape-recorder and asked him my first question. 'I have never met an induna before, could you tell me what official functions you perform in your area?'

Ntombela answered, 'I try cases of people who are in trouble; also I organise meetings of Inkatha, and I try to make peace.'

'Has there been much fighting in your area?'

Ntombela thought about this briefly and said, 'No, but there *were* certain people, UDF people, killing people in 1987, but they just fled themselves and ran away.'

'You didn't chase them out?'

'No, they just left the area, by themselves.'

'They left their houses, belongings, everything?' I asked, to get this quite clear.

'They left their houses,' he confirmed, 'they still stand empty because they fled themselves.'

'And have you ever been attacked yourself?' I asked.

'Once they petrol-bomb my house – everything in flames, furniture, roof, all was ashes. Even today I don't know who did it.'

'And when was this?'

'1979,' he said.

'Have you been attacked more recently,' I asked, 'in the span of this present war?'

'Well, there were the eleven buses full of UDF came to attack me. They use these buses and they don't pay even a cent. Only Inkatha is paying. The drivers are taking UDF youngsters in these buses to go and attack our people. In 1987, you can see the books, Sizanani was making nothing because the drivers were taking the UDF free of charge to make attacks. So, when they came to my house I went outside and I said, "Hey, gentlemen! You come in!" They think I've got lot of people and they have no chance. At the time I was already phoning the police, and the time they saw the eight vans of the police, then they just running in the buses and they just vanish.' Ntombela snapped his fingers dismissively and slapped his palm down on the desk. 'Then they attack me at Daya store,' he continued. 'I didn't notice anybody, when I got into my Kombi, and I'm driving. Then they put in a petrol bomb through the window. And I'm still driving....'

At this point, the door opened and Vitus Mvelase came in holding a copy of *Clarion Call*, the official journal of Inkatha, put out by the KwaZulu Bureau of Communications. 'I thought you might find interesting things in this,' he said, thrusting the magazine into my hands. I thanked him, and he left, trying to close the door noiselessly behind him.

David Ntombela resumed: 'They did that, but I didn't running away. I put on handbrake, I stopped the Kombi. *They* ran away.'

'How many were there?' I asked.

'More than fifty.'

'I take it you were armed.'

'Yes.'

'Did you fire at them?'

'No, I just pulled out the weapon, and they see it and run away. The time I got out of the Kombi they know I'm not scared. They know I got fight, they just running away.'

The door opened carefully and Mvelase returned holding another edition of the magazine, this one headlined 'Pietermaritzburg: Apartheid's Can of Worms'. 'This deals with the things you want to know,' he said, and eased his way out again.

I turned back to Ntombela and asked, 'Has there ever been a time when, in fact, they haven't run away and you've been forced to shoot someone?'

'No, never.'

'You've never shot anyone?'

'Never.'

Vitus Mvelase came in for the third time with a pile of about eight or nine copies of *Clarion Call*, made up of a number of duplicates and some back issues. 'Here, you can take these for some other chaps,' he said.

When he had left, Ntombela asked me sharply, 'You're not distracted?'

Almost at once Mvelase re-entered with a huge bundle of magazines in his arms. He began counting them, 'Fourteen, sixteen, twenty, twenty-five. Here, you can in fact take all of these, I don't mind,' he said, 'you can spread them around lots of chaps for a clear picture of the situation as we know it today.'

As I sat immobilised under the tower of journals on my lap, Ntombela suddenly exploded. 'Even myself now, I am lost,' he expostulated. 'I—I—I—I don't know how to talk now. No, truly!' The two women in the office, Mvelase's associates, who had been sitting silently throughout, giggled.

I said, 'Let me see if I can just take us back—'

'No! I'm tired now, really!' Ntombela broke in. 'I think so, man. I'm tired. You yourself, still playing with those papers. You can't concentrate. You can see yourself that we are disturbed!'

'We have been disturbed,' I agreed, 'but—'

'Yes, really!' he exclaimed again. The women were laughing openly. Ntombela made an effort and said more calmly, 'Anyway, it's all right, do your job, sir. You can continue, sir. I'm prepared to talk to you.'

'You were saying that everyone knows that you always carry a weapon on you. I take it you're armed now. Do you mind if I have a look at your gun?'

Ntombela pulled out a handsome .22 revolver, the barrel rubbed bright by the constant friction of the holster. He snapped open the drum so I could see the gun was loaded. 'Always loaded,' he said. 'You can't have gun without bullets.'

'And you say you've never had to use it?' I asked again.

'No, never.'

'I imagine a weapon like this must have been quite expensive.'

'R600 in 1979,' he said. 'Must be more than a thousand now. And ammunition, very expensive.'

'Although as you've never had to use the gun, that can't have been much of an expense for you,' I suggested.

He laughed mirthlessly and looked at me coldly for the first time. I changed tack. 'At the end of 1987, and the beginning of 1988,' I went on, 'you were named as a respondent in a number of interdict applications brought by COSATU. The specific charges against you were murder and incitement to murder. In your replying affidavits you denied all these charges. If the allegations were simply a bunch of lies, why do you think they would go to the trouble of bringing the applications to court?'

'These people, UDF, they mention my name that I was threatening, which is a propaganda, all lies, as they know I am a strong Inkatha man.'

'Yes, but why would they take it so far?'

'It's because they want to undermine my name, just to show the people that I am a bad man. Which they can't prove – in court. If you are a top leader and this thing happens at night, they'll think, "Who's a strong man?" and say your name. That's why they do it.'

'You've also been called "Inkatha warlord number 1." What do you think of that?'

In spite of himself, Ntombela smirked. 'Well, truly,' he said indulgently. 'They try to give me a nickname which I'm not, and other people hear it and try to hate me now. They say Ntombela is warlord number 1, that's what they call me, warlord number 1.'

'And in your opinion there's no justification for such a nickname?' I asked stupidly.

Suddenly Ntombela seemed to lose his sense of humour and to tire of the interview, as though my flea-bite questions had become too irritating to tolerate. Ntombela snapped back at me: 'Look, sir, there are people who are against me because they know I am a strong man. People, they don't want a straight man. If you are a straight man, you're having enemies; if you change with every man, they say, "No, he's a good man." Some other people they talk all nonsense about Ntombela. They tried to say I'm a bad man, in fact I'm not a bad man; yes, I'm not a bad man. I would be in jail several times, if I'm a bad man. I've never been charged – not even for reckless driving I've never been charged. Otherwise I've never been charged. They even went to the judge, to the Attorney-General. He said, "Ntombela, we can't charge you." I'm telling you, I'm a good man, for God. They just put it out all the time I'm a killer. This thing make me cross. Yes, really!'

On that note he nodded curtly to terminate the interview. I stuffed my briefcase full of Mvelase's magazines, carrying the spill-over in my arms, thanked Ntombela for his time, and made my way with difficulty back to the car.

        ★   ★   ★

Some days later I ran into John Aitchison again and told him about my interview with warlord number 1. Aitchison said, 'Did he handle it well?'

I said, 'I found him like his colleagues: full of conviction but unconvincing.'

Aitchison remarked, 'I think Inkatha have done quite a job on Ntombela – a kind of political beautification. It's as though they've taken the old, wild and dangerous Ntombela, given him a manicure and a position of sober respectability. I think you could read his elevation to the Legislative Assembly as a double message, saying on the one hand, "Well done, here's your reward for services rendered," and on the other, "You've been attracting too much adverse attention in the media. Even the police have been forced to investigate you. We're kicking you upstairs, so keep yourself clean and leave it to other, more obscure people to get their hands dirty."

'I think that what's happened to Ntombela is a manifestation of the fundamentally contradictory relationship between the top Inkatha leadership and the warlords. Inkatha needs the warlords, but can't acknowledge their activities openly. As long as the police turn a blind eye, everything's OK, but when the heat's on – in the media, or the courts – and people start asking questions about the warlords, then the Inkatha leadership needs a way to distance itself. It's a common theme: in Durban, Shabalala was made a member of the Central Committee to calm him down and take him out of the headlines, but that didn't work, so they were forced to repudiate him publicly, which was messy and embarrassing. Here in Maritzburg, they've purged Zuma from his official position in the organisation because he was becoming too much of a liability – too many interdicts, too many column inches in the papers, questions asked in parliament and so on. That was easy because Zuma's young and has no independent source of power, but whether they wanted to or not, they couldn't purge Ntombela because he has his own tribal power base which he could swing against Inkatha if he felt the organisation was treating him badly. So they've sanitised him by making him an MP.'

28
The third force

Monitoring agencies in Pietermaritzburg have received numerous reports of an ostentatious camaraderie existing between warlords and the police. The reports claim that warlords are to be seen in and around local police stations so frequently, and displaying such confidence and complacency, as can only be explained by a relationship of special licence and friendship with the police.

My own researches into the activities of Zuma and Ntombela had shown them to be closely linked to the police. This was true whether the police provided what appeared to be direct assistance in the form of military backstop, detention and disruption of enemies, or indirect assistance, in the form of a failure to investigate complaints *against* the warlords, coupled with an obligingly quick reaction to complaints brought *by* warlords.

With Sichizo Zuma, for example, the police refused either to investigate complaints against him, as in the *Mthembu* and *Ngubane* cases, or to take action against him when caught red-handed in the commission of a crime, as in the case of the abduction of Jaminah Mthiyane. When they were finally pressurised into bringing an action against him for murder, the police made no attempt to assist the already leaky and slipshod prosecution, which resulted in Zuma's quick acquittal.

David Ntombela, too, was only able to carry out his campaign against non-supporters of Inkatha in his and nearby areas, thanks to the certainty that the police would either help him or leave him alone. The illusion of invulnerability he had built up around himself was expanded and reinforced by his apparent immunity from prosecution for such crimes as murder, incitement to murder, arson, incitement to arson, contempt of court and assault. On his own, Ntombela had become a powerful and feared man; but with the aid of the police, he had made himself practically invincible.

I realised it was logically inevitable that a relationship of dependency must arise between the warlords and the police. The police and army have a monopoly over the use of coercive powers in the state, and no other grouping could systematically employ violence – as the warlords and their attendant bands of vigilantes have done – without the sanction of the police, tacit or otherwise.

In the Pietermaritzburg conflict, the police are commonly regarded as a third force, an important participant in the war. Although the police purport to be neutral, committed to ending the strife, there are innumerable allegations of police partisanship in favour of Inkatha – for example, detention figures show that over the two years from July 1987 to July 1989 the ratio of detentions of Inkatha members to UDF and COSATU supporters has been about 1:50. What is more, allegations have also been made of direct police involvement in the fighting in collusion with Inkatha.

According to local commentators, the police first showed their hand in 1986 through their handling of the Mpophomeni killings. In December, an Inkatha rally was held in the township, during the course of which four COSATU supporters were abducted by Inkatha members. Three were killed, but the fourth managed to escape and report the incident, including the identity of the killers, to the police. Despite his statement, the police took no action against the murderers. On the contrary, they patrolled the township to allow Inkatha members, who had been bussed in to attend the rally, safe passage out again.

Shortly afterwards, the funeral was held, preceded by a memorial service in the township church. On this day the police were out in force in full riot gear, and with dogs. Some policemen assaulted and abused mourners on their way to the service, and set their dogs on old ladies making their way to church, reining in the animals on a long leash just as they gathered themselves to spring. Most ominously, they warned the residents that Inkatha was out to get UDF and COSATU supporters, and that they, the police, would not intervene.

The inquest into the Mpophomeni murders, held more than a year later, in February 1988, found that Joseph Mabaso, an Inkatha youth organiser, and eight other Inkatha members were responsible for the killings. The magistrate referred the matter to the Attorney-General, but the police have as yet made no arrests, saying that they 'are unable to find' the perpetrators.

More recently, in April 1989, the police have been named as respondents in an interdict application brought by residents of Mpophomeni, in which an order was sought restraining the police from unlawfully harassing or intimidating people in the township. The application stemmed from an attack by a gang of Inkatha members on residents of Haza, an area of Mpophomeni, and from the police response to the incident. In an article entitled 'Keepers of the Peace are the "Very Cause of Our Fears"' which appeared in the *Weekly Mail* of 5–11 May 1989, Carmel Rickard sets out the main allegations in the affidavit of Stanley Mbambo, a local unionist:

Mbambo, supported by MP Pierre Cronjé who was at the scene, said the police were slow to arrive. When they did, they made no attempts to disperse or arrest the armed gang approaching from Haza, 'and instead attacked and dispersed the residents of Mpophomeni in an undisciplined and unlawful manner.'…

The next day this police behaviour continued, with the SAP allegedly enforcing an arbitrary curfew on the township, whipping people found on the streets, even if they were on their way to work.

Among those beaten in this way was a crippled youth who 'failed to respond to a policeman's instructions quickly enough because of his physical infirmity'.

Over the next weeks, despite repeated requests to the police and local magistrate for protection from threatening gangs, no help was forthcoming and the police continued their attacks on residents.

Bricklayer Vincent Sokhela said he was at the soccer stadium 'when the police began to chase [us]'.

As he ran he saw a policeman assaulting a youth and then ran in the opposite direction.

'When I got to the kitchen door a policeman fired a shot. The bullet struck me in the back of my left thigh … I fell down.

'The policeman came up to me. He turned me over and placed his foot on my leg just above the wound. He pointed a gun at my head … and [another] policeman began to cut at my leg with a small blade and picked at the flesh of my leg.

'As a result of my injury, my left leg was amputated.'

A temporary order was granted restraining the police from carrying out unlawful acts against the residents of Mpophomeni. The police consented to the order and agreed to pay costs, but refused to admit any of the allegations against them.

Other allegations of police partisanship towards Inkatha are based on dozens of examples of a close cooperation between the two forces. For example, many detainees allege that Inkatha members helped the police to track down and arrest them; that they were taken to the houses of Inkatha warlords to be assaulted and interrogated before being taken to a police station or released. On one such occasion, on 3 January 1988, in Madakaneni, a number of people were arrested, forced into a police van and driven to Dambuza where the police were searching for a particular UDF activist. Two of the youths claim they were assaulted by the police when they failed to lead them to their quarry.

Later the van drove over to a white Kombi occupied by Sichizo Zuma and several police officers. The group was made to file past Zuma who declared himself unable to identify any of them. They were then shoved back into the van, sjambokked once again and driven to the Henley Dam turn-off where they were ordered out, beaten again and told, 'This is not UDF country, but Inkatha country!' A black policeman fired a shot into the air and the group fled.

Then there are the allegations that the police provide direct assistance to Inkatha in their war effort, either by neutralising the enemies of warlords by detaining or killing them, or by supporting Inkatha attacks on UDF strongholds. In the notorious Operation Doom attack by Inkatha supporters on the residents of Ashdown township on 31 January 1988, the police allegedly escorted groups of armed men into the township on search and destroy missions, and stood by as members of Inkatha slit the throat of Magic Mandla at the Ashdown bus terminal. In his statement on the incident, Vitus Mvelase, the Inkatha spokesman in Pietermaritzburg, commended the police for not restraining the army of Inkatha vigilantes: 'The police and Defence Force did not disarm the attackers because they had been provoked beyond all endurance,' he said.

In another incident, also in January 1988 in Mpumuza, the police assisted a group of vigilantes to capture a group of comrades, one of whom was killed and his body dumped in the veld overnight. The dead boy's grandmother described what happened:

At midday we saw the Inkatha people appearing. We all went into the house because we were afraid. Two police vans then arrived with five white policemen and two black policemen in them. Both vans stopped near our home and all the white policemen got out … three white policemen ran into my house and tried to get the three boys who were seeking refuge inside, but they ran away. OOne white policeman shot my dog.

The policeman chasing Makhitiza fired three shots. The third shot hit Makhitiza at the top of his back near his neck. He fell down. The policemen came up to him and beat him with their shotguns. They picked him up and dragged him to the van where they put him in the back. He was bleeding slightly from the wound. I asked them if I could take out the bullet, and said I would bring him the next day if he would be charged. The white policeman said no, he was arrested. Mr Agrippa Bhengu, a counsellor of the induna Mr Ntombela, was wearing a police uniform and carrying a gun, though he is not a policeman. He said, 'We will kill him….' Then they drove away with him.

In the morning a girl came to me sent by Mr Mncwabe, my neighbour, to say the boy was outside his homestead, near the bus stop. I went to see him. He was lying on his back on the grass near the road. He was dead. There were many stab wounds in his chest and back and sides.

Direct assistance by the police is said to take several forms. For example, there are many reports in which the police are said to intervene in battles only when the circumstances are disadvantageous to Inkatha, dispersing the comrades with teargas and birdshot. In addition, any collection of comrades is immediately dispersed and individuals are detained and charged with forming an illegal gathering, while gatherings of armed vigilantes are at best ignored or, at worst, actively escorted on raids.

Residents of the Pietermaritzburg townships claim that the police assist Inkatha in other ways, by providing warlords with guns, by turning a blind eye to illegal possession of weapons, and by transporting vigilantes in police vans. When the police deployed two squads of *kitskonstabels* in the area, there were complaints and allegations that many of the new recruits were simply vigilantes dressed in formal police uniform.

Although the *kitskonstabels* have been deployed for little over two years, there have been scores of complaints against them, alleging unprofessional conduct, harassment and intimidation of the population, all stemming from and compounding the fact that in many cases their motivation is suspect and their training period insufficient.

New stories of police impropriety began emerging towards the end of 1989. Various Imbali comrades came forward with allegations against a police 'hit squad' operating out of a red Husky minibus. A temporary interdict was granted against the members of the squad (who had all assumed macho pseudonyms such as 'Rambo' and 'McGyver', taken from American films and TV programmes). The comrades who brought the application accused the squad of engaging in a concerted campaign of harassment, intimidation and torture aimed specifically at Imbali activists.

The police denied the allegations, saying that the members of the squad were 'well aware that they had to act within the law at all times'.

According to local residents, the squad has ignored the terms of the interdict and continues to operate, although the red Husky has now left Imbali and cruises the streets of townships farther afield.

Ultimately, however, there appears to be general agreement among non-Inkatha supporters living in the Pietermaritzburg townships that the most pernicious aspect of police malpractice is the negligent response to requests for help or to complaints brought against Inkatha members. In their *Memorandum on Violence in PMB*, published in November 1987, COSATU and the UDF set out a number of instances in which the police failed to investigate complaints brought by residents, and in some cases even refused to take statements:

In [one] Slangspruit incident ... it was alleged that Sergeant Nene of the Plessislaer Police Station refused to take a statement from the victim, Mrs Makhosazana Hadebe, and advised the complainant that her best course was to join Inkatha.

In a number of instances the police were called while an attack was in progress, but they either did not arrive at all, or only arrived after the event. For example on October 4 1987 the house of Willie Mpulo aged 49 was attacked, allegedly by Inkatha, and his son, Bhekabantu murdered. While the attack was in progress one of Mpulo's children, Busizwe, ran to the Hilton police station to ask for assistance. Help was promised, but never arrived.

I spoke to Matthew Dontzin, of the COSATU legal team, about police response to complaints against Inkatha, and more particularly, about their attitude towards the interdict applications brought by COSATU against members of Inkatha. 'OK, buddy, listen good,' he said. 'You're not going to like what you hear. If you want to know the police attitude to the interdicts, I can sum it up in one word: obstruction. First off, we prepared and provided affidavits of complaint to the police; that's not normal practice, but we did it anyway. Then, when the police failed to trace witnesses we personally escorted witnesses to police interviews; not normal practice. But then at other times – we're talking serious stonewalling here – the police would recall witnesses for interviews up to four times in some cases. We made the point explicitly that the police were not to interview witnesses to the applications without a lawyer present, so what did they do? They would turn up in the early hours of the morning at witnesses' houses, force them to go along to the police stations, take new statements which contradicted their application affidavits, and that's it – witness impeached, case over.'

'If people came to you first, did you advise them to lay a complaint with the police?' I asked.

'Sure we did,' he replied, 'but we said we'd go with them, because if there's one thing this game teaches you, it's how the police treat complaints, and I'm talking specifically about complaints against Inkatha here.

'Here, you want to know about police response, just listen to this passage from the affidavit of Mandla Mkhize, the first applicant in the *Mkhize* v *Ntombela* interdict application.' Dontzin took a file out of his briefcase, flipped through it and unclipped a few pages which he handed to me. 'OK, you know the scenario – Mkhize's mother and sister have been killed and he is told by a cop from the CID that Ntombela and his men have been arrested and the police have finished their investigations. I'm off now, but why don't you read this over and chew on it,' he said, and left.

On the way back I had to pass through Imbali. At a T-junction I saw the first respondent – Ntombela – standing behind his car. I was most surprised to see him at large so I decided to go to the Plessislaer Police Station to find out why he had been set free. I subsequently learned that the other respondents who had been arrested along with the first respondent had also been released.

The following day I went to the police station and asked officer Duma why Ntombela had been released. He told me that the whole matter had nothing to do with me and he left the charge office.

I realised that I would receive no co-operation from Duma so I spoke to another detective in the charge office who works in the C.I.D. He told me that if he were in my position he would immediately move his family to a place where they would be safer. He said that there were some members of the police force who did not regard the first respondent as a criminal. He said that, in his experience, when members of Inkatha committed atrocities, they were arrested but subsequently quickly released and almost never charged and prosecuted. He told me that he was not the only policeman who was of this opinion but that it was difficult to raise these issues in the police force.

* * *

The police deny all these allegations of malfeasance and bad faith, constantly reiterating the refrain that they are a neutral, public body whose only objective is the restoration of peace to these troubled areas and the upliftment of the residents who dwell therein. Inkatha, too, rejects allegations of collusion and collaboration with the police, flinging the accusations back in the face of the UDF and COSATU. Inkatha claims that far from the police favouring Inkatha, some members of the police force are, in fact, in cahoots with the UDF. This fanciful construction is based on a few incidents in which police clashed with vigilantes, and on the fact that on occasion black policemen, harassed by Inkatha recruitment drives, have come out strongly against the organisation, although not necessarily in favour of the UDF.

Conflict between police and Inkatha is rare, although when it has occurred it has been very violent. On 25 September 1987, a policeman and two accomplices set fire to a house in KwaShange in which members of the Inkatha Youth Brigade were holding a meeting. They then shot and killed thirteen youths as they tried to flee. At his trial, the policeman pleaded in mitigation that he and his family had been severely harassed in the past by Inkatha members. He also said that he had earlier arrested some of the Youth Brigade members for arson, but they had been released after the intercession of a senior Inkatha official. He feared that they would kill him in retaliation, so he acted first.

The policeman and his accomplices were sentenced to twelve years' imprisonment, as the judge accepted these to be mitigating circumstances.

In general, Inkatha's claims that it is a victim of police prejudice are patently absurd.

29

Tea with the Brigadier

Protestations of good faith by the police demand closer scrutiny. I wondered how the police would respond to the allegations against them. With this in mind I rang up the offices of the security police, and with surprising ease arranged an interview with Brigadier Jacques Büchner, then head of the security police in the Pietermaritzburg region.

Over breakfast on the day of my interview, I reviewed the few things I already knew about Brigadier Büchner. From a former detainee, I had a picture in my head of a sweating man in full uniform dispensing restriction orders under the impassive eye of the video camera and the glare of studio lights. From John Aitchison I had an impression of a sensitive man, both insulted and hurt by his exclusion from the seminar on violence held at UNP in April 1988. 'He'll probably refer to it,' Aitchison had warned me, 'he's apparently still very touchy on the subject.'

I had also the transcript of the 14 January 1988 edition of *Network*, a news programme on the SABC, which had looked at the violence in Pietermaritzburg. The *Network* interviewer had asked Brigadier Büchner a number of questions about the level of intimidation of the community by the UDF. Büchner replied that the scale of intimidation was very great, not to mention atrocities such as arson and necklacing. Olkers did not point out that there had been no instances of necklacing in the Pietermaritzburg war, but asked a different question entirely:

Olkers: Why do they fear the burning of the body so much?
Büchner: This is a traditional fear. When a person dies, they believe that the spirit of the forefather is re-incarnated – that's what they traditionally believe in. But what we have here is where a person is burnt, especially when he is alive, then the belief is that his spirit perishes with him, so that the children have no mediator between themselves and the forefathers' spirits. That is a very important aspect of traditional culture.
Olkers: So, in other words they fear burning more than they actually fear death.
Büchner: Oh, definitely, yes.

From these sources I built up a composite idea of the Brigadier: a sensitive man with a sense of occasion; a man favouring ethnic theories of analysis; a man moreover with so strong a belief in theory as to assert confidently that both before and at the moment of death, victims of death by fire (who happen to belong to the Zulu ethnic grouping) are more concerned about the spirit of their forefathers than about their own predicament and pain.

I gathered my wits about me and set off for my meeting.

I walked over to the police headquarters, a handsome Victorian brick building in Loop Street, capped by twin cupolas flanking a clock-face. I went in past a sleepy *kitskonstabel* lolling on the steps cradling his rifle like a drunk crooning over a bottle, and signed in with a bored guard at the reception desk. As he laboriously entered my time of arrival and the nature of my business, I looked about me. The entrance hall was dominated by a massive wooden staircase curving upwards in two broad wings. The hall was ill lit and dusty, the scant illumination coming from a small dome, much like a stained-glass pimple, which cast its light from a great height above the entrance. A couple of chairs were scattered about unused on the broad expanse of floor, and near the street door there were a few stuffed animals – a cheetah and a couple of gazelles – looking mangy and shrunken. Set high, above the pelmet near the ceiling, I could just make out a few dry horns mounted in the shadows.

The guard instructed me to go up to the third floor, so I climbed the staircase and at the top came to a steel door with a bell set into the wall beside it. I rang the bell and waited. From the top of the stairs I could see a corridor which overlooked the stairwell. But even the corridor was shut off from the stairs by a wire mesh which stretched from the balustrade to the ceiling. The precaution seemed unnecessary as it would have taken the agility and foolhardiness of a trapeze artist to leap from the top of the stairs to the balustrade.

I stood in front of the steel door, waiting and watching security policemen and administrative staff walk back and forth along the corridor making jokes and teasing each other. They took no notice of me and for an instant I had an impression of being in a zoo, watching caged animals through a mesh fence.

Eventually the door was opened and I was asked to wait outside Brigadier Büchner's office for a few moments. I sat down in the corridor on a solitary plastic chair placed outside his door, my briefcase clutched between my knees and the first sweat of the day trickling down my armpits. Brigadier Büchner appeared and apologised at once for keeping me waiting. He ushered me into his office solicitously, offered me a seat and tea, took a seat himself, and asked, 'Well, sir, and what can I do for you?'

'I'd like to put a few things to you, Brigadier,' I said. 'In my researches into the violence in Pietermaritzburg I constantly hear people tell me that there is a breakdown of law and order in the townships, that their belief in justice has been abused and shattered, and that the police are mistrusted and, if anything, seen as the problem rather than the solution.'

Brigadier Büchner drank some tea and smiled the smile of a man who has been asked the question before and knows the answer. 'At one time perhaps you could say there was a perception in the community that the police – the security branch – were one of the dangers facing the people. But with all due modesty and respect, I can confidently say that that perception in the community has changed. And the main reason for this is that people actively see us out there, helping them. For example, take Boxing Day last year; no, I'm wrong, '87 – I was in a helicopter in the field most of the day, reacting to calls and acts of violence. We could see houses burning, four or five of them at once. In one house a police captain ran in, kicked in the door, found a body, dragged it out. That kind of selfless bravery makes a big impression on people, alters their perceptions.

'You have to realise that there is much friendliness between the police and the black population in the normal run of things. I myself go in and out of the townships as often as I please; I never feel threatened or feel the need to carry a firearm. Remember our function is the preservation of the internal security of South Africa, we are policemen…. To this end I meet with everyone, speak to everyone, black groups, Indians, whites too, although to tell the truth I don't rank that so high because so many whites here have no idea what's going on.

'And I'll tell you something else, and that is that the police are the answer to this violence, the only solution. Remember, we have the smallest per capita police force in the world. If I had treble the force at my command, if I had two policemen walking down every street, I guarantee the problem ends immediately.'

I nodded noncommittally and flipped to a new page of my notebook. 'When people – I mean ordinary residents, not necessarily activists, although they too – talk about their misgivings about the police they back this up with specific claims,' I said. 'For example, they talk about a special relationship between the police and Inkatha warlords, of their immunity from arrest and prosecution, and of various other forms of direct assistance provided by the police. What do you say to these allegations?'

Büchner smiled again, although the question clearly irritated him. 'I'll deal with the small truth in all that first,' he said. 'Inkatha, or some elements in Inkatha rather, were under the impression that they were safe from the police, but they are precisely the people who came short. Nobody is above the law, and that's a lesson that may have been learnt with surprise by some people around here.

'That kind of example may have been the cause of talk, but for the rest I reject all the allegations. What is this "special relationship" you talk about? You must understand that in the tradition of the Zulu, if you are operating as a policeman you cannot speak to the people on the ground, you have to speak to the chiefs, legally appointed representatives of the KwaZulu government, the people responsible for law and order in their own area, the people who mete out justice.

'You see, I hear you use this word "warlord." That immediately makes you take a certain perspective. This "warlord" business, that's a word coined by academics, incessantly used. I don't know who it's supposed to refer to, or why.'

'Well, it's used to label David Ntombela for one,' I replied. 'He's a case in point, arrested for the Mkhize murders in October 1987, and then released. Investigations appear to have ground to a halt, giving the impression that Ntombela can operate with impunity. Likewise, when he was alleged to have threatened a witness in court and, later, in another case was found in court with a loaded weapon, his bail was not revoked. Are these not grounds for a certain cynicism on the part of the residents?'

'Look,' Büchner said, 'I've heard these stories about Ntombela – many times, in fact – and I should say that stories about warlords come from the UDF side. You take a man like Ntombela, a leader, an induna, a card-carrying member of a legal organisation, he can be identified and pin-pointed. The "warlords" on the UDF are nameless and faceless, it's difficult to pinpoint who is responsible on their side. Now you talk about Ntombela's gun. I know that story and I know for a fact he has a firearm licence. He can carry a gun with him wherever he likes—'

'Even into court?' I asked.

'Even into court.'

'Then why was his firearm taken away?' I persisted.

'Because there was an objection,' Büchner said impatiently. 'Look, David Ntombela is a legally appointed representative of the KwaZulu government; he has to rule with an iron hand or he loses respect and authority.'

'But what if he maintains this respect and authority by illegal means?' I asked.

'There is no proof that induna Ntombela was involved in any illegal action.'

'But what about the eyewitness accounts in the Mkhize interdict application? Members of the family actually saw him and his men shoot Angelica and Petronella Mkhize.'

'Those interdicts – well, I won't go into them now – but they were not quite what they might seem. None of the claims have been proved in court, you know. Did you know that? The whole thing was really an expensive propaganda campaign by COSATU against Inkatha. The police investigated every claim, we interviewed the witnesses and often found that the story they told us, the real story, was very different from the one they told the COSATU lawyers. Sometimes, we couldn't even find the witnesses again. They were quick to go to the lawyers but not to the police. Remember there is a suspicion by the local population of the police. Any person seen speaking to the police becomes suspect.'

'Excuse me, I'm a little confused,' I broke in. 'Earlier you said that the police enjoyed popularity and confidence in the community, that perceptions had changed.'

'For most people, yes,' Büchner responded imperturbably, 'but there are always elements who intimidate innocent people and who might attack anyone seen speaking to the police. And the intimidation comes from both sides.'

The phone rang and Büchner went over to his desk to answer it. 'I'm sorry, I asked them to hold my calls,' he said. While he was taking the call I took the opportunity to observe him and his office more closely. The Brigadier was in civilian clothes, a grey suit with a wide black check, matching his pebble-grey hair. His face was smooth with the exception of a few deep lines scored into the flesh around his mouth and nose. His office was divided into two sections: one defined by his desk and the other, where we were sitting, by a group of chairs around a coffee table. Across the room from me, and to his left as he stood speaking at his desk, there was a colonial print of a savage kneeling at a waterfall. The office décor was dominated by an enormous South African flag tacked on to the wall above my head, the first view of a person entering the room or sitting at the desk.

The Brigadier laughed, 'OK, good. *Moet niks doen nie wat ek nie sal doen nie*, hey,' and put down the phone. He came back to his chair, refreshed his teacup and said, 'Sorry about that. Where were we just then?'

'We were discussing allegations of police collusion with Inkatha,' I reminded him.

'Yes, well let's start at the beginning,' he resumed. 'At the end of 1987 Inkatha – no, both sides – embarked on a forceful recruitment drive which alienated the community. The police were reacting to every call they got, but they couldn't get to some places because there was no access to vehicles. These areas became so-called "liberated zones." When I arrived in November I found that we needed more men on the ground. I sent recruits on a six-week training course and saturated the area with policing. The level of violence dropped at that point, it fell completely flat.

'At the beginning of last year Inkatha was in dire straits, but we came in and restored a certain sense of law and order by February.'

'Are you saying, then,' I asked, 'that you intervened on behalf of Inkatha against the forces of the UDF and COSATU?'

'No, we intervened to restore law and order and to restore the rightful authority of the chiefs and indunas, the legal representatives of the Kwa-Zulu government. These people happened to be Inkatha leaders as well.

But at no time did we take sides. The police force is a neutral, public body.'

'But is it neutral?' I asked. 'In January 1988, the Minister of Law and Order said: "The police will face the future with moderates and fight against radical groups." You can't get any clearer than that. And then there's the fact that Inkatha members were recruited into the ranks of the *kitskonstabels*—'

'—special constables—' he corrected me.

'Right – but UDF supporters were barred from joining on the grounds that they were members of an extremist organisation. Surely that implies that the police have taken sides?'

'As I've said, we are a neutral, public body,' he repeated. 'We favour no one political grouping over another, we serve the state.'

'I would like to ask you about allegations that the police have only detained UDF and COSATU supporters in this conflict and left Inkatha supporters alone.'

'This detention business,' Büchner replied, shaking his head and lifting his hands in a gesture of resignation, 'first of all, we don't detain people according to their political beliefs, but according to whether we think they constitute a public danger. Secondly, when we do question them they simply shake their heads and say, "I'm neutral, I'm neutral, I have no politics." But I'll tell you one other thing and that is there are more attacks on people by the UDF than there are by Inkatha.'

'I'd heard exactly the opposite,' I said. 'In fact, the statistics I've seen seem to indicate that the ratio of attacks and murders by Inkatha to the UDF stands at about 4 to 1.'

'I've seen those statistics too,' Büchner commented, 'and I'm sure you're aware that they come from people and groups on the left of the political spectrum, certainly sympathetic to the UDF and antagonistic to Inkatha.'

'Yes, I know that, but that doesn't mean that the statistics aren't accurate,' I said.

'Let me tell you a little about these people – I take it you've met them – and you can judge for yourself just how concerned they are to find the truth of the matter. Last year there was a conference at the University on the subject of "The Violence in Pietermaritzburg." I heard about it and asked whether I could attend. I spoke to a man called John Aitchison – you know him? – right – and he sent over a messenger with a ticket. Then shortly after this he phoned up and said that he would have to withdraw my invitation, because some of the speakers would not attend if the police were present. It's evident what happened: he went to all the goody-two-shoes and so-called Christian brethren who poke around in these matters and told them that Brigadier Büchner would be coming, so they all started bleating like a flock of sheep. I was very insulted by the retraction; I sent a letter to the newspapers about it.'

'But you didn't attend.'

'No, I didn't.'

'Although you would have been entitled to. It was an open seminar.'

'Well,' Büchner conceded, 'I didn't attend myself, but I was there in spirit. Some of my men went along to listen and taped some of the speeches and discussion. They came back shaking with anger and outrage. "Brigadier," they said, "you can't believe the stuff these people are vomiting out. Just lies and more lies about the police."'

'But why would they lie about these things?' I asked. 'Surely it makes more sense for them simply to present the facts.'

'I'm afraid that's rather a naive point of view,' Büchner replied. 'There were certain people there for their own gain, trying to make a name for themselves. A certain section of the academic community trying to make political capital out of the situation.'

'It's a pity you didn't attend,' I commented. 'You could have responded to these claims and debated the role of the police in an open forum.'

'Yes, it is a pity,' he agreed eagerly. 'It's not just that I wanted to hear what people had to say, but I felt I had a real contribution to make. I consider myself an academic too – I don't just act, I think first and act according to my understanding of the situation. I've studied police academics on racial violence in Britain – Toxteth and so on – and I could have drawn parallels with what's going on in Maritzburg. For one thing, the violence here is different from unrest in other parts of the country; it's not an onslaught against the government but a response to basic causes like overcrowding, poverty, the lack of a rosy future, no extramural activities available, a lifestyle where you walk from the lounge straight into the street, no buffer.

'That conference was supposed to try and find a solution to the violence. I said to Aitchison, "You try your way and I'll try mine." So far I've been more successful.'

'In what way have you been more successful?' I asked. 'The fighting is still continuing after eighteen months, the death rate is still high.'

'Well, in many ways things have improved. For example, at first I was attacked by the Pietermaritzburg Chamber of Commerce who commented on the so-called inability of the police to deal with the situation; now I'm *persona grata* with the Chamber. As for the level of violence, it's sporadic and completely under control. By March 1988, major unrest-related conflict had been brought under control. What we are seeing now is a cycle of retribution and revenge which accounts for the monthly death rate of 40 people a month – let's not quibble, call it 50 people. Now this is criminal violence – psychiatrists and legal beagles would simply call it murder – it's no longer politically motivated, so by rights it should not appear in the unrest reports at all.

'No,' he said sadly, shaking his head again, 'no one has worked harder, and with more success, or less acknowledgement than we have to restore peace to this troubled area.'

'It's interesting to me that you say that,' I remarked. 'It reminds me of another complaint about the police, that they've hardly encouraged the various peace talks.'

'I'll tell you this,' Büchner responded, 'those talks were getting nowhere – nothing to do with the police. We couldn't hang around hoping that something might come of a lot of talk, we had to take matters into our own hands to restore peace and security. We couldn't put aside important security considerations for the sake of so-called peace negotiations. The situation in Pietermaritzburg presents a potential threat to the internal security of South Africa, and dealing with that threat is always naturally our first concern.'

'Perhaps you could tell me exactly what it is that constitutes that threat?' I asked.

'Yes, I was coming to that,' he replied. 'You can't understand what's going on here unless you look at the broader picture. First let's start with the ANC. The UDF has taken the position that the ANC had, internally. The UDF executive has held a seven-hour meeting with the National Executive of the ANC – in fact the UDF executive are all ANC people, they've all spent time on Robben Island. In short, the UDF is being used by the ANC to fill in a vacuum inside the country.

'Next, think about this: the ANC claims to represent the people of South Africa. Now there are approximately 28 million people in the country, of which 6 million are white, 6–7 million Zulu, 4 million Xhosa, 2 million Tswana, as well as various other groupings. The ANC doesn't represent the whites, or the Zulus, whose leaders are their king and the KwaZulu cabinet under Buthelezi. This is a legally elected government and Buthelezi is an internationally recognised statesman who's visited Thatcher, Reagan and so on.

'The ANC have a problem, they know that they can only claim to represent the people of South Africa if they could say they represent the Zulu nation.

'The ANC has made a study of the Vietnamese People's War. In 1984 a decision was taken to make South Africa "ungovernable," through a people's war, undertaken in collaboration with the SACP and involving a strategy of action and reaction. To do this they also had to take control of the Zulu nation. They had to break Inkatha, or at least diminish its influence. Now there was no hope of that in Ulundi or traditional areas, so they targeted Pietermaritzburg, the weakest point for Inkatha. The community here has lived here for 150 years, they are more westernised than other Zulus. They've had contact with other ethnic groupings, they are not true blue royalist Zulus as we know them.

'Inkatha had never encountered any opposition before, so they felt no necessity to develop infrastructure in Greater Pietermaritzburg. This gave the ANC their foothold, and certain people in the community were used by them to foment violence and to strike at Inkatha's weakest point.'

At this point I felt compelled to interrupt. 'Excuse me, Brigadier,' I said, 'but are you saying that the violence in Pietermaritzburg has been orchestrated by the ANC?'

'I'm saying that they have had a major hand in it, yes.'

'Now I'm confused again,' I said. 'A few minutes ago you said that it was a local conflict.' I flipped back through my notes and quoted his words back at him: 'You said, "for one thing, the violence is different from unrest in other parts of the country. It's not an onslaught against the government, but a response to basic causes like overcrowding, poverty," and so on. Now you are saying it's part of an ANC grand plan.'

'If you think about it, there's no contradiction there,' Büchner replied. 'Those are the immediate grievances which have been manipulated by the ANC.'

'But why do you say they've been manipulated,' I pursued. 'Isn't it simpler to assume that individuals and organisations react to circumstances without outside prompting? If you're being attacked you don't need someone to tell you that, and to advise you to flee or defend yourself.'

'I'm afraid the political situation here is a little more complicated than you credit,' he retorted.

'All right,' I conceded. 'I accept that it's complicated. For example, there are allegations that Inkatha is in cahoots with the police to break the UDF and COSATU in Natal.'

'Well, that's complete nonsense,' Büchner said dismissively. 'There's no evidence to support such a claim.'

'Well, there's that comment by Minister Vlok last January,' I pointed out. 'He said, "Radicals who are trying to destroy South Africa will not be tolerated. We will fight them. We have a foothold in that direction and we will eventually win in the Pietermaritzburg area." That could be seen as a declaration that the police had decided to intervene on the side of Inkatha.'

'The police is a neutral public body,' Büchner reiterated. 'We don't take sides.'

I asked, 'Why is this conspiracy theory less plausible than the one you've just put forward?'

'Well, obviously the difference is that I have evidence,' Büchner replied irritably, looking at his watch. 'I have information which I cannot divulge to you.'

We both fell silent. The impasse was broken by a head with a cap, followed by an enormous body, which manouevred itself half-way round the door. '*O, jammer,*' it said, and disappeared again.

'I'll be with you now,' Brigadier Büchner called after it. He turned back too me and said, 'I'm afraid that's all we have time for now. There's a very important person coming to see me and we can't keep him waiting.'

I agreed that that would not do and thanked him for his time. I gathered up my notes into my briefcase and shook his hand. 'Remember,' he said by way of a parting admonition, 'don't be fooled about the community's perception of the police. We're not the ogres we're made out to be. For most people we bring comfort and security; we're only reviled by those who have a reason to fear us. As far as the majority is concerned, they love the policemen to be there. I wish you could see sometime the sight of old ladies waving and clapping as we go past, saying, "Thank you for being there when we need you!"'

30
Police work

Apart from Brigadier Büchner's descriptions of his sortie by helicopter over the field of conflict, I had little idea of how exactly the police conducted their day-to-day business. Consequently I contacted Captain Terblanche, the head of the riot police in Pietermaritzburg. I asked whether I might interview him and he said that he would have to check with Brigadier Büchner first and then get back to me. A fortnight passed so I contacted the Captain again and reminded him of his undertaking. He apologised profusely, saying, 'I'm so sorry, sir, it completely flipped my mind. I'll tell you what – we'll make a provisional appointment for Wednesday at 2.00. Meantime I'll speak to Büchner – hell, man, and I saw him only this morning – and get back to you if there's any problem.'

No call came so I drove out to the riot police headquarters in the Pietermaritzburg suburb of Oribi. I parked near a clump of regulation Mazdas and walked over to the main gates. An endless stream of yellow police vans – known as 'mello-yellos' in the townships – were going in and out, disgorging and taking on squads of men in light-blue denim riot gear. I was stopped at the gate by a black policeman in a police track suit, holding a baton. I stated my business and he went to report my arrival. He returned a minute later and ushered me to a low prefab building near the entrance. I looked around at the groups of riot policemen relaxing in the main square of the compound, fiddling with their rifles and swishing their sjamboks against their legs. At the far end of the square a number of young men, new recruits by the look of them, were standing about self-consciously. They seemed to be wearing their civilian gear like a uniform: short moustache and floral short-sleeved shirt, their huge thighs bulging out of tiny shorts. Only the black policemen in blue track suits, criss-crossing from building to building, seemed to be in any hurry.

Captain Terblanche greeted me and said, 'I'm terribly sorry but I won't be able to speak to you. Brigadier Büchner feels it would be better for you to apply for permission through the Commissioner of Police in Pretoria. I tried to get hold of you to tell you, but you had already left.'

There was nothing to do but go away again. As I drove back to my office, I wondered why Brigadier Büchner had shut me out like that. Had he been offended or antagonised by my questions, or did he simply not trust Captain Terblanche to answer my questions satisfactorily on his own? *

★   ★   ★

I was about to petition General Coetzee in Pretoria for the privilege of interviewing Captain Terblanche of the Pietermaritzburg riot police, when I was unexpectedly afforded the opportunity of seeing his men in action.

Sipho Maloko, an Ashdown activist, had been killed by *comtsotsis* in Dambuza, and I was invited to attend the memorial service in the Ashdown Community Hall at 7.00 p.m. on a Thursday night. I drove past the Plessislaer police station, over the bridge, past that part of Ashdown known as Beachfront, and then through the traffic circle to the hall. It was already growing dark as I parked the car and walked over. The lights were on in the hall but the door was shut and access was barred by two riot policemen with rifles at the ready. A large crowd had gathered in front of the hall demanding to go in. A squad of riot policemen, also with the butts of their shotguns nestling in their crotches, stood by with nervous, watchful expressions. The policemen seemed absurdly young – some of them had not even started shaving but still sported a ragged down on their cheeks and upper lips. As I watched, reinforcements arrived; another five vans drove up fast, stopped abruptly and spilled out dozens of riot policemen. They spread out in front of the crowd, sjamboks sprouting from their fists.

The security police were also present in the form of a man in a safari suit a size too small, holding a camera and old-fashioned flash. He moved through the crowd, leering into people's faces – particularly the white faces in the crowd – before photographing them from aggressively close up. Trailing behind him, a man in shorts was videoing the scene, and a blonde woman in high heels and tight trousers stood around hugging herself and chatting to her superior officer. Eventually she went back to a van and sat back with a flask of coffee to watch the action. There was also a tall black security policeman holding a handgun who moved through the crowd with a venomous expression on his face.

More and more vans arrived. I could not understand why this minor occasion should merit such a show of force.

---

* Terblanche was shot dead in March 1990. His body was found in his car, parked alongside the N3 motorway. Within days the police had apprehended a suspect, a black riot policeman in Terblanche's squad. The suspect was killed almost immediately and in highly implausible circumstances 'while trying to escape'. Terblanche was buried in Pietermaritzburg with full honours; the mother of the suspect has threatened to bring an action against the police.

I asked a man in the crowd what was going on, and he told me that the police had cut down the number of people allowed into the hall to 200 – 'and it takes four, five hundred,' he said disgustedly – and had restricted the duration of the service to one hour only. I looked beyond him and saw an attorney from the Pietermaritzburg offices of Cheadle Thompson and Haysom trying to talk to the commanding officer of the riot police who kept turning away, back towards his van.

Eventually the lawyer abandoned his attempt and came back over to the crowd. 'You'll have to disperse,' he said. 'They'll give you five minutes. He's about to give the order now.' The officer called out the order on a crackling loud-hailer and a black policeman repeated it, even more indistinctly in Zulu. I started to walk back to my car which was perhaps twenty yards away, when suddenly I was caught up in a rush of people scattering about me, running and crying out. I bolted for the car and turned to see riot policemen wading into the crowd from all sides, quirts flashing, arms pumping up and down. I heard the commanding officer shout across to his men, '*As jy 'n man sien wat gooi, skiet hom!*', and reckoned that anyone inadvertently stooping or stumbling would earn themselves a bullet in the back.

I estimated that perhaps thirty seconds had elapsed since the order to disperse had been given.

Near me a young policeman stopped indecisively. I could see him quivering, his eyes dilated and his mouth open in a rictus of hysterical excitement. I saw him turn, pause, then plunge like a madman into a group of running people.

Behind the hall came the pop-popping of shotguns and a screen of teargas moved slowly across the grass, but was soon broken and dispersed by the heavy wet air.

I loitered about in my car for a while afterwards wondering whether anything more would happen. In the event the rest of the evening was quiet. The people in the hall emerged on time and quickly scattered into the night. The police vans remained for some time afterwards, slowly patrolling the empty streets like a triumphant army of invasion.

31
Conclusion

The state in its official pronouncements on the situation in Pietermaritz-burg has said either that everything is under control or that there is black-on-black violence taking place. This is a deceptive term coined by the government to diminish the importance of the protests in black townships around the country in 1984–5. Certain sectors of the media latched gratefully onto the phrase, and even some foreign commentators were taken in by it. What is at best a dubious and flawed description is passed off as an explanation. The term is used to reassure white South Africans that the fighting in Pietermaritzburg is merely part of the tribal legacy of the Zulu people and that whites need not concern themselves about it. In this way the government excuses itself from addressing the real political causes of the violence because it claims there are none, only intra-racial and ethnic lines of cleavage which do not require it to interfere.

The government has not been alone in insisting that the causes of the violence are not political. The Inkatha Institute, a sociological research institute based in Durban, has also found that political conflict, in so far as it exists, is merely a subsidiary, aggravating factor in the conflict. According to Gavin Woods, director of the Institute, the causes of the violence in Natal are socio-economic: high levels of unemployment among black youth in the region, together with poverty and general dissatisfaction with their lot and the lack of a rosy future, lead black youth to express their anger through violence which is criminal rather than political.

This argument manages to combine stating the obvious and ignoring the blatantly obvious. Poverty, unemployment and alienated youth are not specific to Natal, whereas the political rivalry between Inkatha and UDF is.

Both Inkatha and the UDF perceive the political nature of the violence. According to Chief Buthelezi and Inkatha, the present war is simply the latest development in an ANC-orchestrated campaign to destroy the movement. The UDF, by contrast, claims to be the victim of a joint strategy devised by Inkatha and the state to destroy all progressive organi-sations in Natal.

It is not surprising that two such incompatible political movements should fall into dispute. Although it adopts an anti-apartheid stance, Inkatha is a strongly conservative organisation which relies on appeals to Zulu nationalism and pride. To create and maintain its constituency at mass rallies and on days of Zulu national celebrations, the Inkatha leadership puts on a spectacular show which employs traditional symbolism and language that hearkens back to a nobler past.

The UDF, on the other hand, presents an aggressively modern image. Its largest support base is found in the urban metropolitan regions (the Western Cape, the Pretoria–Witwatersrand–Vereeniging area and the Durban Functional Region), particularly among the youth, and its campaigns tend to focus on problems facing the urban black population nationwide. The UDF's broad, supra-ethnic appeal directly opposes the narrow nationalist ethic of Inkatha. This challenge is recognised by Inkatha, and many of the anti-UDF denunciations issued by officials in the organisation are of a crudely racist stamp: loyal supporters of Inkatha are warned that the UDF consists predominantly of whites, Indians and Xhosa lawyers intent on creating mischief at the expense of honest and trusting Zulus.

Various commentators, among them Richard Steyn, the former editor of the *Natal Witness*, have ascribed the causes of the violence to tension between older, more traditional Zulus from rural areas fighting to defend their way of life against the encroachments of a younger, urban, more irreverent and cosmopolitan generation. Undoubtedly the rural–urban and generational cleavages do play a part in the war, but they do not explain it. In this conflict the older generation appear to be the aggressors, trying to coerce the youth into traditional patterns of behaviour. However, both sides have displayed impressive cross-generational cohesion: Inkatha Youth Brigade cadres fight alongside older Inkatha members against young comrades who in turn are supported by the elders of their communities. Likewise, around Pietermaritzburg, support for both the UDF and Inkatha straddles the urban–rural divide. In fact, Inkatha's support base in the rural areas is less strong than might be expected.

The causes of the war are more deep-seated and political than the generational or geographical analysis concedes. According to Gerry Maré and Georgina Hamilton in their paper 'Policing "Liberation Politics"', the conflict derives from a basic political difference between the two movements. Although both describe themselves as liberation organisations, Inkatha's version of liberation is the more rhetorical. As the ruling party of a self-governing homeland (whether it is formally independent or not), Inkatha upholds apartheid structures or, at the very least, benefits from them. The Chief Minister's frequent demands for greater powers derive from his desire for greater control over the areas and population which fall within the political ambit of KwaZulu, rather than constituting a real challenge to apartheid.

Maré and Hamilton point out that the KwaZulu Legislative Assembly has ratified the entire corpus of South African security legislation, including the emergency regulations, and has adopted its most iniquitous aspects, such as detention without trial and the banning of organisations and publications deemed undesirable by the KwaZulu government. Chief Buthelezi has frequently called on the South African government to hand over all police stations in KwaZulu to the KwaZulu Police (ZP) on the ground that it is imperative that the KwaZulu government be seen to be responsible for law and order in its townships. In particular, the ZP is expected to counter the activities of 'external subversive agents' whose actions are a threat to freedom and democracy. On closer examination it transpires that these 'agents' are supporters of the ANC and the UDF.

The UDF was formed to protest and campaign against apartheid legislation and its effects on the daily lives of black South Africans. Inkatha, through the KwaZulu government, implements this legislation in Kwa-Zulu. It is therefore inevitable that these two organisations should clash. Inkatha does not welcome even moderate political opposition in its domain – KwaZulu has, in effect, a one-party parliament. The political challenge posed by the UDF is therefore completely intolerable to Inkatha and the KwaZulu government.

The gulf between Inkatha and various organisations such as the UDF is illustrated by a long history of conflict of which the present war is the bloody outcome. Chief Buthelezi locates the antagonism as arising from a clash between Inkatha and the ANC in 1979. Then, when the UDF was formed in 1983, Inkatha was excluded from affiliating to the Front in the unlikely event that it should wish to do so. Chief Buthelezi correctly took this as a particular affront. In the Pietermaritzburg area, the Chief Minister has interpreted the various initiatives of the UDF and COSATU as a challenge and provocation to himself, his honour and the honour of his organisation. Inkatha viewed with alarm the rise throughout the country of UDF-affiliated civic associations and the consequent eclipse of government-sponsored township councils in the mid-1980s. It was anxious to avoid a similar situation evolving in Natal where township councils are dominated by Inkatha.

In May 1985, a milestone in the conflict between Inkatha and the UDF-COSATU was reached when workers at the BTR Sarmcol factory near Howick went on strike, demanding that the firm's management recognise their union. They were all dismissed. In protest, the workers organised a consumer boycott in Howick and Pietermaritzburg, and called for a stayaway from work on 18 July. Inkatha and Chief Buthelezi came out against both these tactics and appealed to people to ignore these calls. Chief Buthelezi claimed that people who broke the boycott were forced to drink washing-detergent and cooking-oil. He also said that the strikers and their campaigns enjoyed no popular support and declared that for the organisers to continue with them in the light of his personal opposition constituted a deliberate challenge and insult to himself. To his chagrin, the stayaway was a success. Almost the entire black working population of the Pietermaritzburg area stayed away from work.

In May 1987, COSATU again called on its members to observe a stayaway in protest against the whites-only general election held on 7 May. Again, Chief Buthelezi called on workers to ignore the call, and again without success.

The UDF and COSATU contest this interpretation of events. They contend that throughout the 1980s Inkatha has consistently opposed all political activity undertaken by the progressive organisations. In 1980, vigilantes assaulted and abducted school pupils out on boycott in the Durban township of KwaMashu. Also in 1980, at the University of Zululand, Ngoye, students critical of Inkatha were beaten up by members of the entourage of Chief Buthelezi, chancellor of the University. In 1983, five students at Ngoye were killed by vigilantes for chanting derogatory slogans about Chief Buthelezi and Inkatha. In 1985, after a wave of arson and looting in the townships around Durban, Inkatha members mobilised to 'stamp out this criminal activity' and used the opportunity to launch a successful search and destroy operation against UDF organisation in the area.

Around Pietermaritzburg, the UDF account continues, Inkatha's opposition has been unstinting. The UDF admits that some people were assaulted and intimidated during the consumer boycott, but points out that in general the Sarmcol campaign enjoyed enormous support among the black population in the region. The boycott and stayaway were not intended as a challenge to Chief Buthelezi – on the contrary, once the strength and fervour of his opposition became known, it was decided to call off the boycott rather than risk a civil war. But Inkatha's opposition was not restricted to the Sarmcol campaign. In mid-1985 the establishment of the UDF-affiliated Imbali Civic Association (ICA) was undermined by Inkatha. Members of the ICA were harassed and the chairman's house was firebombed. In August, Patrick Pakkies, mayor of Imbali and an Inkatha town councillor, together with Velaphi Ndlovu, KwaZulu MP for Imbali, led a march on the Federal Theological Seminary (Fedsem) near Imbali. They accused the seminarians of providing a sanctuary for UDF supporters. The vigilantes ordered them to close the place down immediately. Fedsem was granted an interdict restraining Pakkies, Ndlovu and their followers from further attacking the institution or its associates.

In December 1986, three COSATU supporters were picked up and killed by vigilantes following an Inkatha rally in Mpophomeni, home of the Sarmcol strikers. The vigilantes had been bussed into the township, and the rally was a show of strength by Inkatha in an area heavily supportive of COSATU and the UDF. A large contingent of ZP had been deployed in the township that night, but they did nothing to prevent the abductions and murders, or to arrest the murderers, all of whom had been identified as well-known Inkatha members.

In the same month, township residents who observed the UDF's 'Christmas Against the Emergency Campaign' by switching off their lights and cutting out all festivities, were attacked by vigilantes and their houses stoned.

The May 1987 stayaway was not intended as a slight against Chief Buthelezi, although the fact that 90 per cent of the workers in the area ignored his appeal and stayed away did signal a significant political defeat for him and for Inkatha.

The UDF claims that from August to November 1987, Inkatha warlords and vigilantes conducted a campaign of forced recruitment into the organisation. All those who resisted, refused to join or, having joined, refused to be drafted into the vigilante army were killed or forced to flee. To back up these claims, the UDF has produced affidavits and eyewitness accounts of people approached by Inkatha in this way. The UDF points to this recruitment drive as the immediate catalyst of the war.

Of these alternative histories of a decade of conflict between Inkatha and the UDF and its forebears, the non-Inkatha account is more plausible. It has fewer omissions and fabrications, and unlike Chief Buthelezi's rendition it avoids any appeal to conspiracy theory.

Chief Buthelezi does not appear to take the objectives of the various UDF and COSATU campaigns at face value: protesting aggainst poor education, campaigning for the reinstatement of dismissed workers, establishing structures of democratic community representation, protesting against the disenfranchisement of the black population of South Africa.... Instead he tends to regard all campaigns and initiatives on the part of the progressive organisations (in Natal at least) as part of a wide-ranging and sinister conspiracy dedicated to undermining his person, reputation and organisation. To dismiss the obvious in favour of the devious seems an unreliable approach to history as well as politics. Chief Buthelezi frequently claims that the actions of the progressive organisations are planned as a direct challenge to his political control over the region, but this it can be argued is an inversion of the true state of affairs. It is he himself who issues the challenge by opposing each campaign *after the fact* and by doing so in strong and threatening terms.

*   *   *

These years of chronic antagonism place the present war in historical context, but the fundamental questions remain: why Pietermaritzburg and why September 1987?

At the conclusion of the 1986 Indaba conference, a plan for the establishment of the federal political entity of Natal–KwaZulu was ratified by the various participants. As a political idea, the Indaba won the support of the Inkatha Central Committee, many white residents of Natal, and certain sections of the local media. Certainly Chief Buthelezi and Inkatha stood and, if implemented, stand to gain much from the Indaba proposals, not least of which are the extension of Inkatha's influence beyond the borders of KwaZulu and the elevation of Chief Buthelezi to the premiership of the province of Natal. However, to secure this new dispensation (leaving aside such other obstacles as the opposition of the South African government), the Chief Minister had to prove his credentials by bringing into the scheme the black population of Natal which he claims to represent.

Chief Buthelezi's constituency has always been measured by the size of the membership of Inkatha, and this figure, though large in absolute terms, is small relative to the six million Zulus who live in the province. Inkatha's support, though widespread, is hardly universal among blacks in Natal and the shortfalls are most noticeable in urban areas. Pietermaritzburg, in particular, has never been an Inkatha stronghold and Chief Buthelezi's command over the allegiance of the population of this region is relatively weak compared with the support he carries in the more remote, rural areas of KwaZulu.

Even in Vulindlela, which falls within the borders of KwaZulu, support for Inkatha is passive rather than active. In the townships of Ashdown and Imbali, Inkatha-led town councils have been established in the past but they were so unpopular and unsuccessful that the Ashdown council has ceased to exist. Most alarming of all for Inkatha, in Edendale, the largest urban township in the Natal Midlands, Inkatha's influence is at best tepid.

In his paper, 'Inkatha, Political Violence and the Struggle for Control in Pietermaritzburg', Nkosinathi Gwala attributes the major causes of the present war to Inkatha's desire to win control over Edendale. Gwala points out that blacks have enjoyed freehold rights in Edendale since the early 1840s, a situation that chafes both the South African government and Inkatha: the former because it is faced with an autonomous township which escapes the controls of the Black Local Authorities Act, and the latter because it would dearly like to incorporate Edendale into KwaZulu or, failing that, at least establish a town council in the township.

According to Gwala, Inkatha's political clout relies less on voluntary, popular support than on the organisation's access to bureaucratic entry points in black urban and rural areas of Natal. These entry points consist of control over the distribution of rights and resources such as access to land and employment and trading opportunities. Wherever Inkatha encounters resistance, it seeks to overcome this opposition either by strengthening its bureaucratic entry points where they exist, or where they are absent, through the incorporation of the troublesome area into KwaZulu.

In places such as Edendale, where neither option is available, Gwala contends, Inkatha local officials have used coercive recruitment to draw in new members.

Inkatha denies that its members resort to such measures, and has repeatedly stated that forced recruitment is a prohibited practice. There is no denial, however, that a recruitment campaign took place in the Pietermaritzburg area in late 1987, or that there was a stream of allegations about malpractice on the part of some recruitment officials.

Whether the campaign was indeed a concerted attack, as the UDF claims, and whether coercive measures were used (and certainly there is no reason, on the evidence, to doubt the veracity of these claims), the campaign was an important component of the power struggle that has defined political activity in the region for the last ten years. Both sides are uncompromising in their attitude towards the other – they see their opponents as military enemies rather than political competitors. A recruitment campaign conducted by either side, and by whatever means, is seen as a provocative act of aggression. By the end of 1987, Inkatha and the UDF–COSATU has been circling each other for some time in an atmosphere of increasing tension; Inkatha's campaign took this tension beyond its critical limit and provided the excuse and motive for outright war.

* * *

The national political terrain has changed dramatically since the war started. The eclipse of former State President P W Botha and the advent of F W de Klerk to the state presidency, together with the increasing legitimacy of the ANC in white business and political circles, have ushered in a new era of reconciliation and atonement on the part of the government. The unbanning of the ANC, the release of Nelson Mandela and other political prisoners, the start of the negotiation process – all this changes, too, the nature of the war and the search for peace. The first and most important consequence is that the ANC has become a major player, rather than the minor force giving diplomatic support to the UDF and COSATU, which had been the extent of its involvement in the Natal conflict before its unbanning.

Now, however, the ANC has to address the war as its own political problem. There is no doubt that the organisation wants peace in the region – continuing violence undermines its claim to hold the disciplined support of hundreds of thousands of people in Natal. In general, ANC statements of the subject of the war have been conciliatory towards Inkatha (their harshest criticism is reserved for the police and, in particular, the Minister of Law and Order) and have stressed the need for unity and a commitment to peace. At his first rally in Natal, Nelson Mandela specifically commended Chief Buthelezi and Inkatha for their stand against apartheid over the years and he called on his followers to 'close down the death factories, throw your weapons into the sea'.

However, as that rally grimly indicated, the gulf between intent and implementation persists. Many ANC supporters, comrades for whom the war has become the most tangible aspect of their lives, and for whom enmity towards Inkatha is simply taken for granted, were unimpressed by Mandela's appeal. Many expressed their displeasure by walking out of the stadium during the rally; others explained that although they would like to renounce violence and throw away their weapons, it would be suicidal to do so in the absence of a reciprocal disarmament by Inkatha.

While the ANC faces difficult problems reconciling the militancy of its Natal constituency with peace talks with Inkatha, the difficulties facing Chief Buthelezi are even more stark. Aside from the immediate requirements of the Indaba (which itself seems more and more to be on the decline as political developments overtake it), Chief Buthelezi is concerned to secure his regional power base once and for all. Unlike the ANC, he has no national constituency to fall back on; all his support is concentrated in Natal. Without Pietermaritzburg behind him, he cannot claim to be the pre-eminent force in the region, and until his position in Natal is unassailable, his claim to be a national political leader of stature equal to the leadership of the UDF, COSATU and the ANC will amount to no more than pretension.

After two years and more of warfare, Chief Buthelezi's claims to be the authentic voice of the Zulu nation are looking increasingly threadbare. Inkatha's influence in Pietermaritzburg is no greater than it was before the war began – if anything, it is weaker. The war has seen the rise of local warlords who have established personal power bases. The allegiance which these warlords presently give to Inkatha is based as much on political pragmatism, as on ideological loyalty, and the Chief Minister could face the unpleasant prospect of a warlords' revolt should they conclude that his political clout is on the wane. Add to this the fact that most of the warlords have done well materially out of the war, and it seems less and less likely that they will favour a complete cessation of hostilities.

To add to Chief Buthelezi's woes, the emergence of the Congress of Traditional Leaders of South Africa (CONTRALESA) has placed fresh strain on Inkatha. Inkatha has always been strong in rural areas where the chiefs and indunas have considerable powers and have used them to bring in membership to the organisation. By petitioning the support of these chiefs, CONTRALESA strikes at the very heart of Inkatha. Chiefs and indunas who have supported Inkatha for years are now presented with a political alternative. Within CONTRALESA the Zulu chiefs and their headmen are no longer seen as stooges of the South African state through the proxy of the KwaZulu government: they have been rehabilitated as important traditional leaders with a part to play in the struggle for liberation from apartheid.

Chief Buthelezi and Inkatha have lost support outside the black community too. Many whites who have always cited Chief Buthelezi as the moderate, non-violent hope for the future now reserve their judgement. By now, Inkatha's claim to be a non-violent organisation is being seriously reviewed. Overseas, too, Chief Buthelezi's image has been tarnished and his reputation as an international statesman has been damaged.

While all these negative factors undermine Chief Buthelezi's ability to restore peace (and for that matter, his own image) he still remains an important political actor, without whose involvement no political solution either in Natal or nationally is possible. The South African government continues to endorse Chief Buthelezi and Inkatha, but their previous automatic and undisguised preference for Inkatha ahead of other black opposition organisations has been tempered.

The government is no longer able simply to allow the war to run on. Like the ANC, it too has to show that it can ensure peace and stability. This means that it has to find a solution to the violence in Natal, and the first step along that road is the recognition that both Inkatha and the police have hands as bloody as, if not bloodier than, the UDF and ANC.

The old glib apportionment of blame to the UDF no longer stands. To some extent the government has recognised that simply deploying more policemen in the region is no answer. President De Klerk has already taken steps to 'depoliticise' the police but as yet this has had little effect. Reports of police partisanship and collusion with Inkatha continue to pour in. Until the government takes active steps to redress this, their protestations of concern will continue to ring hollow.

Up to now, politicians and political commentators have tended to focus on joint rallies or meetings addressed by both Chief Buthelezi and Nelson Mandela as the most important step towards peace. They stress the need for a bipartite (or, bringing in the government, tripartite) peace treaty. But such a step, while necessary and welcome, would constitute only the first and easiest stage-post on the road to peace. As has been shown, it is not enough for top leaders to issue calls to their followers from lofty platforms. It is vital that Inkatha and the ANC strengthen their intermediate and local levels of organisation. Talks between Mandela and Buthelezi will have neither influence nor purchase without a formal, disciplined chain of communication relaying messages between national and local levels — and that means communication from the bottom up as well as from the top down.

Inkatha already has formal levels of command, but over the past two years, UDF organisations have been smashed by the state of emergency and by Inkatha. They now need the space and resources to resuscitate themselves.

The government, too, has to face up to its responsibilities. It owes the people in this region enormous reparations for its wilful neglect over the past few years. Its first task is to restore local residents' trust in the processes of law. This entails the revamping of the police force into a professional, impartial body which will arrest and prosecute the perpetrators of violence with dedication. In addition, special courts should be convened to speed up the process. The police and the courts have forfeited the trust that should be their due, and it is up to them to win it back.

Finally, a comprehensive development plan is needed for the region. The government has taken the first steps towards this by putting an unspecified sum aside for revitalising war-torn areas. This is a good start but insufficient; here again, the government will be dogged by the legacy of its cynical role in the past. A viable development plan should have the government as, at best, a junior partner, with the bulk of the decisions taken by the warring organisations through the mediation of a credible third party.

There is no easy solution to be found for Natal, but the measures outlined above at least provide a start, something positive to work towards. And the difficulties notwithstanding, ultimately none of the parties has any choice: without a solution to Natal, the much vaunted negotiations on the future of South Africa will be just so much empty talk.

Postscript

As I packed up to leave Pietermaritzburg, I carried one scene with me in my head, more prominent than any of the other images I had gathered from the flotsam of this war.

The scene takes place at the Plessislaer police station: Mangethe Mkhize and his younger brother and sister have come to report the murder of their mother and sister, Angelica and Petronella Mkhize, by David Ntombela and eight other men. Mangethe is weeping with grief and rage, mocked by an audience of laughing policemen. Once statements have been taken from the witnesses, Mangethe is approached by a policeman who asks him to wash one of the police cars, a white Toyota Cressida.

'We did not want to wash this car,' Mangethe says in his affidavit. 'We did so, however, because we did not wish to antagonise the police.'

Chronology

SEPTEMBER 1987

Tremendous floods destroyed houses in Edendale and Vulindlela. Inkatha was alleged to be making offers of relief and assistance to flood victims conditional on their joining the organisation. Even the mayor of Pietermaritzburg, Mark Cornell, castigated Inkatha for making political capital out of the floods. Reports came in that in Vulindlela, Inkatha had set a final date of 4 October, after which all inhabitants had to have either joined Inkatha or left the area. The UDF claimed the recruiting drive was encountering strong resistance. On 16 September a police officer and two colleagues ambushed and murdered thirteen members of the Inkatha Youth Brigade in KwaShange.

Number of deaths in September: 60.

OCTOBER 1987

Fighting intensified, mainly in Edendale and Vulindlela. UDF supporters and Inkatha members were being killed at a rate of 2 to 1. Defence committees staffed and run by comrades and activists began to operate in the townships. Inkatha was reported to be losing support in many areas. Attention turned from urban areas to rural chieftaincies — traditional Inkatha strongholds. But even here Inkatha support was no longer guaranteed. The pattern continued throughout November and December. The UDF and COSATU established a *de facto* alliance. Each consulted the other on strategy and policy, but maintained separate organisational structures. The alliance coordinated a 'peace talks' strategy, contacting the Pietermaritzburg Chamber of Commerce which offered to play the role of 'honest broker'. Inkatha contacted the Chamber with a similar request. The Chamber tried to set up a meeting with both parties present. COSATU meanwhile sent a legal team to Pietermaritzburg to investigate complaints against Inkatha warlords of assault, intimidation and murder.

Pretoria-based riot policemen were despatched to Pietermaritzburg and stationed at Oribi. Brigadier Kotze, Divisional Commander of the SAP, said, 'There is no need to worry … the situation is normal and under control.' Refugees began pouring out of rural areas into urban townships and 'white' Pietermaritzburg. Skhumbuzo Shezi, aged 4, was decapitated by vigilantes.

Number of deaths in October: 83.

NOVEMBER 1987

The Pietermaritzburg Agency for Christian Social Awareness (PACSA) was inundated with requests for assistance from refugees and other victims of the fighting. Huge increases in the number of homeless people were reported. The Centre for Adult Education at UNP began to monitor the course of the war, setting up a data base in which every incident was entered. The data base was used to compile a range of statistical indices.

An ecumenical service was held in Pietermaritzburg to pray for an end to the violence. Speakers at the service emphasised that the real enemy was apartheid and not Inkatha. However, Inkatha stayed away. Church leaders from a variety of denominations spoke to community leaders and to Chief Buthelezi.

Velaphi Ndlovu, KwaZulu MP for Imbali, told the press that if an Inkatha member was killed by a UDF supporter, it was legitimate for Inkatha to take revenge against the family of the killer. The UDF and COSATU called on members and supporters to refrain from acts of violence against ordinary Inkatha members, but to defend themselves with vigour against warlords. The UDF–COSATU alliance was keen to win over to its ranks disaffected Inkatha members and township residents harassed by vigilantes. The alliance compiled a memorandum on the violence, setting out cases of attack and murder by Inkatha warlords and vigilantes. The memorandum was presented to a meeting of diplomats, journalists, clergymen and white politicians.

The COSATU legal team launched a strategy aimed at forcing the police to investigate complaints against warlords. On 2 November papers were served in three applications for restraining interdicts against Inkatha warlords, including David Ntombela, induna and chairman of the KwaMncane Inkatha branch; Sichizo Zuma, chairman of the Harewood branch of the Inkatha Youth Brigade; and Jerome Mncwabe and Abdul Awetha, Inkatha town councillors in Imbali – who denied the allegations against them. Interim interdicts were granted and the cases referred for oral evidence.

Later in the month the two Pietermaritzburg UDF secretaries, Martin Wittenberg and Skhumbuzo Ngwenya, were detained together with other senior activists. After pressure from the Chamber of Commerce, the press and various embassies, they were released and the alliance agreed to hold peace talks with Inkatha on 24 November. The talks were cordial and some agreement was reached on minor points, but not on the major ones such as the existence or non-existence of warlords.

Number of deaths in November: 61.

DECEMBER 1987

Ten thousand people attended a rally at Wadley Stadium convened by the UDF and COSATU. Activists reported back on peace talks and called on supporters to stop fighting. The corresponding Inkatha rally was poorly attended. The second round of peace talks was held, but Inkatha refused to proceed unless the UDF and COSATU repudiated an article calling for the destruction of Inkatha which appeared in *Inqaba yabasebenzi*, official journal of the Marxist Workers' Tendency of the ANC. The UDF and COSATU protested that they had nothing to do with the article, but complied with the request. Inkatha refused to accept their repudiation and peace talks broke down.

Militarily, the COSATU–UDF alliance appeared to have gained the upper hand. Inkatha supporters were driven out of the township of Ashdown into the neighbouring rural settlement of Mpumuza. Border skirmishes between the two enclaves ooccurred frequently. In the rural areas of Vulindlela, the authority of the chiefs was undermined and Inkatha was forced onto the defensive. This signalled a reversal of traditional patterns of political control in the area.

The police deployed a squad of 150 *kitskonstabels* in the area. Two further interdict applications were brought by COSATU against Inkatha.

Aitchison's figures for the year show that in 1987, altogether 397 people died, of whom 126 were known to be UDF supporters and 62 were known to be Inkatha members. There were 895 events of political unrest, of which 321, or 35 per cent, involved a death. Most of the deaths occurred in Edendale or Vulindlela, but the death rate was high in Imbali, Slang-spruit, Ashdown and Mpumalanga as well.

Number of deaths in December: 113.

JANUARY 1988

The breakdown of tribal authority left a political vacuum in the rural areas. The UDF was unable to capitalise on this opening as it lacked the structures needed to channel support. Inkatha took advantage of this shortcoming to stage a fight-back, regaining much lost ground. There were fears that Inkatha was planning a counter-offensive, known as 'Operation Doom' or 'Operation Clean-Up', to be launched on 19 January. Nothing happened on the day, but on 31 January Inkatha convened a prayer rally at KwaMkhulu at which people were allegedly exhorted to drive non-Inkatha members out of the area and to kill them. After the rally, vigilantes, apparently escorted by the police, attacked Ashdown and killed a number of people.

There were reports of police collusion with Inkatha against the UDF–COSATU. These were given credence by the Minister of Law and Order, Adriaan Vlok, who said, 'Police will face the future with moderates and fight against radical groups.'

The Inkatha Institute, an independent sociological research unit based in Durban, released a report which claimed that unemployment, rather than political antagonism, was the real cause of the conflict. The report was endorsed by Chief Buthelezi who blamed the violence on apartheid. The president of the UDF, Archie Gumede, called again for peace. Chief Buthelezi responded by saying that Gumede supported the ANC and that peace talks would therefore be futile. Chief Buthelezi also declared that he wanted talks to be held between national, rather than local, leaders.

Bus drivers belonging to the Transport and General Workers' Union were murdered by vigilantes. Their colleagues staged a two-day strike, after which they were informed by management that drivers who took further action would be dismissed. Management did not undertake to provide protection for drivers.

Pupils thought to be supporters of the UDF, or who failed to produce Inkatha membership cards, were turned away from schools run by the KwaZulu Department of Education and Culture.

Number of deaths in January: 161.

FEBRUARY 1988

A group of vigilantes attacked and injured people in Retief Street, in down-town Pietermaritzburg. They were arrested and charged with public violence. This was later altered to the weaker charge of constituting an illegal gathering. They received light, suspended sentences.

Further interdict applications were brought against warlords, but these were hampered by the murder of some of the applicants and witnesses on the eve of the applications. Interim interdicts were granted and the cases referred until August for oral evidence to be heard. Various Supreme Court judges became concerned about the situation. Some called in the Attorney-General and demanded to know what was being done about prosecuting the perpetrators of violence. Other judges complained that the interdict applications were wasting the court's time. David Ntombela, an Inkatha warlord cited as one of the respondents in several of the interdict applications, threatened to shoot a COSATU official 'even here in court'. Ntombela received a warning from Mr Justice Booysen.

A delegation of 300 women from Ashdown visited the offices of the Progressive Federal Party (PFP) in Pietermaritzburg to complain about police involvement in the attack on Ashdown on 31 January. After further allegations of police collusion with Inkatha, a police spokesman, Brigadier Leon Mellet, said, 'It is not the duty or the policy of the police to side with political groupings.' The mayor of Pietermaritzburg, Mark Cornell, called on the South African Defence Force (SADF) to send troops to halt the violence, but was told by the Minister of Police that the police were up to the task.

Dr Khoza Mgojo, president of the Methodist Church, tried to organise a fresh round of peace talks but without success.

Chief Buthelezi demanded an explanation from the Chamber of Commerce for remarks attributed to the managing director of the Chamber, Paul van Uytrecht. Van Uytrecht had told a reporter on the *New York Times* that he was not convinced of Inkatha's commitment to the peace process. The Chamber repudiated these comments, but Buthelezi remained dissatisfied. The Chamber continued to push for another round of peace talks, but on 10 February various UDF activists were detained, including the UDF regional secretaries, Ngwenya and Wittenberg. The detentions scuppered any hopes of further talks. The police were accused of undermining the peace process but the Deputy Minister of Law and Order, Roelf Meyer, declared, 'The Chamber of Commerce and church are wasting their time with peace talks.'

By the middle of the month there were reports of up to 60 000 refugees in the region, some of whom had taken shelter in the white suburbs of Pietermaritzburg.

On 24 February the government imposed severe restrictions on 17 extra-parliamentary organisations including the UDF and COSATU. They were prohibited from engaging in any political activity whatsoever. Inkatha condemned the move: the national chairman of the Inkatha Youth Brigade, Musa Zondi, asked, 'Who is there now for us to talk to?'

Number of deaths in February: 50.

MARCH 1988

A further 300 *kitskonstabels* were deployed at the beginning of the month. The men had been recruited in Natal and trained in Cape Town. There was dismay among township residents, who said that the *kitskonstabels* were simply Inkatha vigilantes in police uniform. A group of women from various Pietermaritzburg townships went to see the Attorney-General of Natal to express their fears that these vigilantes would use their newly acquired rank to exact vengeance. The Attorney-General was non-committal.

The police declared that recruits were not screened as to their political affiliation, but while Inkatha members could be policemen, supporters of the UDF could not, as it was an 'extremist organisation'. Activists claimed that many of the *kitskonstabels* were known criminals and some even had cases pending against them. The police denied that anyone with a criminal record had been recruited and said that the *kitskonstabels* were 'extremely popular with the community'. On 10 March a number of the new recruits were discharged for involvement in criminal activities. Among them was the son of a well-known warlord, Abdul Awetha.

In mid-March, the managing director of the Chamber of Commerce, Paul van Uytrecht, was withdrawn from the peace talks after pressure from Chief Buthelezi and from the Associated Chambers of Commerce (ASSOCOM).

Still more interim interdicts were granted against Inkatha warlords, including the chairman of the Sweetwaters branch of Inkatha, Shayabantu Zondi. At the inquest into the deaths of the three COSATU supporters killed in Mpophomeni in December 1986, the examining magistrate found that a number of Inkatha members were responsible for the murders. The matter was referred to the Attorney-General for prosecution, but at the time of writing had not been pursued. At the inquest, David Ntombela arrived armed and had his firearm confiscated during the course of the proceedings.

On 21 March the police rounded up all the men they could find in Ashdown and Sobantu, both UDF strongholds, and detained them briefly. On the same day the Minister of Defence and his Deputy, as well as the Minister of Police and his Deputy, were taken on a tour of the townships.

The death toll for the month was the lowest it had been for nine months. The police took this as a vindication of their policy of saturation policing and of the deployment of *kitskonstabels*.

Number of deaths in March: 14.

★　　★　　★

In the general fortunes of the war, March was unquestionably a turning point. The police presence played an important part in reducing the death rate, but another important factor was a certain war-weariness which had crept up on the antagonists. Whereas in the past whole armies had clashed, now attacks were more sporadic, carried out by smaller groups against indeterminate targets. The number of killings had dropped and those which still occurred seemed unfocused and arbitrary. In April the National Party MP for Pietermaritzburg North, Danie Schutte, said, 'I can now report that calm and peace has returned to the area.' Schutte's statement reflected the hopes of many whites in Pietermaritzburg that the war itself was over and what was left was a residue of vengeance and criminality which would gradually dissipate. The police confirmed this optimistic viewpoint, but in the event they were all wrong.

In April the number of deaths increased to 28, and for the rest of the year the monthly average was 51. The war was far from over; it had simply changed gear and was running at a lower intensity.

★   ★   ★

APRIL 1988

An Inkatha meeting at Sweetwaters was cancelled after residents complained, fearing it would degenerate into violence like the rally held in Mpumuza at the end of January. The KwaZulu Police (ZP) blamed the South African Police (SAP) for the deaths of two Inkatha members who had been arrested, interrogated and then released in Ashdown, a known no-go area for Inkatha.

The Durban Supreme Court declared two former policemen guilty of the murder of thirteen Inkatha Youth Brigade members in September. The judge found mitigating circumstances in the fact that the men had feared an attack by the group and had pre-empted this by attacking first. They were sentenced to twelve years' imprisonment.

In mid-April a seminar which investigated the causes and effects of the war was held at UNP. It was attended by academics, businessmen and diplomats. The police were invited and then disinvited. Brigadier J Büchner, head of the security police in the region, told the press he had been insulted.

The KwaZulu Legislative Assembly (KLA) called for the black areas of Greater Pietermaritzburg to be placed under the jurisdiction of KwaZulu.

MAY 1988

The UDF appealed to the Minister of Law and Order to allow the organisation to participate in peace talks with Inkatha. The Minister did not reply. Chief Buthelezi was refused a visa by the Austrian authorities who were concerned about his controversial role in South African politics. The Inkatha Central Committee decided to suspend any member accused of using violence for political ends.

An Inkatha member, Mlungisi Shabalala, was sentenced to death for the murder of Mganyo Miya, and Jerome Mncwabe appeared in the Pietermaritzburg Supreme Court on three charges of murder. Although the victims were shot in the back, the judge accepted Mncwabe's claim that he acted in self-defence, and he was acquitted. His co-accused, Nkosinathi Mncwabe, was found guilty of culpable homicide and sentenced to five strokes and one year's imprisonment suspended for four years.

Number of deaths in May: 32.

JUNE 1988

Twwo stayaways were called by COSATU. Both were well supported by workers. The PFP called on the police to prohibit a rally in Sweetwaters organised by the Inkatha Youth Brigade. Inkatha claimed it was merely a meeting to discuss strategy and dismissed residents' fears that anyone who failed to attend would have to 'face the consequences'. There was intense fighting in Slangspruit.

Number of deaths in June: 27.

JULY 1988

Sixteen schoolchildren at Siyahlomula High School in Ashdown were shot and injured by *kitskonstabels*. The pupils had been protesting against the presence of the police on the school grounds. A delegation of women went to the (then) PFP offices to ask for a meeting to be set up with the police. Subsequently the *kitskonstabels* were almost entirely withdrawn from Ashdown.

The police released a number of detainees. Many of them had severe restrictions placed on them, designed to prevent them from engaging in any further political activity. In Molweni and Gezubuso, residents fled their homes to escape fresh outbreaks of violence in the area.

Ernest Mthembu, a witness due to give oral evidence in August against Inkatha warlord Sichizo Zuma, was killed at his house in Imbali. In February his brother Simon Mthembu was allegedly killed by Zuma after serving papers on him.

Number of deaths in July: 49.

AUGUST 1988

The first of the interdict applications came before the Supreme Court for oral evidence to be heard. The violence in the region intensified. Brigadier Büchner attributed this to the re-infiltration of the area by provocateurs and agitators who had previously been chased out by the police. Progressive organisations ascribed the upsurge of violence to another forced recruitment drive by Inkatha. Five people were killed at a funeral in Mpumalanga after an attack by an army of 300 Inkatha vigilantes.

The police announced that because of the trouble surrounding the deployment of *kitskonstabels*, they were now being used as interpreters and guards rather than in active policing functions.

Number of deaths in August: 57.

SEPTEMBER 1988

Before the process of hearing oral evidence against Inkatha warlords could be completed, COSATU and Inkatha signed a Peace Accord, under the terms of which all but one of the applications were settled between the two parties. A Complaints Board under the presidency of a retired judge was established to monitor the situation. All those found responsible for acts of violence by the Board would be referred back to their organisation for discipline. The Accord led to some tension between COSATU and the UDF comrades as the latter could not participate in the agreement because of restrictions placed on the UDF by the government in February. The comrades also complained that they had not been consulted by COSATU before the signing.

Number of deaths in September: 54.

OCTOBER 1988

There were reports of over 20 000 refugees in the Greater Pietermaritzburg area alone. Fighting continued in and around Retief Street in Pietermaritzburg, but the majority of deaths were caused by fighting in Mpumalanga township.

Number of deaths in October: 53.

NOVEMBER 1988

Chief Maphumulo of Maqongqo near Table Mountain was summoned to Ulundi to answer an inquiry into the administration of his area. The inquiry followed complaints from Inkatha members that Maphumulo's policy of non-alignment in the war meant that UDF refugees were settling in Table Mountain and living together with Inkatha members there. Maphumulo refused to attend the inquiry as he claimed that the directive he had received was vague and ambiguous.

There were reports that Inkatha had embarked on a new forced recruitment campaign in Trust Feed near New Hanover.

Number of deaths in November: 58.

DECEMBER 1988

Fifteen people were killed at a vigil in a house in Trust Feed. Chief Buthelezi threatened to sue anyone who suggested that Inkatha members were responsible for the murders. He claimed that the dead people were in fact Inkatha members, although survivors and relations of the dead people denied this vehemently.

Shopkeepers in Retief Street, Pietermaritzburg, complained that the continued fighting at the bus and taxi depots in the area was bad for Christmas trade.

The secretary general of Inkatha, Oscar Dhlomo, went on record as saying that he believed the Peace Accord was still in operation. However, Chief Buthelezi declared that the only reason COSATU had signed the Accord was because it knew it would lose the court cases against Inkatha. COSATU denied this.

Number of deaths in December: 87.

JANUARY 1989

There was further fighting between residents of Ashdown and Mpumuza. The SAP station at Mpumalanga was handed over to the ZP. Following the hand-over ceremony, Inkatha members attacked people in Edendale outside Thulani's Garage. A deputation of women went to the PFP offices to complain about the police handling of the incident. Following the arrival of a warlord in KwaMhlaba in the Shongweni Valley, the whole population of the area moved out, turning the settlement into a ghost town. Refugees moved further up the hill to the Albini Catholic Mission, or went to Pinetown.

Number of deaths in January: 72.

FEBRUARY–MARCH 1989

There were several clashes between comrades and *comtsotsis* as well as between groups of vigilantes under the command of different warlords. The regional director of the PFP in Pietermaritzburg, Radley Keys, accused an Inkatha warlord of having murdered up to 25 people. The police and Inkatha denied this. The warlord in question, Sichizo Zuma, was reportedly 'shocked at the idea'. He made a call instead for aggression to be channelled into harmless pursuits, such as soccer matches. The police released a number of detainees, including UDF secretary Skhumbuzo Ngwenya, following a hunger strike. The regional secretary of the Transport and General Worker's Union, Alfred Ndlovu, was, however, convicted of terrorism and sentenced to eight years' imprisonment.

Number of deaths in February: 60
Number of deaths in March: 56.

APRIL–MAY 1989

Brigadier Büchner left his post as head of the security police (Pietermaritzburg) to take up a post in Ulundi as commissioner of police (KwaZulu).

Nelson Mandela sent a cordial letter from the Victor Verster Prison, near Paarl, to Chief Buthelezi. Mandela called for national unity in the struggle and peace in the Pietermaritzburg townships. Chief Maphumulo of the Table Mountain region also called for peace and petitioned the State

President to appoint a judicial commission of inquiry into the causes of violence. Chief Buthelezi rubbished the petition and opposed the idea of a judicial commission. The Minister of Law and Order, Adriaan Vlok, also dismissed the call.

Towards the end of April, 30 people were killed in one weekend. The escalation of the rate of killings galvanised the conflicting parties into making fresh calls for peace. COSATU and the UDF said that they shared a 'common view and commitment to a mass movement for peace' with Inkatha, and called for a peace conference to be convened by church and community leaders. Chief Buthelezi also proposed a peace plan involving a massive media campaign in the townships. Adriaan Vlok reiterated his view that the UDF and COSATU were responsible for all the violence in the region and announced an increase in police personnel and equipment, a move that had been discussed with Chief Buthelezi during a recent visit to Ulundi.

The peace talks were bogged down before they could begin, when Chief Buthelezi demanded that the talks be held at Ulundi, while COSATU and the UDF wanted a neutral venue, such as Durban. Although Chief Buthelezi had said to Archbishop Hurley that he would be prepared to 'go to the ends of the earth if needs be' to stop the violence, he now declared that he had no intention of going to Durban or anywhere else to hold peace talks.

Number of deaths in April: 48.

Number of deaths in May: 53.

JUNE–JULY 1989

The Minister of Law and Order undermined the peace process by placing high-ranking UDF officials, including the president, Archie Gumede, under virtual house arrest, thereby making it almost impossible for them to attend the talks. Vlok declared that his only concern was to bring peace to the region.

In July the first rounds of the 'five-a-side' peace negotiations were held in Durban between representatives of Inkatha and the COSATU–UDF alliance. Chief Buthelezi was not present. Later in the month a series of rallies were held by both Inkatha and COSATU. The former were marked by spectacular effects but low attendances, while the latter were more low key. Chief Buthelezi was incensed by an article in the *Weekly Mail* which described him as enjoying a cult of personality.

The death tally fell in June, awakening hopes that peace was in the offing, but the figures climbed again in July.

Number of deaths in June: 27.

Number of deaths in July: 54.

AUGUST–SEPTEMBER 1989

The peace negotiators agreed on an agenda for a meeting of presidents, a top-level peace conference to be held at some overseas venue and attended by the presidents of Inkatha, the UDF, COSATU and the ANC. The plan was endorsed by all parties, but did not get off the ground as Inkatha accused the ANC of dragging its feet over the proposals.

A 'hit squad' consisting of police members and operating from a red Husky mini-van was reported to be roaming the streets of Imbali, abducting and assaulting comrades and activists. The members of the squad used nicknames taken from American films and TV serials.

In September the UDF and COSATU launched a defiance campaign against apartheid laws; the organisation and administration of this campaign to some extent deflected energy away from peace negotiations. At the same time Inkatha claimed that it had discovered two documents undermining the peace process, one which had been issued by local comrades and the other by the exiled South African Congress of Trade Unions (SACTU). The documents were repudiated by the UDF and COSATU and appear to have been skilful forgeries, but Inkatha remained unsatisfied and called ooff any further negotiations.

Sentencing a former ZP policeman to sixteen years in jail for murder, Mr Justice Didcott found that the accused had committed the crime because he had put his allegiance to Inkatha above his duty as a policeman. He had done this because in training, the accused had been specifically instructed by his superior officers to join Inkatha. Mr Justice Didcott said it was imperative that the police force be impartial in the present climate of political violence.

Number of deaths in August: 50.

Number of deaths in September: 46.

OCTOBER–NOVEMBER 1989

An interim interdict was granted to an Imbali activist, restraining the members of the police 'hit squad' from further abducting and assaulting him. On the same day he was again briefly detained by the squad and interrogated.

An inquest into the massacre at Trust Feed in December 1988 found that three policemen may have been involved in the shooting. The matter was referred to the Attorney-General.

In November there were reports of sporadic violence in Imbali as small groups of comrades and Inkatha supporters clashed with each other. However, the worst of the fighting occurred in Mpumalanga and Hammarsdale, and the focus of the war shifted from Pietermaritzburg to the townships around Durban.

The Zulu king, Goodwill Zwelithini, convened a meeting of the nation at King's Park Stadium in Durban. The convention was attended by 70 000 people. The king complained that he, Chief Buthelezi and the Zulu nation had been spurned by the recently released leaders of the ANC because they had been excluded from homecoming celebrations. Later, Walter Sisulu responded by saying that all were welcome, and the celebrations were open to anyone who wished to attend. He also accepted an invitation to hold talks with the Inkatha leadership on the question of peace and reconciliation between rival organisations in Natal.

Inkatha displayed increasing hostility towards the Congress of Traditional Leaders of South Africa (CONTRALESA) and King Goodwill called the organisation 'an unwelcome newcomer to black politics'.

Number of deaths in October: 68.

DECEMBER 1989

Fighting escalated in Mpumalanga and in the townships around Durban. A group of Hammarsdale industrialists appeared to have engineered a remarkable breakthrough when, through a process of mediation, they secured a ceasefire between Inkatha and the UDF in Mpumalanga. Two unofficial commissions of inquiry into the Pietermaritzburg war were convened, one under the auspices of Chief Maphumulo, and the other under the auspices of local church groups.

The most significant feature of December was the intensity of fighting in the squatter camps of Inanda near Durban, giving rise to the (temporary) impression that the focus of the war had shifted from the Midlands to the coast.

Number of deaths in December: 91.

JANUARY 1990

The new decade began with the massacre of ten people at Wartburg near Pietermaritzburg. Thulani Ngcobo, a small-time Inkatha warlord, was killed in the centre of town by gunmen shooting from a get-away car. In Durban the fighting continued to such a degree that the Minister of Law and Order toured Inanda by helicopter, together with Chief Buthelezi. Later the Minister said, 'Brother is killing brother. If we don't stop hating each other the killing will continue. It will not end until there is a change of heart.' A new development was the targeting of the Indian community on the Natal north coast for attack, for which certain 'inflammatory' editorials in *Ilanga*, the Inkatha-owned Zulu-language newspaper, were blamed.

A combined UDF–COSATU delegation met Minister Vlok, as did a delegation from the Church Leaders Group, comprising senior churchmen active in the Pietermaritzburg region. The Minister agreed to relay their request for a commission of inquiry to the State President, F W de Klerk.

FEBRUARY 1990

In his speech at the opening of parliament, the State President unbanned the ANC, and a few days later, Nelson Mandela was released after 27 years in prison. The ANC stated that the resolution of the conflict in Natal was a priority for all parties. The leader of the internal wing of the ANC, Walter Sisulu, toured Pietermaritzburg towards the end of the month and met with the Inkatha secretary general, Oscar Dhlomo. On 25 February the ANC deputy president, Nelson Mandela, addressed a rally of 125 000 people at King's Park Stadium in Durban. He made conciliatory remarks about Inkatha and Chief Buthelezi, praising their opposition to apartheid over the years. Mandela also called on his followers to throw their weapons into the sea. 'Close down the death factories now,' he said.

The ceasefire in Mpumalanga broke down after Inkatha declared it null and void, and there was an immediate upsurge in violence and in the number of casualties. Towards the end of the month, the fighting shifted from the townships around Durban to the Pietermaritzburg area, with the worst flashpoint being Table Mountain, the chieftaincy of Chief Maphumulo. By the end of the month it became clear that Maphumulo's authority was slipping and that Inkatha was becoming increasingly powerful in the area. Many refugees who had fled to Table Mountain in the early months of the war moved out again to seek refuge in other townships.

Number of deaths in February: 115.

MARCH 1990

This month was the high-water month of the war in terms of number of deaths, surpassing January 1988 with its death tally of 162. Violence escalated around Pietermaritzburg, despite Nelson Mandela's call for peace at the end of February. In contrast to the conciliatory tone of Mandela's speech, Chief Buthelezi in his opening speech to the KwaZulu Legislative Assembly attacked the ANC and the UDF, explicitly blaming the latter for starting the war and keeping it going over the years.

Captain Deon Terblanche, head of the riot police in Pietermaritzburg, was murdered in his car along the N3. Within days his alleged killer was found, who in turn was shot dead almost immediately 'while trying to escape'.

Inkatha held a rally on 25 March at King's Park Stadium which was attended by 8 000 people. A few days later, Inkatha launched a sustained attack in the Pietermaritzburg region which amounted to a full-scale invasion of UDF strongholds in Edendale and Vulindlela. A feature of the attack was the huge size of the armies (up to 3 000 people were reported) and the large number of guns in evidence. Fatalities were consequently high with 35 people killed in a single day and over 80 in a week. Within days 11 500 refugees were being accommodated in makeshift camps in Pietermaritzburg. Eyewitnesses claim that David Ntombela was centrally involved in co-ordinating the Inkatha offensive.

The upsurge in violence dominated local media for over two weeks and received much coverage overseas. Chief Buthelezi repeated his claim that the instigators of violence were the UDF, COSATU and the ANC. Inkatha also claimed that the current attack was retaliation against the stoning of Inkatha buses by UDF comrades. The UDF responded by saying that the retaliation was out of all proportion to the stoning, and that the scale of the invasion was so large that it must have been prepared well in advance. There were many reports of police colluding with Inkatha attackers, and police dispersed a peaceful march of unarmed women on the Plessislaer police station in protest at police involvement in the attacks.

At the height of the fighting, Chief Buthelezi announced that he and Nelson Mandela would address a joint rally in Taylor's Halt, the heart of the war zone. Mandela then withdrew from the rally saying that he had never given his agreement and arguing that a joint rally at such a time could lead to a bloodbath in the stadium.

The Black Sash called for the deployment of troops in the Natal townships, arguing that the police had lost all credibility and that only the army could restore control.

Number of deaths in March: 180.

APRIL 1990

The fighting continued around Pietermaritzburg for some time but then tailed off. Inkatha gained some territory but was beaten back in most areas. The fighting then shifted to Mpumalanga, where it was eventually contained by the deployment of 32 Battalion of the SADF, made up of black Portuguese-speaking soldiers, who, it was claimed, would be entirely impartial in carrying out their duties.

The State President announced a development plan for Natal to be administered by the Minister of Planning and Provincial Affairs, Hernus Kriel. A sum of R250 000 was made available immediately for refugee relief, and further plans are still being drawn up for the long-term socio-economic revitalisation of the region.

Although the level of violence has dropped from the March high point, tensions are still high and the army can only contain, not erase them. It is becoming increasingly clear that a massive peace initiative is needed in

Natal, including but superseding talks between Mandela and Buthelezi. For the first time the possibility exists for this to come about as the government at long last appears ready to assume its responsibilities towards the people in the war zone.

MAY–JUNE 1990

The ANC entered into talks about talks with the South African government at Groote Schuur in Cape Town. The violence in Natal featured prominently in the deliberations and the ANC presented the government delegation with a memorandum containing allegations of malpractice on the part of Inkatha, the SAP and the ZP.

At a May Day rally in Durban, a spokesman for COSATU declared that all avenues towards peace had been exhausted and announced that COSATU now considered itself to be formally at war with Inkatha. Senior COSATU leaders later qualified this statement but did not dispute its thrust. Chief Buthelezi deplored the declaration, saying that the search for peace should continue, and called on ANC deputy president Nelson Mandela to meet him to discuss a joint strategy aimed at ending the violence. The ANC responded by stating that the time was not propitious for such talks.

The ANC and COSATU called on the government to disband the KwaZulu Police (ZP) and strip Chief Buthelezi of his powers as Minister of Police in KwaZulu. The ANC implied that the government's response to this call would influence its decision regarding the continuation or suspension of the armed struggle. Likewise, COSATU declared that if no response was forthcoming within a certain time, it would call a week-long general strike in Natal. Chief Buthelezi dismissed the call, saying that it was no more than a further 'unsuccessful attempt' to undermine him and the authority of the KwaZulu government.

Dr Oscar Dhlomo, secretary general of Inkatha for more than 10 years, announced his resignation from the organisation. He stated that he was resigning in order to devote more attention to private matters. His move triggered a wave of speculation both on his political future, and on the implications of his resignation for the future of Inkatha.

Index